"At a time when the 'good chaps theory of government' seems to be failing British democracy, Chris Monaghan's *Accountability, Impeachment and the Constitution* charts a radical new reform agenda. Evidence-based, provocative and incredibly timely . . . this is the book that could really shape the future of British politics."

– **Matthew Flinders,** *University of Sheffield*, United Kingdom

"An outstanding work on a much talked-about constitutional device that originated in Britain where it is now defunct, but famously continues to operate in the United States. Chris Monaghan makes a powerful case for a revived and reformed impeachment procedure at Westminster, designed to strengthen ministerial responsibility to Parliament and – at a time when judicial review is under threat – buttress the political forms of control and redress over the abuse of executive power and unconstitutional conduct."

– **Robert Blackburn,** *King's College London*, United Kingdom

"In Britain, impeachment is generally regarded as obsolete. Chris Monaghan seeks, however, to show that it can be a powerful weapon in strengthening governmental accountability. His book is both analytical and securely based on comparative evidence. It is also original and provocative and should be read by anyone interested in British government."

– **Vernon Bogdanor,** *King's College London*, United Kingdom

Accountability, Impeachment and the Constitution

This book sets out and explores the case for a modernised impeachment process for the United Kingdom.

The work examines the present law and history of impeachment in the United Kingdom, which today is widely regarded as having fallen into desuetude and its procedures inappropriate for modern conditions. It discusses how impeachment operates in two countries, the United States and Denmark, selected respectively for their marked differences from and similarities to the United Kingdom's political and constitutional system, for the purposes of illumination and possible lessons for a new impeachment process. The book seeks to provide a balanced and independent examination of the case for this, concluding that it would have a valuable role to play in the future development of the United Kingdom's system of politics and government. It concludes by setting out a detailed model for the structure, working and effect of impeachment.

The book will be of interest to students, academics and policy-makers working in the areas of constitutional law and politics.

Chris Monaghan is a principal lecturer in law at the University of Worcester and holds a PhD from the Dickson Poon School of Law at King's College London. He has published widely on aspects of public law.

Routledge Frontiers in Accountability Studies

Series Editors:

Matthew Flinders; *University of Sheffield, UK.*

Chris Monaghan; *University of Worcester, UK.*

Ellen Rock; *University of Technology, Sydney, Australia.*

Thomas Schillemans; *Utrecht University School of Governance, the Netherlands.*

Routledge Frontiers in Accountability Studies series promotes state-of-the-art analyses that reflect and interrogate the shifting accountability landscape from a range of perspectives.

The series welcomes proposals for monographs, edited collections and shorter works by established and early-career academics from a range of disciplines that span the arts, humanities and social sciences. Inter-disciplinary studies are particularly encouraged, as are approaches that seek to challenge dominant frameworks of 'self-evident' truths. The series is designed for a global audience, welcoming contributions that address national, comparative and international issues.

Other titles in this series:

For more information about this series, please visit: www.routledge.com

Accountability, Impeachment and the Constitution

The Case for a Modernised Process in the United Kingdom

Chris Monaghan

Routledge
Taylor & Francis Group
LONDON AND NEW YORK

First published 2022
by Routledge
4 Park Square, Milton Park, Abingdon, Oxon OX14 4RN

and by Routledge
605 Third Avenue, New York, NY 10158

Routledge is an imprint of the Taylor & Francis Group, an informa business

British Library Cataloguing-in-Publication Data
A catalogue record for this book is available from the British Library

Library of Congress Cataloging-in-Publication Data
A catalog record for this book has been requested

ISBN: 978-1-032-21581-5 (hbk)
ISBN: 978-1-032-21584-6 (pbk)
ISBN: 978-1-003-26905-2 (ebk)

DOI: 10.4324/9781003269052

Typeset in Galliard
by Apex CoVantage, LLC

Contents

Cases

Denmark

United Kingdom

United States

Primary Legislation

United Kingdom

Council of Europe

Denmark

Europe

European Union

Iceland

United States

In memory of Sheila Cronin (1925–2022)

Preface

Accountability, Impeachment and the Constitution: The Case for a Modernised Process in the United Kingdom is based on almost ten years of research into the historic, comparative, and contemporary use of impeachment. My interest in impeachment initially arose from studying the East India Company as an undergraduate at the University of Liverpool. It was Warren Hastings, the Governor-General of Bengal and the East India Company's chief administrator in India, whose impeachment trial from 1788 to 1795 is perhaps the most famous example of its use in this country, that sparked my interest in impeachment. I would like to thank Dr Patrick Tuck, who taught me at Liverpool, for introducing me to impeachment and the problems in holding the East India Company to account.

The origin for this book is my PhD thesis that I undertook at King's College London. Working full time, the PhD was undertaken on a part-time basis over the best part of a decade. During this time, I have enjoyed the support and generosity of many individuals, who collectively have been responsible for keeping me going throughout my doctoral studies. I would especially like to thank my primary supervisor, Professor Robert Blackburn QC, who has supported my research throughout my studies and in writing this book and who has and provided the encouragement to develop my initial proposal into a fully fledged thesis and ultimately to publish it as a book. I would also like to thank my two secondary supervisors, Professor Vernon Bogdanor and Professor Catharine MacMillan, who have both been supportive and always encouraging. I would like to take the opportunity of acknowledging the support of Dr Michael Kandiah and Dr Virginia Preston from the Institute of Contemporary British History, Professor Satvinder Juss who acted as the internal examiner for my PhD upgrade, and Professor Eva Pils, the Director of Doctoral Studies at the Dickson Poon School of Law. I would like to thank my external examiners, Professor Lord Norton of Lough from the University of Hull and Professor Philip Schofield from University College London.

I would like to thank Professor Conor Gearty for meeting with me to discuss how impeachment might operate in the United Kingdom, and Oonagh Gay (the then head of the Parliament and Constitution Centre, House of Commons Library) who kindly met with me and was willing to discuss my thesis over coffee in Portcullis House. Oonagh Gay subsequently arranged for me to visit the House of Commons Library and to use the archival material on impeachment. Professor Jim Phillips (University of Toronto) agreed to meet with me in Toronto to discuss historic impeachment in Ontario and colonial history. Jim Phillips subsequently invited me to talk about my research at the Osgoode Society for Canadian Legal History. Professor Roger Mortimore (Director of Political Analysis at Ipsos MORI) met with me to advise on conducting interviews and this really helped in approaching the interview process.

A number of individuals generously gave up their time to be interviewed as part of my research: Lord Phillips of Worth Matravers, Professor Sir Ross Cranston, Chris Bryant MP, and Lord Owen. I would also like to thank the retired senior judge whom I interviewed, but who wished to remain anonymous. In addition, I would like to thank David Shaw (formerly Chief Constable of West Mercia Police) who discussed impeachment and broader issues of accountability with me. The Rt Hon. The Viscount Hailsham QC provided me with a statement as to his views on impeachment, and Henrik Skovgaard-Petersen (Head of Section, Constitutional Law and Human Rights, Danish Ministry of Justice) generously prepared an account of the use of impeachment in Denmark for me. Professor Erik Goldstein (Boston University) kindly read the comparative material and provided invaluable feedback. Finally, Professor Matthew Flinders has been generous with his time and has supported me during the process of turning my thesis into a book.

The publishing team at Routledge has been fantastic and highly supportive during the commissioning and publishing process. In particular I would like to thank Alison Kirk and Anna Gallagher for their support. I would also like to thank Richard George for all his help during the production process. I am grateful to my anonymous academic reviewers for their feedback and helpful suggestions.

Colleagues at the University of Worcester have always supported my research and have been generous with their time. I have had the support of friends and family, and in particular I would like to mention Bill Davies; Matt Wade-Wight; Michael Carleton; Josie Welsh; Stephen Hurley; Sarah Greer; Marcus Levens; Verity Currie; Sheila Cronin; my parents, Michael and Marie Monaghan; my parents-in-law, Nick and June Haralambous; and my brother, Jonathan Monaghan. Finally, I would like to take this opportunity to thank my wife, Nicola, who has supported me over the course of my studies and the writing of this book and has provided constant encouragement. The book is dedicated to Sheila Cronin.

1 Introduction

Impeachment is arguably most closely associated in popular culture with the United States. The circumstances around President William (Bill) Clinton's impeachment and President Donald Trump's two impeachments have certainly generated considerable public interest on both sides of the Atlantic. However, impeachment within the United Kingdom is arguably less well known. I first encountered the term whilst studying A-level history and I then re-encountered impeachment as an undergraduate while studying the East India Company in my final year at university. This second encounter was within the context of the impeachment and trial of Warren Hastings, the first Governor-General of Bengal, and the problems with holding a powerful corporate body and its officials to account. Impeachment is a product of English, and then British, political history and developed in truly remarkable circumstances to create a way for the Commons to hold royal advisors to account. It is within the spectrum of accountability that this book is concerned.

The purpose of *Accountability, Impeachment and the Constitution: The Case for a Modernised Process in the United Kingdom* is to explore whether impeachment, reimagined and modernised might offer a way to enhance the political accountability of the executive within the United Kingdom. I seek to place impeachment within a political context and set out a case for how impeachment could serve as a way to protect the existing constitutional norms. This may be a controversial idea, in as much as it is drawing upon something perceived by many as a historical relic to address a contemporary problem. However, *Accountability, Impeachment and the Constitution: The Case for a Modernised Process in the United Kingdom* will set out how impeachment could be reimagined and deployed as a mechanism to enhance political accountability and to protect the constitution from being ignored or abused by the executive.

This first chapter is designed to establish the groundwork for the argument advanced. It will set out the central question that will be addressed throughout, before then considering the aims of the book and the research methodology used, and providing a definition of impeachment. Finally, this chapter will provide an overview of the eight other chapters within this book.

DOI: 10.4324/9781003269052-1

Central question

Accountability, Impeachment and the Constitution: The Case for a Modernised Process in the United Kingdom explores the use of impeachment as a form of political executive accountability and whether this could serve a beneficial purpose in the contemporary United Kingdom. The inclusion of accountability is an acknowledgement that impeachment originated as a way for the House of Commons to hold the king's advisers and ministers to account, one which predated the notion of responsible government. The book will question whether impeachment could be used in conjunction with the existing mechanisms that are available to ensure executive accountability within the United Kingdom, as a way of improving executive accountability, and whether the usage of impeachment would be a feasible proposition. Therefore, it asks whether impeachment could buttress the existing political accountability mechanisms. The focus here is the accountability of the executive within the Westminster system, and this book will restrict the scope of impeachment to cover only the Prime Minister and other ministers.

In order to answer the central question it is, first, necessary to consider examples of how impeachment has been used in English and British history, to show its historical purpose and how its usage developed over time. It is, second, necessary to consider impeachment within a comparative context and to see how it has been used in both presidential and parliamentary systems. The consideration and analysis of the comparative use of impeachment will demonstrate the strengths and weaknesses associated with its use as an executive accountability mechanism.

Finally, this book will critically consider whether, within the context of the United Kingdom, impeachment is obsolete, and, if it is not, whether it is appropriate to be used again, and, if so, how this might work and whether it would be expedient to revise how impeachment would operate and if it could play a positive role in the enforcement of accepted constitutional norms. It will be necessary to test the feasibility of modernising the procedure of impeachment, to consider the views of experts and informed commentators as to its status and merits and finally to test whether it could co-exist with and complement existing accountability mechanisms. The intention of the book is not to ignore the difficulties associated with impeachment, or the arguments that it is now obsolete and superseded by the confidence vote and ministerial responsibility to Parliament; rather, it is to explore whether impeachment, or a modified form of it, could add something different and valuable to the existing executive accountability mechanisms within the UK Constitution.

The aims of the book

My intention when writing this book was to provide an original contribution to the academic literature on impeachment by:

(1) Seeking to provide a definition of impeachment for the purposes of this book. This definition will be informed by the historical usage of impeachment

and its comparative use in Denmark and the United States, and by the proposed reforms that will be outlined for a revised form of impeachment.

(2) Considering the operation of the UK unwritten constitution and reviewing the political accountability mechanisms and then considering whether impeachment could serve a role in buttressing these existing mechanisms. There will be a discussion of the perceived limitations of the political accountability at Westminster and how a revised form of impeachment could reassert the authority of Parliament and respect for accepted constitutional norms.

(3) Examining the case for impeachment, which takes the form of a revised model within this book. It will then take into account the counter-arguments against impeachment, before seeking to address these criticisms. The discussion draws heavily upon the existing literature and takes into account views of politicians and senior former members of the judiciary who were interviewed as part of this project. The aim will be to provide a balanced and independent examination of the argument that a new impeachment procedure would buttress the existing political accountability mechanisms at Westminster.

(4) Drawing upon the comparative usage of impeachment and by considering two case studies, Denmark and the United States, which were chosen due to both their differences from and their similarities to the United Kingdom. The case studies will be used to help inform the discussion as to what form the revised procedure of impeachment should take and, where appropriate, look at possible scope for a partial constitutional transplant.

(5) Bringing the arguments and discussion in the book together by putting forward a blueprint for a revised procedure for impeachment in the form of a proposed Impeachment Act. Once the Impeachment Act has been outlined there will be detailed consideration of how the Act and impeachment might operate in practice within the contemporary United Kingdom. The emphasis will be on the exceptionalism of impeachment, in that it is not perceived that it will be used often, but its existence serves as an incentive to follow the accepted norms of the constitution.

It is hoped that *Accountability, Impeachment and the Constitution: The Case for a Modernised Process in the United Kingdom* will add to the debate surrounding the accountability of the executive and be of interest to those interested in the status of impeachment within the United Kingdom.

Research methodology

This section concerns the research methodology used to undertake the research upon which the book is based. *Accountability, Impeachment and the Constitution: The Case for a Modernised Process in the United Kingdom* addresses impeachment as a form of accountability from a contemporary and comparative analysis, and it explores the use of impeachment as a form of political executive accountability. The central question posed by my research was whether impeachment could ever be effectively used again in the United Kingdom and whether it might serve a useful purpose as a form of executive accountability today and for the future. To understand what was meant by impeachment, I conducted a review of its historical use in this country, before considering two comparative case studies. This enabled me to approach the question with an awareness of how impeachment had been used, the problems associated with its use, and how effective it had proved as a form of executive accountability. The approach adopted in my research was not to set out to make a case for the future use of impeachment in the United Kingdom, but rather to question whether this was possible, needed, or capable of academic, political, and judicial support and then to propose a blueprint for its use.

My research methodology was approached in two ways. The first approach was a desk-based method where I used a variety of resources to undertake my research. This is a more traditional approach and incorporated the use of online and physical archives. There is a considerable volume of literature on how impeachment works in the United States, and this often considers the use of impeachment in England and Great Britain. There are also a number of books from the twentieth century considering the use of impeachment in England and Great Britain, although these focus on distinct periods of time or particular impeachments. Academic journals, such as *Parliamentary History*, have proved invaluable in order to access articles on impeachment, and this particular publication has published recent pieces on the impeachment of Viscount Melville and the Duke of Buckingham. A number of online resources have also been invaluable to obtain out-of-print books, Google Books, and the University of Toronto's archive.org database. The online database of parliamentary proceedings, Hansard, has enabled me to follow parliamentary debates on impeachment. I have used a number of libraries at the following organisations: King's College London, the London School of Economics and Political Science, the University of Greenwich, the University of Worcester, and the House of Commons Library. Whilst there is a wealth of material on impeachment, there is very little on how it would work today in the United Kingdom, apart from observations that it is obsolete,[1] or referencing the procedure set out in the original edition of *Erskine May*.[2] In terms of the history of impeachment and its purported use in 2004, there tends to be only brief coverage on this in recent works published in this country.[3]

1 W McKay and CW Johnson, *Parliament and Congress: Representation and Scrutiny in the Twenty-First Century* (OUP 2010); O Gay and N Davies, 'Impeachment' (House of Commons Library, Standard Note, 16 November 2011). Note that an updated version is available.

2 T Erskine May, *A Practical Treatise on the Law, Privileges, Proceedings and Usage of Parliament* (1st edn, Charles Knight and Co 1844).

3 G Rangwala and D Plesch, 'A Case to Answer: A First Report on the Potential Impeachment of the Prime Minister for High Crimes and Misdemeanours in Relation to the Invasion of Iraq' (August 2004); R Singh QC and C Gearty, 'In the Matter of an Impeachment of the Prime Minister: Arising from the War Against Iraq' (Legal Opinion, 22 September 2004); Gay and Davies (n 1).

Where material was particularly limited, I contacted institutions and organisations for assistance. Henrik Skovgaard-Petersen (Head of Section, Constitutional Law and Human Rights, Danish Ministry of Justice) generously prepared an account on the use of impeachment in Denmark and Oonagh Gay (the then head of the Parliament and Constitution Centre, House of Commons Library) arranged for me to visit the House of Commons Library and to use the archival material on impeachment. I supplemented my research with discussions with experts, such as Professor Jim Phillips (University of Toronto), who has published on the use of impeachment in colonial Canada, and Professor Erik Goldstein (Boston University), who kindly read my comparative chapters and provided invaluable feedback.

The qualitive interviews

The second approach was to adopt an empirical method in the form of qualitive interviews. This approach was designed to address my research question by testing the workability of impeachment and gauging the problems that might be encountered with using impeachment again.

Before I conducted the interviews, I met with a number of leading experts in order to discuss impeachment: Professor Conor Gearty (London School of Economics and Political Science), who co-authored the 2004 legal opinion (with Rabinder Singh QC, now a Court of Appeal judge) on impeaching Tony Blair; Professor Vernon Bogdanor (King's College London), who was my second supervisor from 2013 to 2017; and Oonagh Gay. These preliminary discussions helped to shape my research and the direction of the thesis.

I conducted a number of empirical qualitative interviews with leading experts, for which I obtained ethical approval. This method was needed for my research given the limited amount of material available on impeachment and whether impeachment as a procedure might be used again, and, if so, its feasibility as a form of constitutional justice and the practical obstacles that would need to be overcome. In terms of guidance, I met with Professor Roger Mortimore (King's College London and Director of Political Analysis at Ipsos MORI) who provided comprehensive guidance on undertaking empirical interviews. The key requirements for the qualitive interviews were to interview in depth a small number of leading experts from politics and the judiciary, with the verbatim transcripts available for use in my research.

Based on my meeting with Professor Roger Mortimore and my own research into conducting interviews, I decided to adopt the following approach. First, I needed to determine whom I would interview as part of the select number of qualitive interviews that I would conduct as part of my research. Second, I identified the ideal number to be six, as this would ensure that I could travel to an agreed location and have at least a one-hour interview with each interviewee; that I could arrange the administration and selection process effectively; that I could interview a sufficient number of politicians, senior judges, and leading political scientists; and that I could have the interview professionally transcribed.

Determining whom to interview

Once I had determined that I would aim to interview six individuals, I set about deciding whom I would interview. As previously stated, I had decided to interview politicians, senior judges, and leading political scientists. The choice of politicians was justified on the basis that, as the users (and potential targets) of impeachment, it would be expedient to gain their understanding of the process, the arguments for and against its use, and their view as to whether it could be revised. I sought to interview experienced politicians, that is those who have written about impeachment or parliamentary practice and history, who have had long-term experience as a Member of Parliament or member of the House of Lords, or who have held ministerial office. I drew up a list of individuals who would fall within this range and devised a shortlist. I then approached one individual at a time.

The choice of senior judges was justified on the basis that senior judges have traditionally played a role in impeachment proceedings (as advisors on points of law), that judges often chair public inquiries, and that a possible format of a revised impeachment process could include senior judges as part of a Court of Impeachment. Therefore, it was expedient to include the opinions of senior judges. As with politicians, I drew up a list of potential interviews and contacted one individual at a time.

The choice of a senior political scientist was justified on the basis of the nature of the thesis. I discussed my research and the aims of my thesis with Professor Vernon Bogdanor, a political and constitutional historian, formerly Professor of Government at the University of Oxford and currently a research professor at the Centre for British Politics and Government.

Once I had identified whom to interview, I sent out the initial request using an email, or where there was no email address stated for an individual, then by letter. The response rate was positive in as much that a majority of individuals responded to indicate that they were willing to be interviewed, were not willing to be interviewed, or whilst not willing to be interviewed recommended someone who might be. In total, I interviewed five individuals and it is necessary to briefly explain why each individual was selected.

I interviewed Lord Phillips of Worth Matravers, who was formerly the President of the Supreme Court. Before this he was the Senior Law Lord in the Appellate Committee of the House of Lords, served as the Lord Chief Justice of England and Wales, and the Master of the Rolls. Lord Phillips had chaired a public inquiry, had spoken extrajudicially about the rule of law, and had given an opinion in *R v Chaytor*,[4] a case concerning parliamentary misconduct in relation to parliamentary expenses. I approached Lord Phillips due to his considerable judicial experience. I interviewed Sir Ross Cranston, who is a Professor at the London School of Economics and Political Science. Sir Ross Cranston was formerly a

4 *R v Chaytor* [2010] UKSC 52.

High Court Judge, a Member of Parliament, and served as the Solicitor-General. He therefore was both a former politician with ministerial experience and a former senior judge, and this is why I approached him for an interview. Chris Bryant is a Member of Parliament for the Rhondda and was formerly Under Secretary of State for Foreign Affairs. I interviewed Mr Bryant due to his parliamentary activity, his authoring of a two-volume history of parliament,[5] and prior ministerial experience. I interviewed Lord David Owen CH because he had written about the use possible use of impeachment in twentieth-century history and had spoken in Parliament on the impeachment of Tony Blair.[6] Lord Owen was formerly the Secretary of State for Foreign Affairs and leader of the Social Democratic Party, and therefore his inclusion would allow me to interview someone with considerable parliamentary and ministerial experience. I also interviewed a retired judge who wished to remain anonymous. The judge was very senior and was chosen for their judicial experience and the possible use of senior judges in any revised impeachment process.

In addition to the empirical interviews, the Rt Hon. The Viscount Hailsham QC provided me with a statement as to his views on impeachment. He had co-drafted the motion in 2004 to impeach Tony Blair. Viscount Hailsham was unable to meet personally, but kindly agreed for me to quote the views he outlined in our email exchanges.

Summary

The desk-based and empirical qualitive research enabled me to achieve a thorough and comprehensive understanding of the subject matter. The consideration of comparative legal scholarship, legal history, constitutional history, and contemporary scholarship in the political sciences and constitutional law has ensured that my research took into account the key sources and, where appropriate, responded to the academic debate. The empirical qualitative research provided a mechanism to address my central question and the broader issue of executive accountability. The desk-based review formed the basis for much of the book, whilst the empirical research was important in shaping Chapter 9 and the proposed blueprint for how impeachment could operate in the contemporary United Kingdom.

Understanding impeachment within a British context

Impeachment originated during the Good Parliament of 1376 as a way for the Commons to proceed against those individuals deemed to be blameworthy for the state of England's misfortunes. It was 'revived' by the House of Commons in 1621, and the last impeachment took place in 1806 with the acquittal of

5 C Bryant, *Parliament: The Bibliography, Volume 1: Ancestral Voices* (Doubleday 2014); C Bryant, *Parliament: The Bibliography, Volume 2: Reform* (Doubleday 2014).

6 HL Deb 12 July 2016, vol 774, col 167.

Viscount Melville in the same year. In essence, impeachment permits the House of Commons to find that an individual has acted in such a way as to amount to high crimes and misdemeanours and then to demand that that individual be tried before the House of Lords. The charge against those impeached often included treason.

The definition of precisely what type of behaviour amounted to high crimes and misdemeanours developed incrementally and depended on the circumstances of the time. Raoul Berger, in his seminal work *Impeachment: The Constitutional Problems*, was clear that there was no requirement that the high crimes and misdemeanours constituted an indictable offence, just that they were 'a crime by the "course of Parliament"', and this meant that a wide range of otherwise ordinary non-criminal conduct could be treated as criminal.[7] However, this view was countered by Clayton Roberts, who criticised Berger's approach and held that an impeachable offence was limited to 'the known law of the land' and needed to fall under an 'existing law'.[8] Roberts argued that the phrase 'high crimes and misdemeanors' was first used in 1642.[9] He was clear that an impeachable act needed to be unlawful, as there could not be an impeachment if the act was lawful.[10] The Lords safeguarded against impeachments that were based on political conduct, rather than a breach of the known law. Roberts gave examples of the Commons frequently abandoning impeachments despite a trial being arranged, such as the impeachment of Lord Somers, Lord Halifax, and Lord Orford in 1701, where the Commons knew that it could not prove criminal conduct.[11] Furthermore, when 'the House of Commons did seek to create a category of political offenses which were not violations of the known law . . . the House of Lords resolutely opposed this theory of impeachment.'[12] It is clear that just because the Commons impeached an individual, it does not follow that a trial took place.[13] Equally, just because an article was worded to proceed on the basis of political conduct, it does not mean that this could be proved to be illegal or accepted by the Lords. Roberts' thesis is to be preferred, as it narrows the scope of impeachable offences to criminal conduct recognised by the known law, albeit this might be wider than the common law.[14] One consequence of this is Edmund Burke's failure to persuade the House of Lords to accept broad allegations against Warren Hastings that were not of an established criminal nature. In their recent account of impeachment, Tribe and Katz noted that there was sympathy with Burke's approach in America, as Burke 'had charged Hastings with rampant subversion

7 R Berger, *Impeachment: The Constitutional Problems* (Harvard University Press 1973) 67–9.

8 C Roberts, 'The Law of Impeachment in Stuart England: A Reply to Raoul Berger' (1975) 84(7) *Yale Law Journal* 1419, 1419, and 1439.

9 ibid 1431.

10 ibid 1432.

11 ibid 1435–6.

12 ibid 1436.

13 ibid 1433–4.

14 ibid 1430.

of England's unwritten constitution' but not of a specific criminal offence.[15] The debate over whether an impeachable offence must be limited to a criminal offence remains a moot point in the United States.[16]

The impeachment trial involved the House of Commons acting as the prosecutor, the Lord Chancellor (or Lord High Steward) presiding over the trial and being assisted by judges on points of law and evidence, and the Lords serving as the jury. There is a distinction, one that was being reinforced at the end of the eighteenth century, between the House of Commons voting to prosecute and the trial governed by the ordinary common law rules of procedure and evidence. It will be argued throughout this book that impeachment should not be seen purely through the lens of history, as this will distract from the normative purpose of impeachment. This purpose evolved over time. At the start of the eighteenth century this was to proceed against political opponents in a manner that would destroy their chances of recovery; however, within several decades impeachment was used only to proceed against those who were accused of treason, financial misconduct, and abuse of position. It is important to consider the range of sanctions, as impeachment could result in loss of life, liberty, or office, and financial penalties.

Defining impeachment for the purpose of this book

The definition provided for impeachment in this section reflects the geographical scope of the research undertaken. Impeachment is concerned with the ability of Parliament, or more precisely the House of Commons, in its capacity as the guardian of the constitution, to have the means of proceeding against ministerial conduct that is perceived to be contrary to accepted constitutional norms. Ministers are, in terms of the democratic exercise of executive power, arguably agents of the House of Commons, and it is the Commons operating within the uncodified constitution of the United Kingdom that are responsible to ensure the integrity of the constitution and to protect it from the effects of ministerial misconduct.

The discussion is informed by English, British, and then UK history, and also by the use of impeachment at a federal presidential level in the United States and within a parliamentary system of government in Denmark. The rationale and justification for the choice of the comparative case studies will be advanced in Chapter 3. Therefore, it should be noted that the inclusion of alternative countries could potentially have altered the definition provided here. Nonetheless, there is a linkage between the three jurisdictions chosen and the origins of the form of impeachment, namely, the influence of the English and British use of impeachment on the drafters of the US Constitution, and the influence of the

15 L Tribe and J Matz, *To End a Presidency: The Power of Impeachment* (Basic Books 2018) 45–6.

16 ibid Chapter 2 'Impeachable Offenses'.

Westminster model of parliamentary government on the drafters of the original Danish Constitution.

The present focus of the definition is on executive accountability and the ability to hold senior ministers to account, to question their decisions, and to seek a determination as to wrongdoing. It would be possible to expand upon this, as impeachment includes judicial accountability in the United States. However, it is submitted that the impeachment of judges is distinct, in terms of rationale and justification, from the impeachment of senior ministers within the executive. In terms of accountability of the judiciary and the mechanisms to remove judges from office in the United Kingdom, this has already been achieved as a result of the Act of Settlement 1701 and the Senior Courts Act 1981.

In the United Kingdom and the United States, the wrongdoing relates to high crimes and misdemeanours, treason, and bribery, although there is considerable uncertainty about the precise scope of what could be an impeachable offence. Broadly speaking, impeachment relates to performance of duties by the office holder, although as a matter of English and British history this could be wider. By way of comparison, in Denmark, impeachment relates to the performance of obligations and duties that are established in law, being the Ministerial Responsibility Act 1964. For the purposes of this book and the application of an impeachment process in the United Kingdom, the wrongdoing, as addressed by a revised form of impeachment, will be solely related to the performance of official duties and the integrity of the constitution. In the United Kingdom, if, by a majority of the House of Commons, the allegations are found to have occurred, those allegations, framed as articles of impeachment, will then at present be delivered to the House of Lords, as the forum for the trial and to determine wrongdoing.

The determination of wrongdoing will combine forms of political and legal accountability. In the United Kingdom and the United States, it is the upper chamber that acts as a jury and determines guilt on the articles of impeachment. The members of the upper chamber, in their capacity as the jury, will be assisted by judges, with the Lord Chancellor or High Steward presiding in United Kingdom, and the Chief Justice of the Supreme Court presiding in the United States. As an alternative format, the Danish Constitution allocates the task of the determination of any wrongdoing to a Court of Impeachment, which consists of both judges and lay members, the latter having been appointed by politicians. For the purposes of this book and the application of impeachment to the United Kingdom, the core requirement that the accusation be separated from any determination is essential, as what impeachment can offer is a way to empower parliamentarians to bring forward allegations, which can then be referred to a separate body (either a specially constituted court or an upper chamber).

In terms of what is achieved if wrongdoing has been determined to have occurred, impeachment can offer a range of sanctions. In the United States, a guilty verdict will result in removal from office and a possible restriction from holding public office in the future, whereas in Denmark, a guilty verdict could result in a custodial sentence. For the United Kingdom, the sanctions for impeachment could include a custodial sentence, a fine, and removal from office. It will be argued in *Accountability, Impeachment and the Constitution: The Case for a Modernised Process in the United Kingdom* that the sanctions in a modernised impeachment process for the UK Parliament should reflect its own indigenous concept and scope of impeachment, which is countering unconstitutional conduct, and be limited to sanctions such as removal from office or being compelled to apologise.

Chapter outline

Accountability, Impeachment and the Constitution: The Case for a Modernised Process in the United Kingdom is divided into three parts: part one on the foundations and use of impeachment, part two on the UK Constitution and accountability, and part three on whether there is a justifiable case for impeachment. Overall, there are nine chapters. The first, which is the present chapter, sets out the central question to be explored and the definitions of impeachment for the purpose of the book.

The purpose of Chapter 2, which addresses the English and British history of impeachment, is to inform the understanding of impeachment for the analysis in Chapter 9 of whether impeachment could operate in the contemporary UK Constitution. The history of impeachment is important for any scholar or constitutional lawyer, both within the United Kingdom and in the United States, wishing to understand what is meant by impeachment. In the case of the British reader, the history is a matter of understanding the past, whilst for the American reader, it is part of understanding the present and the influences upon impeachment within the federal constitution of 1787. The literature on the history of impeachment is considerable. In terms of publications by British scholars, the most recent are *inter alia* Colin Tite on its use in the seventeenth century[17] and the bicentenary collection of essays on Warren Hastings,[18] which was preceded in the 1920s to 1960s by a debate amongst scholars on the origins of impeachment in the fourteenth century.[19] More recent publications tend to focus on one particular impeachment or 'revival' in the 1620s,[20] Dr Henry Sacheverell,[21]

17 CCG Tite, *Impeachment and Parliamentary Judicature in Early Stuart England* (University of London: The Athlone Press 1974).

18 C Nicholson and G Carnall (eds), *The Impeachment of Warren Hastings: Papers from a Bicentenary Commemoration* (Edinburgh University Press 1989).

19 See MV Clarke, *Fourteenth Century Studies* (LS Sutherland and M McKisack eds, Clarendon Press 1968); TFT Plucknett, 'The Origin of Impeachment' (1942) 24 *Transactions of the Royal Historical Society* 47; B Wilkinson, *Studies in the Constitutional History of the Thirteenth and Fourteenth Centuries* (Manchester University Press 1937).

20 A Thrush, 'The Fall of Thomas Howard, 1st Earl of Suffolk and the Revival of Impeachment in the Parliament of 1621' (2018) 37(2) *Parliamentary History* 197.

21 M Knights, *Faction Displayed: Reconsidering the Impeachment of Dr Henry Sacheverell*, Parliamentary History (Wiley-Blackwell 2012).

Warren Hastings,[22] and Viscount Melville.[23] In terms of recent accounts of the history of impeachment, a brief narrative was considered as the second chapter of a report into the proposed impeachment of Tony Blair, and a House of Commons Library briefing note does the same.[24] Earlier accounts such as Hatsell's *Precedents*[25] are invaluable to understanding impeachment. Likewise, impeachment is mentioned as part of general histories, such as Holdsworth's *A History of English Law*[26] or *The Oxford History of England*.[27] In light of the considerable literature on impeachment, Chapter 2 will consider a number of examples of how impeachment has been used, in order to provide an account of the origins, disuse, revival, and abeyance of impeachment, and to construct a historical narrative. The purpose of *Accountability, Impeachment and the Constitution* is not to advance an original account regarding the historical use of impeachment, but rather to put forward examples of how it has been used to inform our understanding as to what is meant by impeachment.

Chapter 3 and Chapter 4 will consider the comparative use of impeachment in two case studies, the United States and Denmark, respectively. The inclusion of such chapters is required in order to gauge how impeachment operates from a comparative perspective and to ascertain how similar to, or indeed different from, the impeachment processes are as regards the model that was last used in the United Kingdom in 1806.[28] In light of the absence of impeachment within the United Kingdom for more than 200 years, it is necessary to address its comparative use. This is because whilst impeachment is arguably still a term known to many people within the United Kingdom, it is most likely to be associated with the use of impeachment in the United States, namely, the impeachment of President Clinton and the two impeachments of President Trump. Therefore, impeachment as a term will carry connotations of its usage

22 J Murray, 'Company Rules: Burke, Hastings, and the Specter of the Modern Liberal State' (2007) 41(1) *Eighteenth-Century Studies* 55.

23 GD Hutchinson, '"The Manager in Distress": Reaction to the Impeachment of Henry Dundas, 1805–7' (2017) 36(2) *Parliamentary History* 198.

24 Gay and Davies (n 1).

25 J Hatsell, *Precedents of Proceedings in the House of Commons under Separate Titles with Observations, Volume IV Relating to Conferences and Impeachment* (2nd edn, Luke Hansard and Sons 1818).

26 Sir William Holdsworth wrote 12 volumes which were published by Methuen in the early twentieth century.

27 For example, see M McKisack, *The Fourteenth Century 1307–1399: The Oxford History of England* (OUP 1959, reprinted 1988).

28 The impeachment of Henry Dundas, Viscount Melville. For a contemporary account of Melville's impeachment and procedure adopted see *The Trial, By Impeachment, of Henry Lord Viscount Melville, for High Crimes and Misdemeanors Before the House of Peers in Westminster Hall, Between the 29th of April and the 17th of May 1806* (Longman, Hurst, Rees and Orme 1806). For the most recent, if brief, description of impeachment, see M Hatton et al., *Erskine May: Parliamentary Practice* (25th edn, Lexis Nexis Butterworths 2019). See also Gay and Davies (n 1) 'Impeachment' and J Simson Caird, 'Impeachment' (House of Commons Library, Briefing Paper CBP-7612).

in the United States and in other jurisdictions, and it is necessary to appreciate how impeachment works. The United States was chosen as a case study for a number of reasons. First, the framers of the US Constitution were aware of the British use of impeachment, and some of the American colonial assemblies had engaged in impeachments prior to the revolution. Second, impeachment was included within the constitution, and this had many similarities to the British process, although there were also many differences, and these will be discussed ahead. Third, one of the most, if not *the* most, high-profile impeachments within living memory, were those of Presidents Clinton and Trump. Fourth, the scholarship by US academics is considerable and draws upon the English and then British practice of impeachment in determining the scope of US federal impeachments.

Denmark was chosen as a case study for the following reasons. First, Denmark is a constitutional monarchy with a parliamentary system of government. Second, Denmark's Constitution was heavily influenced by the 'English' Constitution. Third, Denmark is a Contracting State to the European Convention on Human Rights ('ECHR') and a member of the Council of Europe and is a member of the European Union. Fourth, Denmark has a provision for impeachment within its constitution. Finally, because of the factors previously mentioned, Denmark was chosen as a case study because it demonstrated how impeachment could co-exist in a parliamentary system of government alongside other parliamentary mechanisms of ministerial accountability. These reasons will be considered ahead in far more detail.

It is submitted that Chapter 3 and Chapter 4 will help inform the development of the argument advanced in this book by offering an analysis of how impeachment operates in a comparative perspective. These chapters offer an opportunity to gauge how impeachment might work in the United Kingdom. In the case of the United States, impeachment is limited to removal and/or disqualification from holding office, whereas in Denmark impeachment can result in a custodial sentence. In the United States, impeachment is used as a political weapon and is overwhelmingly dependent on arithmetic in Congress, for example Bill Clinton was impeached because the Republicans controlled the House of Representatives. Thus, impeachment carries connotations of partisanship and being a political weapon and any use of impeachment in the United Kingdom would risk increased partisanship and combative dialogue. The comparison of Denmark within the context of UK impeachment is unique and adds a new understanding of how, by way of a constitutional transplant, impeachment could operate again in the United Kingdom. The Danish experience of impeachment permits a tentative comparison with how the United Kingdom has proceeded against conduct that led to an impeachment in Denmark.

Chapter 5 will, in light of the importance of the theory and practice of executive accountability within the United Kingdom, review the literature on executive accountability, ministerial responsibility, and the debate about whether Parliament is in a state of decline.

Chapter 6 will set out the existing political accountability mechanisms that exist in the United Kingdom and addresses their effectiveness. Chapter 7 will then provide the context for the consideration of whether impeachment could buttress the existing accountability mechanisms. It will do so by setting out an account of the UK Constitution, with its key features, underpinning principles, and characteristics. Finally, Chapter 7 will endeavour to advance a theoretical underpinning for impeachment undertaking such a role, and this will be further developed in Chapter 9. This consideration of theory will draw my argument together and justify the scope and aims of the book.

Chapter 8 will consider the counter-arguments to the use of impeachment in the United Kingdom. These arguments will be addressed, with consideration of how they can be overcome and how these concerns can be mitigated against. Attention will be paid to how impeachment has been perceived in recent history and its attempted use against the then Prime Minister, Tony Blair, in 2004. In particular Chapter 8 will explore how constitutional and legal historians have viewed the emergence of ministerial responsibility to the House of Commons, with the possibility of a vote of censure or no confidence, as superseding impeachment and rendering it obsolete. It is submitted that impeachment is still available and should not be considered obsolete. Rather by revisiting what is meant by impeachment and assessing what such a revised mechanism could provide today, it will be argued not only that impeachment is not obsolete, but also that it potentially offers a way to achieve greater accountability. Chapter 8 will address the contemporary understanding of impeachment, accountability within the constitution, and how a revised form of impeachment could function. It will be argued that impeachment does still exist in the United Kingdom. The argument that the passage of time, or the development of other forms of accountability or responsibility, renders impeachment obsolete in the sense that it is no longer available is a misunderstanding of the origins and use of impeachment. Historically, there were distinct periods of time in which impeachment had been used before falling into abeyance and then being 'revived' at a later date. It may well be argued that both of these previous points render impeachment obsolete in the sense that it is no longer appropriate. However, this is not to be confused with whether it is still actually available to the House of Commons.

Chapter 9 will consider how a blueprint for a modernised form of impeachment would operate in the United Kingdom. It draws upon the review of the political accountability literature in Chapter 5, the arguments set out in Chapter 7 that make a case for the use of a modernised form of impeachment in the United Kingdom, the counter-arguments to impeachment addressed in Chapter 8, the historical review in Chapter 2, and the two comparative case studies in Chapter 3 and Chapter 4, to examine how impeachment might work in the United Kingdom. Chapter 9 will set out how impeachment would operate, the differences between the historical and the proposed modernised form of impeachment, and the justification for how it has been redefined and its purpose subject to necessary constitutional evolution. Finally, in Chapter 9 I will propose an Impeachment Act that sets out the process and procedure, the bodies and institutions that would be involved with the impeachment process, the scope of an impeachable offence, and how safeguards would be built into the process to prevent inappropriate impeachments and respect natural justice, due process, and the human rights of those involved.

Finally, it is important to reflect on the fact that sometimes what has previously been an antiquated concept or procedure can be reformulated for later circumstances. An interesting example is whether treason should be revived. A proposal by Policy Exchange has called for the use of a modernised form of treason to proceed against UK nationals who were members of the Islamic State in Syria. In this case, the proposal was a considered, and not a 'knee-jerk' response, supported by Lord Judge, the former Lord Chief Justice of England and Wales.[29]

29 K Rawlinson, 'Renew Treason Laws to Jail Enemies of the State for Life, Says Thinktank' *The Guardian* (25 July 2018). See R Ekins, P Hennessey, K Mahmood, and T Tugendhat, 'Aiding the Enemy: How and Why to Restore the Law of Treason' *Policy Exchange* (2018). The proposal has been criticised: K Malik, 'If We Want to Build Trust in Society, a New Treason Law Is No Way to Do It' *The Guardian* (29 July 2018).

Part One

Foundations and use of impeachment

2 The history and politics of impeachment

This chapter seeks to place impeachment within its historical context and show through the use of examples how impeachment operated at different times in English and British history and the purpose that it served. This will help inform the discussion on what form a revised procedure of impeachment should take. This chapter consists of four examples that have been selected to demonstrate the changing nature of impeachment in the seventeenth to early nineteenth centuries. It is not intended as a history of impeachment, rather an account of how it was used and for what purpose at a given time in history. Impeachment originated at the end of the fourteenth century during the reign of Edward III and was first used by the Good Parliament of 1376. The last person to be impeached was Viscount Melville in 1806 and he was acquitted by the House of Lords in that same year. Since 1806 there have been several attempts to impeach leading political figures, most recently the Prime Minister Tony Blair in 2004. The four examples illustrate the operation of impeachment following its rediscovery by the House of Commons in 1621. They are, first, the debate surrounding the revival of impeachment in 1621; second, the decline of the party impeachments in the mid-eighteenth century; third, the impeachment of Warren Hastings and the parliamentary efforts to hold the East India Company to account; and, fourth, the impeachment of Viscount Melville.

The focus of this chapter is to inform the understanding of impeachment for the purposes of this book and its role in buttressing accountability at various stages of English and British history. When considering each example, a number of questions will be addressed. First, whether impeachment enabled the House of Commons to hold the executive to account. Second, whether it was used as an alternative to, or in conjunction with, the other accountability mechanisms. Third, how the impeachment was perceived at the time and what this tells us about the nature of impeachment. Fourth, how the use of impeachment in the example can inform our understanding of impeachment for the twenty-first century. These questions will help reflect on the changing purpose of impeachment and the perceived strengths and weaknesses with its use.

DOI: 10.4324/9781003269052-3

The 'revival' of impeachment in early Stuart England

This first example will consider the use of impeachment during the reign of James I and its revival in the 1620s. Impeachment had originated in the Good Parliament of 1376 and, with one exception, had fallen into disuse during the Lancastrian monarchy. The rediscovery of impeachment in the 1620s marked the development of the House of Commons' asserting its position against the monarchy and demanding a far more active role in the developing of policy, the approval of finances, and the conduct of the James I's ministers and favourites. Anderson considers the development of the House of Commons' attempts to hold ministers responsible to Parliament in the late sixteenth and early seventeenth centuries.[1] This phenomenon of an assertive House of Commons using its role in granting money to the Crown as an attempt to define the Crown's policy had originated during the reign of Elizabeth I.[2] Anderson provides examples of how the Commons sought to do this during the 1580s and 1590s.[3] By the time that impeachment was rediscovered by parliamentarians, the relationship between king and Parliament had become strained, a position that would be further stretched during the next two decades until the outbreak of armed conflict.

The example being considered here is the rediscovery of impeachment in the 1620s and what exactly its status was. The original medieval impeachment that had originated during the reign of Edward III had been based on the House of Commons, as a collective body, alleging that royal ministers and other officials had abused their position and demanding that the accused be tried before the House of Lords. This was very much the House of Commons taking the initiative, although the role of the House of Lords in challenging the Council headed by John of Gaunt, the king's son, and being receptive to holding a trial, cannot be underestimated.[4] With some exceptions the impeachments were brought en masse by the House of Commons, protecting individual members from personal liability which they could have incurred had they brought the charges in their own name.[5] Crucially, the House of Lords had refused to condemn the first person to be impeached, Lord Latimer, without a trial, and this secured the role of lawyers in the impeachment proceedings. Therefore, impeachment could be reduced to specific charges drawn up by the House of Commons relating to misconduct and misgovernment, which were presented to the House of Lords, and the House of Lords would then agree to the trial of the accused. It must be remembered that the constitutional developments during the fourteenth century had rendered the

1 CB Anderson, 'Ministerial Responsibility in the 1620's' (1962) 34(4) *The Journal of Modern History* 381.

2 ibid.

3 ibid.

4 See B Wilkinson, *Studies in the Constitutional History of the Thirteenth and Fourteenth Centuries* (Manchester University Press 1937) 88–94.

5 Richard III had tried to seize control of impeachment and use it as a way to proceed against his opponents.

House of Commons a powerful body, as the monarch had conceded that their approval was needed before any taxation could be approved.

Returning to the seventeenth century, in terms of the number of impeachments that took place between 1621 and 1681, Hatsell noted that there were 39, although some instances involved more than one individual being impeached.[6] An important consideration when viewing an impeachment by the House of Commons is whether the House of Commons, in its role of prosecutor, brought the accused before the House of Lords for trial. Roberts argued that many of the impeachments were not actually prosecuted before the House of Lords.[7] To Hatsell, '[t]he forms of proceeding, even in these early instances, particularly in the case of the Duke of Suffolk, in 1450, were much less different from the present, than what at periods so distant might be expected.'[8] This is a contentious point, and one which will be considered when addressing whether impeachment was revived as a continuation of the procedure which was last used in the fifteenth century. It is interesting to note the reason for the each instance of impeachment, which can be summarised as four for corruption, bribes, or embezzlement; nine for misconduct, malversation in office, or offences in administration; five for sedition, publication of a book, false imprisonment, or illegal patents; three for religious reasons; and 14 for treason and/or high crimes and misdemeanours.[9] Of those impeached, seven were senior ministers, four were either ambassadors or navy administrators, five were judges, four were senior religious officials, one was a Member of Parliament (MP), and there were three other individuals.[10]

There is considerable academic debate surrounding the precise nature of the impeachments of 1621. Thrush argued that 'the Commons seems to have come perilously close to rediscovering impeachment in 1610' when it sought access to medieval records in order to proceed against Cowell.[11] Interestingly, Thrush suggests that Sir Francis Bacon, who was then Attorney-General, may have deliberately chosen not to give too much detail about the impeachment of royal ministers.[12] In light of the relationship between James I and the House of Commons, it would be unsurprising that Bacon would be restrained in reacquainting Members of Parliament with, for example, the impeachments of two royal advisors, Lord Latimer in 1376 and the Duke of Suffolk in 1450.

6 J Hatsell, *Precedents of Proceedings in the House of Commons Under Separate Titles with Observations, Volume IV Relating to Conferences and Impeachment* (2nd edn, Luke Hansard and Sons 1818) 104–7.
7 C Roberts, 'The Law of Impeachment in Stuart England: A Reply to Raoul Berger' (1975) 84(7) *The Yale Law Journal* 1431, 1435–6.
8 Hatsell (n 6) 71.
9 ibid 104–7.
10 ibid.
11 A Thrush, 'The Fall of Thomas Howard, 1st Earl of Suffolk and the Revival of Impeachment in the Parliament of 1621' (2018) 37(2) *Parliamentary History* 197, 199.
12 ibid.

The debate surrounding the 'revival' of impeachment is of academic interest, as it goes to the root of what the purpose of impeachment was and whether the House of Commons had, by right and without restriction, the authority to demand that the accused be tried before the House of Lords. It will be argued that impeachment in the form it took in the 1620s was a powerful weapon and one that gave the House of Commons the ability to proceed against those they viewed as exploiting their positions and mismanaging the country, without having to proceed directly against James I.

So, the question is whether the impeachments in the 1620s were direct revivals of the procedure that had last been used against the Duke of Suffolk in 1450. This remains a moot point. It is clear that the personalities of those behind the impeachments were of considerable importance for why and how it was rediscovered. Clarke argues that in 1621 the use of impeachment was not a direct revival as 'the procedure was dead and forgotten.'[13] This meant that Sir Edward Coke, the former Chief Justice of the King's Bench, and other members of the Commons 'were forced to rediscover for themselves essential parts of the medieval process'.[14] Clarke was critical of Coke and his particular understanding of the constitution, as he had not demonstrated an accurate understanding of the procedure and this led to confusion in 1621.[15] Hatsell had observed that Coke had embarked on a precedent hunt in 1620.[16]

By way of placing the use of impeachments in context, White argues that 'Coke's primary objective in the parliaments of 1621 and 1624 was to remedy specific grievances and not to expand parliamentary power, attack royal authority, or engage in constitutional controversies with the king or court.'[17] Furthermore, White argued that 'one should not overestimate the importance of constitutional conflict in James I's last two parliaments', even if '[i]n retrospect, Parliament's prosecutions of important crown servants like Bacon and Middlesex look like attacks on the crown.'[18] White is clear that James I had no intention to defend those impeached, even if he did unsuccessfully suggest a different way of trying Bacon than a trial before the Lords.[19] White's assessment of the relationship between James I and his last two Parliaments is a sound one, as the civil wars of the 1640s were not an inevitable outcome of the testy relationship between the

13 MV Clarke, *Fourteenth Century Studies* (LS Sutherland and M McKisack eds, Clarendon Press 1968) 266.

14 ibid.

15 ibid 267.

16 Hatsell (n 6) 108–9.

17 SD White, *Sir Edward Coke and the Grievances of the Commonwealth* (Manchester University Press 1979) 142.

18 ibid.

19 ibid 144. See also JP Kenyon, *The Stuart Constitution: Documents and Commentary* (2nd edn, Cambridge University Press 1989) 88, for James' willingness to let the Commons proceed against his officials.

two, and therefore any disagreements should not be overplayed. Indeed, JR Tanner observes that

> [t]he revival of impeachment in 1621 was not a far-sighted political measure aimed at the removal of Ministers of State but a natural result of the exercise of the traditional function of the Lower House in searching out and redressing grievances.[20]

The House of Commons' target in 1621 was Sir Giles Mompesson and his control of a controversial monopoly.[21] This was not high constitutional accountability, but specific grievances being pursued through a novel mechanism.

Ogilvie highlights the danger that impeachment posed, as it could challenge the Lancastrian model of government and permit the Commons to trespass upon the idea that ministers were responsible only to the king and not to Parliament.[22] However, as Ogilvie observes, Mompesson's impeachment focused on monopolies, as opposed to his role as a minister.[23] The Commons by themselves could use the argument that Mompesson was in breach of parliamentary privilege.[24] The Commons had initially found Mompesson guilty and had passed sentence on him.[25] This action was the precursor to the rediscovery of impeachment. What came next was that the House of Commons, realising that their powers were limited, formed a committee 'to search for precedents "to shew how far and for what offences the power of this House doth extend to punish delinquents against the State as well as those who offend against this House" '.[26] This led to the rediscovery of impeachment. Tanner argues that it was the Commons' 'discovery of their own impotence' that led to the revival of impeachment.[27] This is a sound observation and reflects the increased assertiveness of the Commons and its frustration with its present powers.

According to Plucknett, 'The revival of impeachment under James I was an astonishing feat of antiquarianism.'[28] This was true: it was bringing back a procedure that had not been used since 1450, and before mainly confined to the last decades of the fourteenth century. However, in 1621 the House of Commons was very willing to accept that there had been a time when it had exercised the power

20 JR Tanner, *Constitutional Documents of the Reign of James I: 1603–1625* (Cambridge University Press 1930, reprinted 1961) 321.
21 ibid.
22 C Ogilvie, *The King's Government and the Common Law* 1471–1641 (Greenwood Press 1981) 141.
23 Tanner (n 20) 321.
24 ibid 321–2.
25 White (n 17) 145.
26 Tanner (n 20) 321–2.
27 ibid 322.
28 TFT Plucknett, 'Impeachment and Attainder' (1953) Fifth Series (3) *Transactions of the Royal Historical Society* 145, 157.

to accuse its opponents and demand judgment by the Lords, and that not only had this power been asserted, it was also accepted by the House of Lords and the king. It is interesting to note how Adams perceives the rediscovery of impeachment:

> No statute was passed against monopolies by the parliament of 1621, but the investigation of them led to a much more important constitutional result, the revival of impeachments, and their revival in such a way, so clearly for the punishment of acknowledged corruption, that the king, even if he had wished to do so, could find no ground on which to object. Thus, without appearing openly to attack the king, the most effective weapon which the middle ages had invented for combatting an arbitrary government was restored to the hands of parliament.[29]

This restoration can be best seen as a by-product and one seized upon in the Long Parliament to proceed directly against Charles I's leading advisors.

White argued that the discovery of Parliament's judicial powers, whilst amounting to 'a sharp break with the practices of Tudor parliaments', was an extension of the Commons' 'more traditional attempts to remedy grievances' by placing the blame on a scapegoat.[30] However, it would soon allow the Commons to attack the king's key advisors and be used 'as a political weapon'.[31] According to Tite, 'It is important to emphasise that impeachment did not, as is often assumed, re-emerge in its full form in 1621. Such an assumption obscures the very important developments in judicial procedure which occurred in both Houses in the 1620s.'[32] Tite argues that the use of the word impeachment presents 'a terminological problem' due to the difficulty in comprehending its meaning.[33] The first use was in 1626 and the proceedings of 1621 and 1624 were not described as impeachments.[34] Tite notes that the word impeachment was used in the Commons' proceedings against Floyd in 1621,[35] but not those of Mompesson, or Francis Bacon, the Lord Chancellor:

> [T]here is little justification for describing the trials of 1621 – with the possible but curious exception of Floyd's – as impeachments. . . . What is much more important to notice . . . is that various procedures were tried and that the Commons learnt from their mistakes. . . [and yet] whatever the precise character of the cases of 1621 parliamentary judicature had been revived.[36]

29 GB Adams, *A Constitutional History of England* (Jonathan Cape 1921) 280.
30 White (n 17) 144.
31 ibid, see Kenyon (n 19) 89.
32 CCG Tite, *Impeachment and Parliamentary Judicature in Early Stuart England* (University of London: The Athlone Press 1974) 219.
33 ibid 41.
34 ibid.
35 Tanner (n 20) 319–21.
36 ibid 146–7.

This point has been challenged by Stacy:

> Tite's study . . . is in part misleading. If impeachment, loosely defined, was revived in 1621, parliamentary judicature was not . . . [as since the fifteenth century] both Houses of Parliament had continued to share parliamentary judicature . . . in the form of bills of attainder.[37]

Stacy continued to argue that the Commons chose to impeach rather than use attainder in order to overcome previous difficulties, and that had the Lords decided to proceed against the individual it would have used attainder.[38] Alongside Mompesson, Sir Francis Mitchell was also impeached because of his use of monopolies and was also found guilty by the House of Lords.

The next person to be impeached in 1621 was Francis Bacon, Viscount St Alban, who was accused of accepting bribes from litigants in his capacity as Lord Chancellor. It had become clear that the king would not save him from being tried before the Lords and therefore Bacon confessed that he had indeed been corrupt.[39] Ogilvie is clear that James I allowed Bacon to be treated as a scapegoat and, although he was guilty, he had not acted differently from other Lord Chancellors.[40] The impeachment was viewed by his biographer as 'a political campaign against the king's chief favourite, Buckingham' and 'orchestrated by Edward Coke and Sir Lionel Cranfield, who were both his enemies'.[41] In a recent article, Thrush argues that Coke, who was '[responsible] for the rediscovery of impeachment', may have always intended to use this procedure against Bacon:

> There are several reasons for supposing that Coke had Lord Chancellor Bacon in his sights from the outset. . . . By late February 1621, Coke had the means, the motive, and the opportunity, to destroy Bacon. He hated the lord chancellor, whose success contrasted with his own disgrace and dismissal. He also knew that there were men waiting in the wings ready to complain to parliament that Bacon was corrupt. . . . However, these factors do suggest that the parliamentary attacks on Mompesson and Mitchell, and the Commons' uncertainty about how to proceed, provided Coke with an opportunity that was simply too good to miss.[42]

37 WR Stacy, 'Impeachment, Attainder, and the "Revival" of Parliamentary Judicature Under the Early Stuarts' (1992) 11(1) *Parliamentary History* 40.

38 ibid 55.

39 M Peltonen, 'Bacon, Francis, Viscount St Alban' in *Oxford Dictionary of National Biography* (OUP 2004, Online 4 October 2007).

40 C Ogilvie, *The King's Government and the Common Law 1471–1641* (Greenwood Press 1981) 142.

41 Peltonen (n 39).

42 Thrush (n 11) 210–11.

Clarke regards the impeachment of Mompesson, Bacon, and Mitchell as more akin to the petition against Lee in 1368[43] than the impeachments of 1376, as 'the Commons had done little more than to demand inquiry' and therefore had been observers during the actual trial.[44] Kenyon observed that '[t]he very word "impeachment" was not used in 1621, nor in 1624, and the Commons were not invited to act as prosecuting counsel until 1626, against Buckingham.'[45] Indeed there were no trials in the case of Mompsesson who escaped, or Bacon who had 'pleaded guilty', while Mitchell's guilt 'was obvious enough'.[46] It is clear that caution must be used in seeking to describe the proceedings of 1621 as impeachments in the sense that they reflected the medieval practice. However, there is a danger in not accepting that they were in part impeachments, even if not achieving the full medieval powers of the Commons until 1626, as otherwise there is a risk of obscuring the procedural innovation that had occurred in 1621. What we can see here though is that the House of Commons quickly developed what was meant by impeachment within a few years.

In 1624 Lionel Cranfield, the Earl of Middlesex, was impeached. As Cranfield had disagreed with the Duke of Buckingham's policy of going to war, the Duke of Buckingham had decided to use Parliament to remove him.[47] This demonstrated the ability of impeachment to be used as a tool by the Crown and its advisors, who as in the 1380s, could see possibilities for proceeding against their own opponents. Buckingham was successful in achieving his aim, as Cranfield was accused of corruption and fined £50,000. Cranfield's biographer regarded the evidence against him as 'incomplete' and that he was 'harshly dealt with'.[48] Tanner argues that the impeachments of Bacon and Middlesex were important as they were 'an assertion of the responsibility of ministers to the law' and not just the monarch.[49] Clarke argues that the impeachment of Middlesex in 1624 moved closer towards an indictment, with the formalisation of the charge against the accused.[50]

Anderson views 1624 as a crucial year because 'the house of commons had an opportunity to implement . . . various proposals for parliamentary control over the expenditure of subsidies.'[51] This opportunity arose from Prince Charles and the Duke of Buckingham's attempts to counter the king's foreign policy, which they disagreed with, and they used Parliament as a way to do this. To achieve this, they 'browbeat [the king] into summoning parliament in 1624 and asking

43 Clarke (n 13) 267–8.
44 ibid.
45 Kenyon (n 19) 88.
46 ibid.
47 MJ Braddick, 'Cranfield, Lionel, First Earl of Middlesex' in *Oxford Dictionary of National Biography* (OUP 2004, Online 23 September 2004).
48 ibid.
49 Tanner (n 20) 322.
50 Clarke (n 13) 267–8.
51 Anderson (n 1) 381.

it for advice on foreign policy. Parliament urged the king to break off the treaty negotiations and to declare war on Spain. But James resisted this advice.'[52] Anderson is clear that James I understood the dangers to the Crown of an assertive parliamentary involvement in the development of policy, whereas Prince Charles and Buckingham, 'like King Henry VIII before them . . . did not hesitate to enhance the power and prestige of parliament by making it an instrument of their policy'.[53] This analogy is important, as whilst Henry VIII had been able to control his Parliaments, as evidenced by the key role they played during his reign in implementing his policies and proceeding against his enemies, Charles could not. Having succeeded in forcing the king to change his policy towards Spain, Prince Charles and Buckingham failed to deliver military success against Spain and Charles married Princess Henrietta Maria of France.[54] The consequence of these events was that the Parliament of 1625 was hostile to both the Crown's policy and Buckingham's influence.[55] The House of Commons was critical of the policy and the king's choice of advisor.[56] Anderson observes that the House of Commons 'were raising the question of ministerial responsibility and challenging the sovereignty of the crown, because Buckingham had the unqualified support of Charles'.[57] Buckingham had to defend the policy before Parliament.[58]

Consequently, the Parliament of 1626 saw the House of Commons conduct investigations into the Crown's policies, demanding records and the attendance of witnesses and scrutinising how the subsidy granted in 1624 had been spent.[59] As part of its investigation, the House of Commons sought to examine the Councillors of War on the advice that they had given to the Duke of Buckingham. This was refused by Charles I, and it hindered the House of Commons' attempt to proceed against Buckingham. It was not until the impeachment of the Duke of Buckingham in 1626 that 'the full procedure of impeachment was finally recovered' and it could be seen as a criminal indictment presented by the Commons.[60] Tite observed: '[a]s the records describe Buckingham as having been impeached . . . it is legitimate to suggest that Buckingham's case may have been the first impeachment in England in the seventeenth century.'[61] This was the first instance of the Commons indicting rather than presenting articles to the Lords; the Commons prosecuted and received Buckingham's answers to their charges.[62] The impeachment of Buckingham was different because the charges against him stemmed from

52 ibid 382.
53 ibid.
54 ibid 384.
55 ibid 381.
56 ibid.
57 ibid 384.
58 ibid.
59 ibid 385.
60 Clarke (n 13) 268.
61 Tite (n 32) 205.
62 ibid 205–6.

his perceived incompetence in office, rather than 'crimes and grievances committed in office' as in the case of the others.[63] Tite observed that '[h]itherto, the attack had been largely legal in nature; now it had become mainly political.'[64]

The 1620s saw the rediscovery of impeachment by the House of Commons, although there is much debate over whether this was a direct revival and just when it could be properly regarded as an impeachment. It is clear that historians have either downplayed or highlighted the constitutional significance of impeachment. Whilst impeachment could be used to proceed against leading officials within the executive, this was not why and how it was used at first, even though Bacon was the Lord Chancellor and Mompesson a senior advisor. Impeachment did however allow for senior members of the executive to be impeached by the House of Commons, where there was a real disagreement over policy, as in the case of the Duke of Buckingham, and it was used in this way once more against the Earl of Strafford and Archbishop Laud during the first years of the Long Parliament. We can see that impeachment presented a unique opportunity to demand that those accused by the House of Commons were punished and held to account, as without impeachment the Commons could frustrate policy by refusing to approve taxation but could not demand that certain officials be tried. In terms of how impeachment in the 1620s could inform how we understand impeachment today, it is important to appreciate why it was used again and the purpose it served before its later association with party impeachments. It was a product of its time, being used by the House of Commons for a specific purpose, a purpose that over time would change. It is possible to see a core purpose of facilitating greater accountability and giving the House of Commons, as the representatives of the people, a greater role in challenging conduct or policy that was seen as contrary to the national interest. Its rediscovery in 1621 demonstrates how impeachment can lay dormant for a long period of time, only to be rediscovered when the House of Commons seeks greater powers and a clearer role in pursuing grievances. If impeachment were to be used again today, it would be argued that it would be concerned with the failure to abide by the accepted norms of the constitution, something that the House of Commons might appreciate that at present it has limited powers to proceed against and that is arguably at present frustrated by the state of the relationship between Parliament and the executive.

The decline of the party impeachments and the development of the need for a ministry to maintain the confidence of the House of Commons

The next example is the use of impeachment at the start of the eighteenth century and how within four decades it had been stopped being used as a politically partisan weapon to proceed against former ministers. This is not to say that there

63 ibid 206.
64 ibid.

were not political calculations made by those who supported later impeachments, but that the main motivation was not to punish political rivals and instead focus on specific grievances. This is very important in understanding the evolution of impeachment in the eighteenth century, as the other impeachments that took place since the decision not to impeach Walpole in 1742 related to the 1745 Jacobite Rebellion,[65] the perceived abuses that took place in the administration of territory controlled by the East India Company in India,[66] and allegations of corruption.[67]

A reflection on contemporary literature at the start of the eighteenth century

It is first important to consider how impeachment was regarded by contemporary commentators. The first anonymous pamphlet to be considered in this section is *The Justice of Parliaments: On Corrupt Minister, in Impeachments and Bills of Attainder, Considered*[68] which was a direct response to an earlier publication, *An Enquiry Into the Origin of Parliamentary Impeachments: With A History of the Most Remarkable Proceedings of That Kind From the Beginning to Our Time.*[69] Both publications set out contemporary knowledge of impeachment and how this type of procedure had developed alongside bills of attainder and trial by peers. It is important to consider how contemporary writers viewed impeachment and its place in the early eighteenth century. With such pamphlets, one of which is dedicated to a leading noble, the context must be considered, namely, that the author was expressing their agenda, at a time when impeachment was used as part of party politics.

The author of *The Justice of Parliaments* argued in support of impeachment and set out five reasons in support. The first was:

> [T]hat Trials by Impeachment must be more just and impartial than those of an inferior jurisdiction in any court whatsoever . . . because the prosecutors upon an Impeachment have neither personal Malice, nor personal interest, to satisfy; too often the motives of inferior prosecutions. They are only the Agents for an injured Nation to demand justice upon an offending Minister; and to present the Complaint and prepare the Proofs, in order to

65 Lord Lovat was impeached in 1747; for more details see EM Furgol, 'Fraser, Simon, Eleventh Lord Lovat' in *Oxford Dictionary of National Biography* (OUP 2004).

66 Warren Hastings, the first Governor-General of Bengal, was impeached in 1787.

67 Viscount Melville, a member of Pitt's government, was impeached in 1806.

68 Anon, *The Justice of Parliaments: On Corrupt Minister, in Impeachments and Bills of Attainder, Consider'd* (London: J. Roberts in Warwick-Lane 1725). Please note that the original spelling has been kept.

69 Anon, *An Enquiry into the Origin of Parliamentary Impeachments: With a History of the Most Remarkable Proceedings of That Kind From the Beginning to Our Time* (London: J Peele at Locke's Head, in Pater-Noster-Row 1745).

> his Conviction; and all they can get by the consequence of the Trial, is the Satisfaction of doing their Country Justice, and bringing a transgressor of its Laws to Punishment.[70]

The fourth was:

> BECAUSE though *Parliament* has a *Legislative* Capacity, yet in their *Judicial* [capacity] they act according to the known Laws of the Realm . . . and the Measure of the One being what was legally just; and the Other, what was prudentially and politically fit; yet that these were not to be confounded in Judgment, nor must they piece up want of Legality with Matter of Convenience.[71]

Here we can see impeachment being portrayed as the fairest way of achieving justice and that those who prosecuted from the House of Commons were not biased against the accused. This would appear to present impeachment as devoid of political bias. This interpretation of impeachment is perhaps misleading in its simplicity and ought to be regarded as normative in nature, as opposed to accurately describing the motivations of those who sought to impeach individuals in the seventeenth and eighteenth centuries. Nonetheless, the concept of justice (and consequentially doing one's country an injustice through unpopular ministerial decision-making) is relative, and it would be far too simplistic to view any factional impeachment against political rivals as being devoid of any concern for the national interest and the need to hold their rivals to account. We can also see the distinction being made between law and politics, and that the impeachment trial must be founded in law and not political expediency. This need for legality, in terms of the offences contained within the articles of impeachment, and the rules of evidence followed during the trial, were certainly taken seriously in the later eighteenth century as evidenced by the trial of Warren Hastings.[72] The requirement for evidence was not required to enact an Act of Attainder.[73]

This view that impeachments were impartial and should be welcomed as an opportunity for investigating potential wrongdoing by ministers was a point made by the anonymous pamphlet concerning the Peace of Utrecht negotiated between 1713–14, which brought the War of the Spanish Succession to a close. The use of 'Without Passion' in the pamphlet's title seeks to argue that it is impartial: *Reasons (Without Passion) for the Impeachment of Corrupt Ministers.*[74] The author argued, 'THE Design of Impeachments in Parliament in general, being only an Honest Desire to be rightly informed, where Miscarriages in

70 Anon (n 68) 22.
71 ibid 25.
72 See ahead.
73 Anon (n 68) 35.
74 ibid.

GOVERNMENT lye',[75] and he called for a bipartisan impeachment, by Whigs and Tories, to impeach those responsible for negotiating peace.[76] However, it is clear that the author was partisan against those he wished to see impeached, as this would 'satisfy their late Allies, for the most barbarous, and inhuman Breach of Faith'.[77] Another anonymous pamphlet, published in 1715 by David Scott in Edinburgh and by J Roberts in London, *Arguments Pro and Con in Several Speeches for and Against an Impeachment*, sets out the speeches that could be made to advocate or counter the impeachment of those ministers responsible for making peace with France, which perhaps offers an account of the arguments that would have been familiar to its contemporaries.[78]

The political consequences of the accession of George I in 1714

The death of Queen Anne in 1714 gave rise to the impeachment of the leading Tory ministers who had served in her government. The main rationale for the impeachments was the decision to make peace with France and its allies in the Treaties of Utrecht, which were controversial with the Whig opposition. Pincus observes that to the Whigs, 'the tory-negotiated peace of 1713. . . threw away Marlborough's battlefield gains.'[79] Therefore, the Tory ministers were impeached by the new Whig government upon the accession of George I in 1714. It is important to consider that political impeachments had occurred in the seventeenth century, as during the reign of William III and Anne the Tories and Whigs had used their positions in government for their political advantage and to proceed against their opponents.[80] Hoffer and Hull observe that '[t]hroughout the 1690s and 1700s Whigs sought to prevent Tories from entering government and Tories sought revenge against Whigs, resulting in articles of impeachment based upon the defendants' political miscalculations and mistaken policy.'[81] Plumb concludes that 'it is impossible to deny the ferocity of party strife, Whig versus Tory, in Parliament and in the constituencies' and the impeachments that took place 'were all party impeachments'.[82] Pincus observes that '[p]arty divisions cut deeply into British society' at all levels and not just the 'rarefied metropolitan elite'.[83] The

75 ibid 5.
76 ibid 5–6.
77 ibid 13.
78 *Arguments Pro and Con in Several Speeches for and Againft an Impeachment* (London: J. Roberts, near the Oxford Arms in Warwick Lane 1715).
79 S Pincus, 'Addison's Empire: Whig Conceptions of Empire in the Early 18th Century' in M Knights (ed), *Faction Displayed: Reconsidering the Impeachment of Dr Henry Sacheverell*, Parliamentary History (Wiley-Blackwell 2012) 99.
80 For commentary see JH Plumb, 'The Rage of Party' in *The Growth of Political Stability in England 1675–1725* (Macmillan 1967).
81 PC Hoffer and NEH Hull, *Impeachment in America, 1635–1805* (Yale University Press 1984) 7.
82 Plumb (n 80) 157.
83 Pincus (n 79) 101.

essential problem was that from 1689 no government could manage the House of Commons 'for more than a session or two'.[84] This was changed with Sir Robert Walpole and the development of a 'Venetian Oligarchy'.[85]

The use of impeachment at the beginning of the eighteenth century clearly demonstrates the politically motivated use of impeachment. The impeachment of Lord Somers, the Earl of Portland, Lord Halifax, and the Earl of Oxford, all of them former Whig ministers in 1701, was brought by the Tories, but proved to be unsuccessful. The impeachment of Dr Henry Sacheverell was brought by the Whigs on the grounds that he had preached seditious sermons.[86] According to Speck,

> [the] Whigs were outraged that so far from linking 5 November 1688 with the Gunpowder Plot [the sermon] had actually denied that there was any such link by denying that there had been resistance in the revolution. The whig government determined to bring him to book.[87]

Hoffer and Hull regard Sacheverell's impeachment as '[t]he most notorious of these political impeachments'.[88] Speck observes that 'the trial was more a political than judicial process. Brute votes in a very partisan house of lords were to decide the outcome' and the sentence was far more lenient than what the ministry had originally wanted.[89] The impeachment, albeit successful, backfired and led to the Tories returning to government.[90] Holdsworth referred to the Whigs embarking on the 'suicidal step of impeaching Sacheverell' against the advice of Lord Cowper, the Lord Chancellor.[91] Therefore, it is possible to see how impeachment had been used as a political weapon and that the misconduct of the essentially amounted to political grievances, and this arguably risked discrediting the impeachment process.

The parliamentary action against Queen Anne's former ministers is important, as it was a way for the Whigs to proceed against their political opponents, without

84 Plumb (n 80) 158.

85 ibid. See generally 'The Triumph of the Venetian Oligarchy' in Plumb (n 80).

86 For commentary on different aspects of the trial see Knights, *Faction Displayed: Reconsidering the Impeachment of Dr Henry Sacheverell.* Cowan presents the impeachment trial as allowing the Whigs and Tories to set out different views of the Glorious Revolution, B Cowan, 'The Spin Doctor: Sacheverell's Trial Speech and Political Performance in the Divided Society' in M Knights (ed), *Faction Displayed: Reconsidering the Impeachment of Dr Henry Sacheverell*, Parliamentary History (Wiley-Blackwell 2012) 32–3.

87 WA Speck, 'Sacheverell, Henry' in *Oxford Dictionary of National Biography* (OUP 2004).

88 Hoffer and Hull (n 81) 7.

89 WA Speck, 'The Current State of Sacheverell Scholarship' in M Knights (ed), *Faction Displayed: Reconsidering the Impeachment of Dr Henry Sacheverell*, Parliamentary History (Wiley-Blackwell 2012) 22.

90 Plumb observed that '[i]mpeachments, as Sacheverell's had shown, could boomerang' (n 80) 160).

91 W Holdsworth, *A History of English Law, Volume XII* (Methuen & Co Ltd 1938) 196.

permitting them to rely upon the fact that the policy was authorised by the monarch. According to Robertson, 'The Whigs emphasised the doctrine of ministerial responsibility. They refused to admit the late Queen's authority as an adequate reason for exonerating her Ministers from liability, and thereby the precedent laid down in Danby's 1678 case was made good.'[92] The Earl of Danby had unsuccessfully attempted in his defence to rely upon the fact Charles I had authorised the decisions for which he was now being impeached. In 1715, 'the ministers, backed, if not driven by their whig majority, determined to clinch their victory by effectively depriving their chief adversaries of all power in the future.'[93]

It is interesting to consider the way that the House of Commons proceeded against the former ministers. Henry St John, Viscount Bolingbroke, was jointly responsible for the Treaty of Utrecht in 1713 which ended the war.[94] Bolingbroke had failed to have James II's son succeed Anne in 1714, as his colleagues, including Oxford, supported George I.[95] The new king dismissed Bolingbroke from government. Realising that the Whigs were now going to proceed against him on the basis of his ministerial conduct, Bolingbroke left England to avoid impeachment, and this led to his having an Act of Attainder passed against him.[96] Another individual to be impeached in 1715 was James Butler, the Duke of Ormond. The Duke of Ormond had commanded British troops against the French and had been instructed to restrain from actively fighting the enemy.[97] Ormond had also been in contact with James II's son in order to arrange for him to succeed Queen Anne.[98] Upon the death of Queen Anne he was proceeded against by the Whigs and fled to France.[99] Thomas Wentworth, the Earl of Strafford, was also impeached for helping to negotiate the Treaty of Utrecht.[100] There was also an attempt to impeach Robert Harley, the Earl of Oxford. However, this was

92 C Grant Robertson, *England Under the Hanoverians* (Methuen & Co Ltd 1953) 20. Unlike attainder, impeachment did not require the monarch's permission for the accused to be convicted and sentenced. However, the monarch could intervene by way of a royal pardon and bring the impeachment to an end. This would frustrate the Commons as it could prevent a trial taking place before the Lords. This occurred in 1679 when the use of a royal pardon by the Earl of Danby was challenged by the House of Commons. The Act of Settlement 1701 abolished the ability of the Crown to pardon prior to judgment by the Lords, although the Crown could grant a pardon to mitigate against the sentence. The Act states: '[t]hat no Pardon under the Great Seal of England be pleadable to an impeachment by the Commons in Parliament'.

93 B Williams, *The Whig Supremacy 1714–1760: The Oxford History of England* (2nd edn, OUP 1962, reprinted 1987) 156.

94 ibid.

95 ibid.

96 ibid.

97 S Handley, 'Butler, James, Second Duke of Ormond' in *Oxford Dictionary of National Biography* (OUP 2004).

98 ibid.

99 ibid.

100 Williams (n 93) 156.

unsuccessful due to the 'use of a technical point of privilege'.[101] Oxford had served as Anne's 'Prime Minister' and in conjunction with Bolingbroke was responsible for the Treaty of Utrecht.[102] Oxford was dismissed in 1714 because he had clashed with Bolingbroke and the queen had sided with his opponent.[103] George I disliked Oxford because '[h]e was associated with the treaty of Utrecht, which in the new king's view had been a betrayal of the allies – of which the electorate of Hanover was one.'[104] In 1715, he was impeached by the Commons and imprisoned in the Tower of London. Although there were 22 articles of impeachment presented in the Commons, he was never tried.[105] He was 'eventually released as the ministry failed to find sufficiently damaging evidence against him'.[106] Despite being acquitted by the Lords, Oxford was ostracised by the king.[107] The attempted impeachment of Oxford is important, as Robertson observes that it was

> the last example of a purely political impeachment – the transition from the legal to the moral responsibility of Ministers, from the criminal liability of a politician arraigned by political foes for political blunders to lose his head to the political liability to lose his office.[108]

The significance of this transformation is telling, as ministers could lose office without facing criminal liability for the policies that they pursued whilst in office. Williams considers the impeachments to be 'unnecessary' as the king did not have confidence in the Tories and that they 'were the last of that series of purely political impeachments' used to proceed against the king's servants.[109] This meant that the ministers would have been dismissed by the king and replaced their opponents, without the need to use impeachment.

The decision not to impeach Walpole in 1742

The next attempted impeachment was that of the first Prime Minister, Sir Robert Walpole, now the Earl of Orford, who had resigned his position after losing the confidence of the House of Commons in 1742. Langford observed that 'what truly created a consensus against Walpole was not so much his reluctance to go

101 Grant Robertson (n 92) 37.
102 WA Speck, 'Harley Robert, First Earl of Oxford and Mortimer' in *Oxford Dictionary of National Biography* (OUP 2004).
103 ibid.
104 ibid.
105 ibid.
106 HT Dickinson, 'St John, Henry, Styled Viscount Bolingbroke' in *Oxford Dictionary of National Biography* (OUP 2004).
107 Speck (n 102)
108 Grant Robertson (n 92) 37.
109 Williams (n 93) 156.

to war [with Spain] as his lack of enthusiasm for waging it.'[110] In 1741, there were motions from the House of Commons and House of Lords requesting that the king dismiss Walpole.[111] The motion was defeated by 290 to 106 votes in the House of Commons.[112] However, despite the support shown in the previous motion, it had now become apparent that Walpole had only a slim majority in the Commons.[113] This majority was increased later that year.[114] However, in 1742, the government almost lost its majority on a vital vote, which was 'essentially a motion of confidence was so small – 253 votes to 250 – that it was clear that normal government business could no longer be conducted in parliament'.[115] Soon afterwards Walpole resigned as Prime Minister, and his opponents sought to impeach him. The attempt was unsuccessful and, according to Todd, '[s]ince then there has been no instance of an endeavour to proceed by impeachment against a minister of the crown for political offences not affecting his personal character.'[116] This is significant, as the impeachment of Viscount Melville in 1806 was not for a political offence, but for allegations of financial misconduct. Holdsworth observes that '[a]fter [Walpole's] resignation there was some talk of an impeachment or a bill of pains and penalties; but it is a testimony to the new spirit which Walpole had infused into party politics, that this talk came to nothing.'[117] In order to encourage evidence to be presented to the select committee that was established to put together a case for impeachment, the Commons passed an indemnity bill, but this was rejected by the Lords.[118] Walpole's decision to resign after realising that he had lost control of the House of Commons is an important development in the emergence of ministerial responsibility to the House of Commons. Robertson notes that 'the collapse of the retributive measures one more decisive step was taken towards substituting for impeachment deprivation of office as the penalty for failure to retain the confidence of the representative Chamber of the Legislature.'[119]

Impeachments became less political during the course of the eighteenth century. According to Thomas, impeachment, after the Whig attack on Queen Anne's former ministers, 'ceased to serve political purposes, and was retained primarily for use against rebels, traitors, and men accused of misuse of public

110 P Langford, *A Polite and Commercial People: England 1727–1783, the New Oxford History of England* (Guild Publishing 1989) 52.

111 ibid 56.

112 ibid.

113 S Taylor, 'Walpole, Robert, First Earl of Orford' in *Oxford Dictionary of National Biography* (OUP 2004).

114 ibid.

115 ibid.

116 A Todd, *On Parliamentary Government in England: Its Origin, Development, and Political Operation*, Volume II (Longmans, Green, and Co. 1869) 125–6.

117 W Holdsworth, *A History of English Law*, Volume X (Methuen & Co Ltd 1938) 76.

118 ibid.

119 Grant Robertson (n 92) 89.

funds'.[120] It can be seen that the impeachment of Lord Macclesfield in 1724 for misusing litigants' money and selling judicial offices,[121] and the impeachment of the Jacobean Lords in 1717 for siding with the pretender, James Stuart, were brought for purposes that were not entirely dictated by political considerations. Impeachment, Thomas observed, 'was complex, time-consuming and unsuited to an age when incompetent or unpopular politicians no longer risked the loss of life, liberty or property'.[122] This move towards the confidence vote is evidenced by the failure of Walpole's opponents to procure his impeachment.[123] The conflict between the Whigs and Tories, that played out at the start of the century and had seen multiple impeachments, was eventually superseded by the emergence of ministerial responsibility. This required that a government needed to retain the confidence of the House of Commons, and failure to maintain this confidence would lead to the obligation to resign and a new ministry to be appointed by the king.[124] The early eighteenth century was a time of significant constitutional development and secured the acceptance of Parliament's legal sovereignty following the events of the Glorious Revolution between 1688 and 1689. This does not mean that it universally accepted that impeachment against ministers no longer served a purpose, as Thomas cites an 'eccentric protest' in 1730 by Edmund Bacon MP, who had argued that impeachment was better than the House continually criticising a minister.[125] It can be seen though that with the decision not to impeach Walpole, that impeachment was no longer viewed as an appropriate way to proceed against a former minister.

Finally, it is interesting to note how writers on the British constitution viewed impeachment by the point at which the House of Commons had declined to impeach Walpole. In his book, *The Spirit of the Laws*, Baron de Montesquieu observed that the use of impeachment could be justified in order to ensure that those running the country could be held to account and tried before a body able to try them without partiality and passion.[126] This observation

120 PDG Thomas, *The House of Commons in the Eighteenth Century* (Gregg Revivals 1992) 36.

121 For a commentary on the Earl of Macclesfield's impeachment see AA Hanham, 'Parker, Thomas, First Earl of Macclesfield' in *Oxford Dictionary of National Biography* (OUP 2004). Macclesfield had sought to defend his conduct as being common practice. However, every one of the 93 Lords present voted to find him guilty. Holdsworth observed: 'I think that there is no doubt that he was justly condemned. There is still less doubt that his impeachment and condemnation had the most salutary effects' (Holdsworth, Volume XII (n 91) 206).

122 Thomas (n 120) 36.

123 See Thomas (n 120) 37–40 for the development of the confidence vote and the censure of ministers.

124 See for example Hoffer and Hull (n 81) 8, who observed that 'the English experiment with impeachment was over. Even the notorious case of Warren Hastings . . . failed to reawaken the Parliament's old fascination for impeachment.'

125 Thomas (n 120) 37.

126 C de Secondat, 'Baron de Montesquieu' (1748) *The Spirit of Laws* 180–1.

arguably related to the ideal, rather than the reality, a state of affairs driven by overt political considerations. Whether impeachment could be used without partiality and passion was tested with the later impeachments of Warren Hastings in 1787 and Viscount Melville in 1806. These two impeachments will be explored ahead.

Sir William Blackstone, the leading jurist of the eighteenth century, provided a historic account of impeachment within the English system of government in his *Commentaries on the Laws of England* published between 1765 and 1769. Blackstone observed:

> [T]he true excellence of the English government, [is] that all the parts of it form a mutual check upon each other. . . . [The] executive power is . . . checked and kept within due bounds by the two houses, through the privilege they have of inquiring into, impeaching, and punishing the conduct (not indeed of the king, which would destroy his constitutional independence; but, which is more beneficial to the public) of his evil and pernicious counsellors.[127]

The executive was kept in check from making treaties 'which shall afterwards be judged to derogate from the honour and interest of the nation'[128] and engaging in 'improper or inglorious conduct, in beginning, conducting, or concluding a national war',[129] or from assisting 'the crown in contradiction to the laws of the land' by the threat of impeachment.[130] The last example was important, since because the king was above the law, there needed to be a way to hold someone to account for the king's policies and to provide redress, and this was impeachment.[131]

The importance of impeachment was clear to Blackstone even though he was writing after the last partisan impeachments that had occurred following the death of Queen Anne. Blackstone wrote:

> [A]n impeachment before the lords by the commons of Great Britain, in parliament, is a prosecution of the already known and established law, and has been frequently put in practice. . . . A commoner cannot however be impeached before the lords for any capital offence, but only for high misdemeanours. A peer may be impeached for any crime.[132]

127 W Blackstone, *Commentaries on the Laws of England, Book One* (Clarendon Press 1765) 151.
128 ibid 249.
129 ibid 250.
130 ibid 237.
131 ibid.
132 W Blackstone, *Commentaries on the Laws of England, Book Four* (The University of Chicago Press 1979) 256–7.

The fact that the trial took place in the House of Lords was justified as

> though in general the union of the legislative and judicial powers ought to be more carefully avoided, yet it may happen that a subject intrusted with the administration of public affairs may infringe the rights of the people, and be guilty of such crimes as the ordinary magistrate either dares not or cannot punish.[133]

Blackstone argued that the use of the House of Lords was needed, as there was a danger that an ordinary court 'would naturally be swayed by the authority of so powerful an accuser'.[134]

Blackstone's account of impeachment is couched in the language of checks and balances upon the power of the government and the utility of the House of Commons being able to proceed against those accused of misconduct. It is important to appreciate that Blackstone was writing at a time when later criticisms of the earlier use of impeachment as having been politically motivated were not the accepted view. Therefore, it was possible to see the benefit of impeachment and the important purpose that it could serve. It was important to consider Blackstone's views, as it showed how impeachment could still be regarded as serving an important purpose well into the middle of the eighteenth century.

The second example has shown how impeachment had been used at the beginning of the eighteenth century to hold ministers to account to the House of Commons. The decision not to impeach Walpole in 1742 marked the decline of impeachment as a mechanism for holding ministers accountable, as it was superseded by the requirement that ministers retain the confidence of the House of Commons. Impeachment was used as the main parliamentary mechanism to proceed against opponents, although acts of attainder were occasionally used. It is evident that impeachment was perceived by contemporary commentators as serving a purpose, and that this purpose should not be detracted from by concerns over the use of impeachment as a political weapon. In terms of informing our understanding of impeachment for the twenty-first century, the use of impeachment in the beginning of the eighteenth century reveals that impeachment was still perceived as a viable mechanism, even if it was gradually replaced by the need for ministers to retain the confidence of the House of Commons. Its use as a political weapon requires attention, as there is a concern that if impeachment were to be used again today it would be used for partisan purposes and those using impeachment would do so with the aim of damaging or punishing their political opponents. Therefore, if impeachment were to be used again it would need to show that it could not only buttress existing accountability mechanisms and to provide a purpose that is currently not yet satisfactorily achieved, but also be grounded in a procedure that, whilst retaining the initiative of Members of

133 ibid 258.
134 ibid.

Parliament to impeach ministers (and former ministers), sufficiently safeguards against inappropriate impeachments. These safeguards will be discussed in Chapter 9 when the blueprint for a revised form of impeachment will be considered.

The impeachment of Warren Hastings

The third example to be considered in this chapter is the impeachment and subsequent trial of Warren Hastings, the former Governor-General of Bengal, which was arguably the most famous impeachment in the eighteenth century. The legacy of Hastings' impeachment should not be underestimated as a means of comprehending why impeachment fell into disuse during the nineteenth century. For example, Fitzjames Stephen's view was:

> The impeachment of Warren Hastings is, I think, a blot on the judicial history of the country. It was monstrous that a man should be tortured, at irregular intervals, for seven years, in order that a singularly incompetent tribunal might be addressed before an excited audience by Burke and Sheridan, in language far removed from the calmness with which an advocate for the prosecution ought to address a criminal court.[135]

This is certainly an extreme opinion as to the impeachment of Hastings and not one that I would endorse, as it deflects from the purpose of impeaching Hastings, namely concerns over his conduct in India and the mismanagement of the East India Company. However, it does demonstrate the strength of feeling that continued to exist over the impeachment into the nineteenth century, at a time when Hastings was presented by many within the Imperial metropolis as a benevolent co-founder of what would become the British Raj.

Parliamentary action against the East India Company and officials

To understand why Hastings was impeached by the House of Commons in 1787, it is necessary to appreciate, first, parliamentary concerns over the economic performance and conduct of the East India Company, and, second, the controversy surrounding Hastings' conduct as the Governor-General of Bengal. This will help to provide the context and rationale for the penultimate impeachment, and why it was deemed necessary by a majority of the House of Commons. This next section will consider attempts by the House of Commons to proceed against Hastings, who had been appointed to his position after it had been created by the Regulating Act 1773.[136] Hastings had a long career working for the Company in India and had been the governor of Bengal prior to being appointed as Governor-General.

135 JF Stephen, *A History of the Criminal Law of England*, Volume I (Macmillan 1883) 160.
136 13 Geo. III. c.63.

The attempts to proceed against Hastings are linked to parliamentary and contemporary dissatisfaction with the management of the East India Company, the conduct of its servants and their treatment of the Company's subjects and the rulers of neighbouring Indian states, and the dangers posed by these servants using their ill-gotten fortune to purchase influence in Great Britain.[137]

It is first necessary to consider the importance of the dispute in how to manage the Company's territory in India, which occurred in Bengal. Hastings had been instructed to tackle corruption upon his appointment as Governor-General and had clashed with the members of his council, several of whom believed that he had failed to do this.[138] His most significant opponent was Philip Francis, who was a member of the council, and whose opposition to Hastings in Calcutta eventually led to a duel between the two men.[139] Upon Francis' return to Britain in 1781, he played an instrumental role in encouraging Edmund Burke to investigate Hastings' conduct.[140] According to CH Phillips, 'In October 1781, Philip Francis, whose hatred for Warren Hastings and consequently for the Company had become with him a mania, reached England and openly demonstrated that the Regulating Act had broken down.'[141] Weitzman argued that Francis played a significant role in highlighting the failures of Hastings and how the Company was administered in India, and upon his return he adopted a 'plan of campaign [that] was subtle: to present India affairs in such a light as to rouse the public indignation; by attributing all evils to the personal ambition of Hastings and to his disregard of the Directors' orders'.[142] Francis implemented his plan through his publication of an anonymous pamphlet criticising Hastings. The pamphlet 'had the desired effect' and therefore Francis was 'instrumental in inspiring' the establishment of the Select and Secret Committees that were established by the House of Commons to enquire into the Company's conduct.[143] The interpretation given by Weitzman and Phillips to Francis' conduct and motivations cast him as instrumental in presenting Hastings as the epitome of the Company's failings. Travers, in his more recent study of British rule in Bengal, notes the treatment of Francis by Imperialist historians and the recent reassessment of Francis' ideology

137 This could include purchasing country estates, stock in the East India Company, or funding an effort to win election to the House of Commons (such as John Scott or Sir Elijah Impey). See CH Phillips, 'The East India Company "Interest" and the English Government, 1783–4' (1937) 20 *Transactions of the Royal Historical Company* 83. Phillips considered the importance of Indian affairs in domestic politics and the parliamentary attempts to reform the Company and investigate its perceived failings. He also discussed the role of the Nabobs (Phillips, 88–100).

138 For a brief commentary on the allegations against Hastings see JP Greene, *Evaluating Empire and Confronting Colonialism in Eighteenth-Century Britain* (Cambridge University Press 2013) 308–9.

139 See S Weitzman, *Warren Hastings and Philip Francis* (Manchester University Press 1929).

140 Greene (n 138) 308–30.

141 Phillips (n 137) 84.

142 Weitzman (n 139) 137.

143 ibid 137–8.

and how this caused his opposition to Hastings.[144] Travers observes that Francis was driven to protect the ancient Mughal constitution from the Company's rule, which he regards as 'distinctively Whig'.[145]

Crucially, for Francis, upon returning to Britain he was able to gain the support of the prominent Whig politician and philosopher, Edmund Burke, and through Burke, gain the support of other prominent Whigs including Charles James Fox and Richard Sheridan. Burke, who would lead the impeachment against Hastings, regarded Hastings as having deliberately failed to implement the Company's instructions to tackle corruption and the conduct of its servants, for acting as a despot, using force against Indian rulers, and for misgovernment.[146] According to Lawson and Phillips, 'Burke was not an anti-imperialist; he did not question the Company's mission to govern parts of India, but he denied emphatically their right to misgovern.'[147] Indeed, Burke condemned the effect of the Company's rule, as '[u]nder the British, in his view, Indians had been the unwitting victims of all the evils associated with what modern analysts have termed colonialism.'[148] Hastings defended himself through his agent, Major John Scott, who sought to demonstrate his achievements and that the excesses levied against the Company's servants were exaggerated.[149]

It is now necessary to consider the background to Burke's involvement with Indian affairs and the political concerns in the metropolis over the management of the Company. Even before Parliament had turned its attention to Warren Hastings, it is important to consider that reform of the East India Company had been politically contentious, as the reformers could be presented as wishing to usurp the patronage of the Company. Sir William Holdsworth observed:

> The Crown had assumed control in 1773, but some power was still left to the Company. The system of government established in 1773 had not worked well. . . [as] all sorts of abuses in the government were rampant. It had become clear that the Crown must exercise an increased control.[150]

Reform of the Company had proved detrimental to the career of the leading Whig politician, Charles James Fox, who had come into government in 1783 through a coalition with his former political opponent Lord Frederick North.

144 R Travers, *Ideology and Empire in Eighteenth-Century India: The British in Bengal* (Cambridge University Press 2007) 142. Travers presents an authoritative and reasoned assessment of the differences between Hastings and Francis and also highlights where their views converged.

145 ibid 179.

146 Greene (n 138) 311.

147 P Lawson and J Phillips, '"Our Execrable Banditti": Perceptions of Nabobs in Mid-Eighteenth Century England' (1984) 16(3) *Albion* 225, 237

148 Greene (n 138) 312.

149 ibid 313.

150 Holdsworth, Volume X (n 117) 111.

Contemporary caricaturists, such as Thomas Rowlandson[151] and Edward Topham,[152] had presented the coalition between the two men as being facilitated by the devil.

The coalition government between Lord North and Charles James Fox had attempted to reform the Company, with a bill known as Fox's East India Bill being introduced into the House of Commons in 1783. It was condemned by contemporaries as a naked attempt to seize patronage and a violation of the Company's charter. King George III was not supportive of his new government and was instrumental in ensuring that the Bill was defeated in the House of Lords, after he personally intervened to persuade the Lords to defeat it.[153] The result of the coalition's defeat in the House of Lords was the dismissal of the ministry by the king and a general election that resulted in William Pitt the Younger being invited to form the next government. There were allegations that money from India had been used to support Pitt's allies in gaining their seats, provided by men such as Paul Benfield, who was a controversial Company servant, and who had acquired his fortune by exploiting the local ruler of the Carnactic, the Nawab of Arcot.[154]

Now out of government, the Whig opposition, most notably, Edmund Burke, would prove critical in ensuring that the House of Commons proceeded to combat the abuses of the Company's servants. However, it must be emphasised that a senior member of the government, Henry Dundas, played an instrumental role, and even Pitt the Younger would prove significant in ensuring that Hastings' impeachment passed the House of Commons.[155] Finally, it is clear that the conduct of the Company's servants was controversial, especially Paul Benfield and his position as the creditor to the Nawab of Arcot. It was this that first attracted the concern of Edmund Burke. Pivotal to the parliamentary action against Hastings was the establishment of the Secret Committee of Inquiry in 1780, chaired by Henry Dundas (which was concerned with southern India), and the Select Committee in 1781, whose members included Edmund Burke and other opposition figures (which was concerned with Bengal).

151 *The Loves of the Fox and the Badger – or the Coalition Wedding*, 7 January 1784, published by William Humphrey. Rowlandson depicts the role of the devil in bringing about the coalition between Fox and Lord North.

152 *The Union "Whom Has Join'd Let no Man Put Asunder"* (11 March 1783), published by Elizabeth Darchery. Topham depicts the devil marrying Fox and Lord North.

153 For a comprehensive treatment of the events described here see J Cannon, *The Fox-North Coalition: Crisis of the Constitution, 1782–84* (Cambridge University Press 1970). See also Holdsworth, Volume X (n 117) 111–12; L Sutherland, *East India Company in Eighteenth Century Politics* (OUP 1962) 400–406; Phillips (n 137) 83.

154 See PJ Marshall, 'Benfield, Paul' (1741–1810) in *Oxford Dictionary of National Biography* (OUP 2004). Marshall argued that the allegations that eight Members of Parliament owed their seats to Benfield were 'fanciful'.

155 See ahead.

The impeachment of Warren Hastings

This next section will consider the impeachment of Warren Hastings. It will begin by discussing the impetus to impeach Hastings, the charges against him, and the subsequent trial before the House of Lords. In terms of the political impetus to impeach Hastings, it is important to note that whilst Burke played an important role, it is necessary to take into account the significant role played by Dundas, who had previously failed to persuade the House of Commons to proceed against another company official, Sir Thomas Rumbold. This setback did not diminish Dundas' drive to tackle the corruption within the East India Company, indeed 'his activity [in the House of Commons] exposed to the public something of the disorders which prevailed in India and prepared the way for effective reform.'[156] In May 1784, Dundas introduced a motion into the House of Commons calling for Warren Hastings to be dismissed by the East India Company. The motion was supported by a majority of the House of Commons and, but for the intervention of the Court of Proprietors which represented the Company's shareholders, the Directors of the Company would have succeeded in dismissing Hastings.[157] However, in response to the hostility he was encountering at home, Hastings resigned his position and returned to Britain in 1785. Hastings then set about attempting to justify his own conduct and present a counter-narrative to that advanced by Francis.[158]

Edmund Burke led the campaign to impeach Hastings with the support of Burke's allies including Charles James Fox and Richard Sheridan.[159] William Pitt the Younger and Henry Dundas also supported Burke in ensuring that there was sufficient backing for the impeachment in the House of Commons. Weitzman argued that the person who played the leading role in the impeachment was Francis, who had been Hastings' opponent on the council, and that the impeachment had been 'conceived by the tortured brain of Philip Francis'.[160] This observation can be viewed both as revealing attitudes towards the motivation for the impeachment in the early twentieth century and the important role played by Francis. As discussed earlier, Francis had been a constant opponent of Hastings and whilst he had served on the council, Francis had sought to remove Hastings

156 C Matheson, *The Life of Henry Dundas, First Viscount Melville 1742–1811* (Constable and Co Ltd 1933) 82.

157 ibid.

158 See W Hastings, *The Defence of Warren Hastings, Esq (late Governor General of Bengal,) at the Bar of the House of Commons* (J Stockdale 1786).

159 For a discussion of their differing motivations see BW Hill, 'Fox and Burke: The Whig Party and the Question of Principles, 1784–1789' (1974) 39 *The English Historical Review* 1. Hill observed that Fox was motivated by using 'Burke's campaign against Hastings as a means of embarrassing the Government on an issue which might be expected to evoke some sympathy in the country' (Hill (n 159) 12). Fox also had doubts over whether Hastings was 'the chief culprit in India' or that the case against him was 'tenable' (Hill (n 159) 10–12).

160 Weitzman (n 139) 171.

so that he might replace him.[161] The failure to remove Hastings in India and Francis' return to the metropolis resulted in Francis 'continuing the campaign in England'.[162] More recent historians, such as Bowyer, regard Francis' rationale for removing Hastings was to enable Francis to implement his own vision for reforming India.[163]

The articles of impeachment were introduced to the House of Commons in 1786 and included charges relating to Hastings' mistreatment of Chait Singh, the ruler of Benares, encouraging the seizure of the property belonging to the Begums of Oudh, and the acceptance of presents.[164] The House of Commons voted on each charge in turn. The first charge, that relating to the Rohilla War, was defeated on 1 June 1786 by a majority, including Pitt.[165] On 13 June Pitt voted to support the charge against Hastings relating to Benares and his treatment of its ruler, Chait Singh. Pitt's vote was 'practically decisive . . . the measure before despaired as a party cry became a national one'.[166] There has been academic debate surrounding Pitt's decision to vote for the Benares charge, when he had not supported earlier charges.[167] It is interesting to note CC Davies' observation on the evolution of Pitt's attitude towards impeaching Hastings, as Davies states that '[the] younger Pitt's attitude to Warren Hastings, especially the reasons he gave for voting for the impeachment on the Benares charge, surprised, almost astounded his contemporaries [and it] has puzzled historians.'[168] In terms of whether Dundas was instrumental in Pitt's change of mind, Davies discounted the significance of Dundas' 'pleading' for Pitt to support the impeachment:

> Historians have referred to Pitt's change of attitude. Perhaps it would be nearer the truth to contend that Pitt had all along been hostile to Hastings. . . . It looks as if Pitt had decided that Hastings was deserving of punishment long before he voted for an impeachment on the Benares charge. Whether he had always intended to resort to the cumbersome method of

161 TH Bowyer, 'Philip Francis and the Government of Bengal: Parliament and Personality in the Frustration of an Ambition' (1999) 18(2) *Parliamentary History* 1, 7–8.

162 ibid 10.

163 ibid 18. Bowyer had observed that '[t]he enduring sense of mission retained by Francis showed itself in an excessively personalized sense of indispensability and responsibility for India' (ibid 19). This was accompanied by Francis' willingness to use 'low practices' to achieve this vision (ibid 21).

164 See PJ Marshall, *The Impeachment of Warren Hastings* (OUP 1965) for comprehensive commentary on the charges against Hastings (chapters 5–8). See also Weitzman (n 139) for a succinct account of the charges (176–82).

165 Weitzman (n 139) 184.

166 ibid 185.

167 See GM Ditchfield, 'The House of Lords and the Impeachment of Warren Hastings' (1994) 13(3) *Parliamentary History* 277, 289–90 for a discussion of Pitt's motivations and whether this was a ploy to distract the opposition.

168 CC Davies 'Warren Hastings and the Younger Pitt' (1955) 70 *The English Historical Review* 609, 609–10.

impeachment must remain a matter of opinion. The evidence seems to suggest that he would have voted for an impeachment on one or other of the charges without Dundas's advocacy.[169]

A contemporary account observed that '[w]hatever may be the event of the impeachment, the proper exercise of such a power is a valuable privilege to the British constitution, a formidable guardian of the public liberty, and the dignity of the nation.'[170] Although that author observed that those who had impeached Hastings had overlooked his achievements:

> [O]verlooking his confessed and effectual services for thirteen years, which, at a critical period, saved that empire from destruction, they have preferred the vindication of the national character, to the advancement of the public interest; and erecting, in the eyes of Europe, a THRONE OF MERCY for the oppressed inhabitants of India, proceed to display their justice, and vindicate their honour, before the tribunal of the world.[171]

Whether Hastings was deserving of impeachment is a moot point and divided the opinions of his contemporaries and even twentieth-century historians.[172] Lionel Trotter's biography of Hastings published in the late nineteenth century offered an 'impartial account of the great Governor' and noted:

> Few men of equal desert have undergone such cruel injustice at the hands, not only of contemporary assailants, but even of critics who wrote long after the fiery eloquence of Burke and Sheridan had passed into 'the dream of things that were.'[173]

169 Davies (n 168) 614–15. Weitzman (n 139) considered the reasons for Pitt's position and observed that 'Pitt . . . was not prepared to champion Hastings indefinitely merely to defeat Opposition', which demonstrates how the impeachment could not be regarded as a partisan affair (187).

170 J Logan, *A Review of the Principal Charges Against Warren Hastings Esquire, Late Governor General of Bengal* (John Stockdale and John Murray 1788) 3–4.

171 ibid 9.

172 Hastings has had his detractors who have supported Edmund Burke's campaign against him. These have included Conor Cruise O'Brien, *Edmund Burke* (Vintage 2002) and the Whig historian and colonial administrator Thomas Babington Macaulay, *Warren Hastings* (1841, republished, John Long 1905). There have been those supportive of Hastings, such as Penderel Moon, *Warren Hastings and British India* (Hodder and Stoughton 1947). A more modern defence of Hastings has been offered by J Bernstein, *Dawning of the Raj: The Life and Times of Warren Hastings* (Ivan R Dee 2000).

173 LJ Trotter, *Warren Hastings: A Biography* (WH Allen & Co 1878) iii. Trotter, who was a captain in the Indian Army, described Hastings as man 'whose genius had saved from ruin the empire' (380). However, '[a] governor who held so high and arduous an office as Warren Hastings did for thirteen years, must in his time have made not a few mistakes. . . . Few statesmen indeed have paid so dearly for the faults of other men, have suffered such cruel injustice from the passions and the prejudices of their own age' (382). Trotter described

PJ Marshall, in his authoritative study of the impeachment, concluded that 'some of the charges against Hastings were not without foundation', such as the Benares charge (which Pitt supported), his treatment of the Begums of Oudh, and the award of 'extravagant contracts'.[174]

Nonetheless, it is clear that this impeachment, the first since 1746, was not entirely politically motivated, rather it was the culmination of parliamentary attempts to tackle the threat posed by the conduct of the Company's servants. Marshall observes that amongst Members of Parliament there was 'a self-conscious desire to do justice and to uphold the reputation of the House seems to have counted for more than normal political calculations'.[175] This act of public disapproval and repudiation of the Company's wrongdoings was not (primarily, at least for Burke and Dundas) motivated by partisan politics. Greene has observed that 'Burke's relentless efforts to bring Warren Hastings to justice as a final act of public repudiation of the misdeeds of Britain's Asiatic plunders', meant that for seven years the impeachment trial of Hastings captured public attention.[176] According to Epstein,

> The opening of proceedings against Hastings, highlighted by Burke's impassioned prosecution, increased public awareness of India . . . it also generated unease about the effects of 'oriental despotism' not only as practiced in India but as threatening Britain's own political culture.[177]

Burke's speeches as 'all a sad display of hysteric fury about imaginary crimes. The great orator raved and screeched like a madman, or a raging fishwife, against a gentleman whose alleged misdeeds were as nothing to his acknowledged merits' (306). Trotter observed '[h] ow grossly he exceeded the license of fair invective, even on points *that might still be open to question*' (307) (emphasis added).

174 Marshall (n 164) 189.

175 ibid 62–3.

176 Greene (n 138) 316.

177 J Epstein, *Scandal of Colonial Rule: Power and Subversion in the British Atlantic during the Age of Revolution* (Cambridge University Press 2012) 71. The caricatures of James Gillray offer a contemporary perspective on how Indian affairs, Nabobs, and the proceedings against Warren Hastings were viewed at the time: see for example 'State-jugglers' (SW Fores, 16 May 1788), 'Market-day' (SW Fores, 2 May 1788), 'Blood on Thunder fording the Red Sea' (SW Fores, 1 March 1788), 'The political-banditti assailing the saviour of India' (W Holland, 11 May 1788), and 'The Bow to the Throne, alias the Begging Bowl' (SW Fores, 6 May 1788). James Sayers, 'The Princess' Bow alias the Bow Begum' (T Cornell, 1 May 1788) had presented the affair as being steered by Philip Francis, whereas Gillray's response in 'The 'Bow to the Throne' was critical of Hastings and presented Hastings as using his fortune to purchase government and royal support. Overall, Gillray presented the opposition as opportunists, Thurlow as any ally of Hastings, and the government and king as having been bribed by his fortune. The idea that Hastings had purchased the support of the Crown was exemplified by an anonymous caricaturist in 'What a Man buys he may sell' (1786), with Hastings pushing the king and Thurlow along in a wheelbarrow.

The trial 'offered the most spectacular staging if expiating justice' which served as 'a warning' and 'a national cleansing of imperial sins'.[178]

The trial of Warren Hastings before the House of Lords

This next section will consider the trial of Warren Hastings before the House of Lords. The impeachment trial took place in Westminster Hall, which had previously served as the venue for the treason trial of Charles I. The prosecution was brought on behalf of the House of Commons by managers, including Burke and Sheridan. Hastings was defended by counsel. The trial was initially presided over by Lord Thurlow, the Lord Chancellor, until 1795, and the House of Lords acted as the jury.

A number of observations will be made about how the trial was perceived by contemporaries. First, it was very much a public affair, with tickets being sold for those who wished to attend the trial. These tickets permitted those either sufficiently connected to be gifted a ticket, such as Sarah Sophia Banks, or wealthy enough to pay the admission price, to access specific galleries that had been constructed around Westminster Hall. Second, the trial was headline news and written and pictorial accounts of the trial were shared widely. In a recent account of the trial, Chiara Rolli describes popular excitement about the trial and how it was reported by the press and satirists in caricatures.[179] One example of this is James Hook's *The Trial*, which draws analogies between the Hastings trial and Shakespeare's *Merchant of Venice*.[180] Third, the trial was a spectacle and represented high-end theatre. Trotter's description the opening day of the trial gives some impression as to the drama of the proceedings:

> At noon the Court was opened, and the Sergeant-at-Arms summoned 'Warren Hastings, Esquire, to come forth' and save his bail. Hastings advanced to the bar, and on bended knees awaited the Chancellor's permission to rise. That promptly granted, he listened to the Proclamation charging him with high crimes and misdemeanours, and made brief but becoming answer to Lord Thurlow's opening address.[181]

A key issue in terms of the trial was the standards that the House of Lords would follow. The managers favoured relying on earlier precedents of impeachments, the

178 Epstein (n 177) 72.

179 See in particular 'The Reception of the Hastings Trial in the Newspapers and Satirical Prints' in C Rolli (ed), *The Trial of Warren Hastings: Classical Oratory and Reception in Eighteenth-Century England* (Bloomsbury Academic 2019). See also 'A View of the Court sitting on the trial of Warren Hastings Esqr in Westminster Hall' 1 May 1788, *Lady's Magazine*. This pictorial representation of the trial demonstrates the grandeur of the trial and just how packed the galleries were.

180 17 May 1788, published by SW Fores.

181 Trotter (n 173) 305.

law of Parliament, which would give the manager greater freedom in their prosecution of Hastings. The alternative view was that Hastings' trial should follow the standards of the common law, which applied to the ordinary courts. The legal view of how the trial should be conducted was to follow the common law's standards and not to 'revive an anachronism' of the form taken by previous impeachments.[182]

Thurlow played a significant role in ensuring that Burke and the other impeachment managers would be expected to prove their case to the standards expected in an ordinary court. Burke could not seek a conviction on the basis of morality, rather, he must show that an offence known to the law had been committed, and furthermore, the ordinary rules of evidence must apply. Thurlow determined the procedure, with the prosecution setting out their entire case and only then would Hastings be expected to offer his defence.[183] This ensured that Hastings would have the opportunity of knowing the full case against him. Hastings' impeachment trial is regarded as a victory for the common law and the procedures of the ordinary court over the ad hoc customs of Parliament that would arguably have seen the managers achieve a conviction.[184] This ruling by Lord Thurlow ensured that Hastings' trial followed the standards expected by common law lawyers and that it made it more difficult for the managers to secure a conviction. Thurlow had declared, 'I shall hold Mr. Burke to the proof of all he has asserted', thereby by requiring that the ordinary rules of evidence would apply; Thurlow reiterated the presumption of innocence until proven guilty. Thurlow also determined the procedure for the trial, one that would require the prosecution to make their entire case before Hastings was required to respond. This worked to Hastings' advantage as he did not need to make his defence until after each of the articles had been presented by the prosecution managers. Thurlow was clear that 'he never could consent to a mode of procedure, unfair to the defendant in the highest degree, and contrary to the fundamental principles of justice.'[185] Furthermore, Thurlow held:

> There was not a single impeachment, during the last century, in which there were not the strongest marks of tyranny, injustice and oppression; and even

182 Marshall (n 164) 64.

183 The managers had sought for Hastings to make his defence after the prosecution had presented each article. See Ditchfield (n 167) 279. Ditchfield noted: '[a]t the very outset . . . the Lords, asserting the supremacy of the common law over the custom of Parliament drawn from previous impeachments, decided by 88 votes to 33 to hear the whole of the prosecution case on all of the articles before proceeding to the defence. . . . This has rightly been presented as a vital factor in Hastings' acquittal.'

184 See Marshall (n 164) 65–76 for a detailed overview of the arguments surrounding the legal procedure at the trial. Marshall provided a thorough commentary on the conflict over whether the custom of Parliament or the common law standards of a trial in an ordinary court would apply to the trial and the success of those who wanted to ensure that the standards of an ordinary court would apply, as opposed to expediency of parliamentary custom and the ability to frame offences that would be rejected by the ordinary courts.

185 W Cobbett, *The Parliamentary History of England, from the Earliest Period to the Year 1803*, Volume XXVIII (TC Hansard 1816) 55.

> the impeachment of Sacheverel[l], in the present century, contained an instance of injustice, which he trusted would never happen again; when the House of Lords determined upon a point of law contrary to the unanimous opinion of the judges. In the present impeachment, he trusted their lordships would not depart from the known established laws of the land. The Commons might impeach, their lordships were to try the cause; and the same rules of evidence, the same attention to the laws, which obtained in the courts below, would, he was confident, be preserved by their lordships.[186]

Holdsworth observed that Thurlow enjoyed 'the King's favour [which] gave him a secure position [and despite serving under Pitt] he continued to pursue a political line of his own [as] [f]rom the first he defended Warren Hastings'.[187] It is true that Hastings had an ally in Thurlow, but even when Thurlow was succeeded as Lord Chancellor by Lord Loughborough, who was opposed to Hastings, in his summing up at the end of the trial he 'condemned the "looseness and inaccuracy" of the articles'.[188]

Burke had criticised the use of the rules of law and evidence: '[t]hese rules such as they were might serve for rules to the courts below, but were not to shackle the House of Commons nor that High Court.'[189] Indeed, Conor Cruise O'Brien in his biography of Burke credits Thurlow for ensuring that Burke had 'no hope of real success'.[190] This may be the case, however, by ensuring that appropriate safeguards were in place to guarantee the integrity of the trial, Thurlow provided a trial that could not be criticised for being conducted as a purely political exercise. The approach taken in the Hastings impeachment informed the final impeachment, that of Henry Dundas, Viscount Melville, in 1806. In Melville's impeachment, Thomas Erskine presided over the trial as Lord Chancellor and Lord High Steward: 'where he applied his strictures on the Hastings impeachment by insisting on continuous sittings and abidance by legal rules of evidence and procedure'.[191]

A key problem in the prosecution was that the managers could not prove their charges. Marshall notes that Burke's charges were never designed to be tried before the Lords and had never been aimed at a legal audience.[192] Therefore, the central issue was that the charges were not sufficiently legalistic, too broad, and badly drafted.[193] In terms of evidence, the prosecution struggled to find material

186 ibid 62.
187 Holdsworth, Volume XII (n 91) 319.
188 Marshall (n 174) 70.
189 *History of the Trial of Warren Hastings*, Part 5, 84, 25 February 1794. Quoted in Holdsworth, Volume XII (n 91) 509.
190 CC O'Brien, *Edmund Burke* (Vintage 2002) 200–1.
191 David Lemmings, 'Erskine, Thomas, First Baron Erskine (1750–1823)' in *Oxford Dictionary of National Biography* (OUP 2004).
192 Marshall (n 164) 70.
193 ibid 71–2.

to support them and had difficulties in relying upon witnesses.[194] This was a theme central to the manager's insistence, without success, that the prosecution 'was not bound by ordinary rules'.[195] The oratory of Burke and Sheridan may have initially persuaded the wider audience, yet it could not make a legal case before the Lords.

In terms of procedure the prosecution had made its case first. However, even by 1791 when they had finished their case, the managers had left 'sixteen articles untouched'.[196] Counsel for Hastings then delivered his defence to the case put forward by the prosecution and completed this in 1793, some five years after the trial had commenced. Hastings' impeachment trial lasted seven years and spanned the lifetime of more than one Parliament. The fact that it spanned the lifetime of more than one Parliament was significant, as 'the long duration of Warren Hastings' impeachment raised the question in 1791 of whether or not a dissolution of Parliament terminated an impeachment', the answer being in the negative.[197] Ditchfield observed that the opposition had argued that this was a constitutionally important issue as the Crown could prevent an impeachment by simply dissolving Parliament.[198] The trial dragged on because of 'the infrequency of the sittings of the court and the brevity of its sessions' and, as a consequence, the public and Lords lost interest which impacted upon attendance, as well as adding to Hastings' legal expenses.[199] In response, Hastings lobbied members of the Lords to speed up the trial and reach a decision.[200]

Marshall made an important observation about the trial: '[t]o contemporaries, the most disturbing feature of Hastings's impeachment, apart from its length, was the atmosphere in which the case was tried.'[201] The length, which was largely the fault of the court in stretching out the trial, was arguably excessive and demonstrates why there was little public appetite once the novelty of the trial wore off. Public support for the prosecution was also eroded by the language used and their personalised attacks on Hastings' character and accusing him of all manner of disturbing crimes. It would be correct to conclude that the prosecution managers had little realistic chance of success in the Lords, that their best chances of success would have been to exploit the popular interest in the trial, and that they would have arguably achieved this, had the trial concluded before public and political attention drifted to more current issues, such as the French Revolution. This draws a distinction between the legal outcome and the court of public opinion, something which the prosecution arguably failed to achieve on both accounts.

194 ibid 72–3.
195 ibid 74.
196 ibid 80.
197 Holdsworth, Volume XII (n 91) 339.
198 Ditchfield (n 167) 283–4.
199 ibid 279–82.
200 ibid 282–3.
201 Marshall (n 164) 83.

Hastings was eventually acquitted in 1795 by a majority of the 29 Lords who took part in the final vote.[202] These 29 Lords who determined his guilt were the only ones who had followed all of the sessions and were therefore tasked with reaching a verdict.

In terms of its legacy, the trial of Warren Hastings is a moot point. First, did the trial cement public alarm with the conduct of the Company? It is telling that the initial repulsion felt by many contemporaries towards the conduct of the Company and its employees could be argued to have been replaced by a belief that the business of empire could be conducted properly and without disdain. Dirks' commentary on the notoriety and legacy of the impeachment is attractive as it demonstrates how little it achieved at the time:

> For if the scandals of Clive and Benfield were spectacular on their own, the scandal of Hastings became literally, the greatest spectacle of late-eighteenth-century Britain, and the symbol for many of what the imperial relationship between Britain and India had become. And yet the greatest irony . . . was not that the trial fizzled out after nine long years, but that it *led to the regeneration of the imperial idea. Empire emerged stronger than ever.* The imperial enterprise cleansed of corruption. [203]

Second, did the trial and the public exposure of the perceived wrongdoing lead to the reform of the Company? It is questionable as to whether Hastings' impeachment resulted in reform of the Company. Indeed, Pitt's India Act 1784 predated the impeachment, although it was a product of the criticism against the perceived shortcomings of Hastings' conduct as Governor-General and the behaviour of other employees. One outcome was that the Hastings impeachment led to the demise of this form of parliamentary accountability, as the trial had proved ineffective and many contemporaries regarded the conduct of the managers as excessive. It is significant that there would be only one more impeachment, that of Viscount Melville in 1806. Marshall observed:

> Their disappearance was undoubtedly hastened by certain features of Hastings's trial. In the first place, impeachment had proved ineffectual and liable to serious abuse. Secondly, the victory of the common lawyers in the House of Lords over the prosecution's claims to special rules of procedure did much to make sure that impeachment would not outlive their constitutional usefulness, to be employed, as they had so often been in the past, as political weapons.[204]

202 Marshall (n 164) 85–6. See also Ditchfield (n 167) for the rationale for this verdict and the role of Pitt and the opposition in the outcome of the trial.

203 NB Dirks, *The Scandal of Empire: India and the Creation of Imperial Britain* (Permanent Black 2008) 85 (emphasis added).

204 Marshall (n 164) 87.

Marshall concluded: 'the judges performed a considerable service in making a repetition of such a trial unlikely.'[205] According to Holdsworth, the legacy of Hastings' impeachment 'whatever we may think of its justice, had the beneficial result of burning [the principle of trusteeship over India] into the national conscience.'[206]

A review of Hastings' impeachment

The impeachment of Warren Hastings did not concern a member of the government being impeached, rather it concerned the prosecution of a senior colonial administrator. The trial was not about the accountability of the executive, but about the accountability of the East India Company to Parliament. The core issue was the concern that accountability, in terms of the Company and its servants, was ineffective despite legislative reforms that had been intended to improve accountability. The impeachment of Warren Hastings demonstrated that impeachment offered a unique mechanism in terms of prosecuting the person deemed to be most responsible, as it would not have been possible, due to the legal shortcomings discussed earlier, to have prosecuted Hastings before the ordinary courts. Impeachment offered an option that was unique in terms of empowering the Commons to prosecute, but also demonstrated that the Commons were taking seriously the problem with the deemed unaccountability of the Company and its servants. In terms of how the public viewed the impeachment, this evolved over the course of the trial and divided opinion. The conduct of the trial, the scarcity of evidence, the reliance of rhetoric, and the duration of the trial played a significant role in undermining the initial impeachment. The impeachment of Warren Hastings and the trial before the Lords offers lessons to a modern use of impeachment in the twenty-first century. The supremacy of legal form and procedure over precedents of previous impeachments is key. Any impeachment must be fair and require due process and sufficient evidence to convict. The legacy of the Hastings impeachment goes some way to undermining the use of impeachment and is still cited as an example against its use.

The final impeachment of Henry Dundas, Viscount Melville

The final example to be considered is the impeachment of Henry Dundas, Viscount Melville, in 1806 and his subsequent trial, later that year. Melville's impeachment was selected as an example as it was the last impeachment brought by the House of Commons, and therefore he was the last individual to be faced with an impeachment trial in the House of Lords. Furthermore, Melville was a senior member of government and whilst the impeachment was brought by his

205 ibid.
206 Holdsworth, Volume X (n 91) 122.

political opponents, it related not to overtly political considerations, as had often been the case a century earlier, but rather to allegations of corruption.

The impeachment of Viscount Melville

There is some irony that Melville, the person who had played an active role in the parliamentary proceedings against Rumbold and Hastings in the 1780s, would himself be impeached. Melville had been a chief ally of Pitt the Younger and had played a significant role in Indian affairs as President of the Board of Control in the 1790s and early 1800s. In 1804, Melville was appointed as the First Lord of the Admiralty and pursued a policy of increasing the size of the British fleet: 'since there was no chance of challenging Napoleon on land, a bigger and better navy offered the only chance of renewing offensive operations. He was promptly vindicated by Nelson's victory at the battle of Trafalgar.'[207]

Prior to being appointed as the First Lord of the Admiralty, Melville had previously served as the Treasurer of the Navy. However, Melville was accused of financial irregularities because of how he had handled the Navy's money. The problem was that he had not separated his own money from that of the Navy's, which by law should have been kept at the Bank of England, and this contravened legislation[208] that Melville himself had introduced to the House of Commons to prevent 'the Treasurer from appropriating any part of the money passing through his hands to his own private use'.[209] Melville had observed: 'little did I conceive that I should be the object of attack as Treasurer of the Navy.'[210] The attack came from his predecessor, the Earl of St Vincent, who drafted an anonymous pamphlet that declared: '[w]e denounce and proclaim the high crime and misdemeanour of Viscount Melville' for using the Navy's money whilst as Treasurer for 'his own profit'.[211]

Lovat-Fraser observed:

> It was alleged, however, that, in spite of the Act, corruption still continued in the administration of the Navy, and in 1802 an Act was passed by which five Commissioners were appointed to inquire into the frauds and irregularities which were still believed to exist.[212]

The Commission of Inquiry set up to investigate these allegations delivered its tenth report in March 1805. Michael Fry, Melville's most recent biographer, has observed that '[the commission's] political colour could not thus be mistaken . . .

207 M Fry, 'Dundas, Henry, First Viscount Melville (1742–1811)' in *Oxford Dictionary of National Biography* (OUP 2004).
208 1785 st. 25 of the King, c.31, Treasurer of the Navy Act 1785.
209 JA Lovat-Fraser, 'The Impeachment of Lord Melville' (1912–13) 24 *Jurid. Rev.* 235, 236.
210 Quoted in M Fry, *The Dundas Despotism* (John Donald 2004) 262.
211 Quoted in Fry (n 210) 262.
212 Lovat-Fraser (n 209) 236.

it never did much more than try to put flesh on St Vincent's charges, without troubling to master evidence or consider alternative views.'[213] The problem was that Melville had contravened the Act by placing any unspent money in his own private account, which would have been acceptable prior to his own reforms, but was no longer the case.[214] Furthermore, there was a deficit between the unspent money and that which remained in his accounts.[215]

The commission's tenth report '[w]hile it stopped short of saying that Melville had lined his own pockets, . . . blamed him for what had been going on.'[216] This proved to be the end of Melville's once high-flying career, as he was forced to resign from office and from the Privy Council. The scandal was not just confined to Melville, as it 'threatened . . . to bring down the government'.[217] Melville's ally, William Pitt the Younger, proposed that a parliamentary inquiry be established to investigate the allegations. However, Samuel Whitbread, who played the leading role in the parliamentary proceedings against Melville, refused to accept this and argued that Melville should face a motion of censure.[218]

The report was also critical of the Paymaster of the Navy, Alexander Trotter, who had placed naval funds in his own account and had used these as a source of personal investment.[219] The amount of money removed by Trotter into his own accounts at Coutts was £6,000,000, and this had enabled him to purchase stock in companies such as the East India Company.[220] Melville had denied profiting from his position or from Trotter's conduct and he had refused to answer the Commissioner's question as to 'whether he had advanced any of the money applicable to naval services for any other public service than that of the Navy'.[221] Fry described him as 'cagey' when responding to the commissioners' question and not giving a clear answer.[222] However, Fry noted that 'ministers routinely employed and let others employ, unspent public money for private purposes' and such use of public money was common practice and considered acceptable by contemporaries.[223]

On 8 April 1805, the House of Commons rejected the government's proposal to establish a Select Committee of Inquiry and instead voted to censure Melville, who consequently resigned on 9 April.[224] According to Lord Fitzharris, Pitt's response to the defeat was to 'immediately put on the little cocked hat that he was

213 Quoted in Fry (n 210) 262.
214 ibid.
215 ibid 262–3.
216 Fry (n 207).
217 ibid.
218 ibid.
219 Lovat-Fraser (n 209) 236.
220 Fry (n 210) 264.
221 Lovat-Fraser (n 209) 237.
222 Fry (n 210) 264–5.
223 ibid 265.
224 Fry (n 207).

in the habit of wearing when dressed for the evening, and [jam] it deeply over his forehead, and I distinctly saw the tears trickling down his cheeks'.[225] Lovat-Fraser considered that the commission's report was a factor in causing Pitt's premature death in 1806.[226] Whitbread led the impeachment and there were ten articles of impeachment, nine of which concerned Trotter and only one concerned charges of corruption against Melville.[227] Melville had been accused of an offence that could have been indictable in the ordinary courts. This meant that Whitbread could have prosecuted him before the King's Bench, rather than bringing an impeachment in the House of Commons. However, the choice of impeachment over prosecution before the ordinary courts was considered as the favourable outcome by Melville, as '[b]oth Melville and Pitt thought this better than any form of prosecution, since the peers were more likely than the courts to acquit.'[228]

The proceedings against Melville have been described as being 'pursued with such venom and bitterness that the nation became disgusted' and led even those hostile to him, such as the king, to be critical of his treatment.[229] Fry regarded Whitbread as being vindictive and intent on dishonouring Melville.[230] The effect on Melville was considerable, with friends noting the toll that the proceedings were having on his health and appearance.[231]

The impeachment trial began on 29 April 1806 and lasted just 15 days.[232] Compared with the trial of Hastings, this was extremely brief. The opening day of the trial, held in Westminster Hall, amounted to an impressive spectacle. One observer wrote: 'I never knew what earthly magnificence was',[233] whilst another observer, Lord Minto, was left unimpressed with proceedings, '[t]he scene is horrid. Lord Melville looks like death.'[234] Dundas' defence were clear that he had not committed a criminal offence.[235] The articles were criticised by leading Whig Lords, with Lord Holland describing the articles as 'so ill drawn that it was difficult to ascertain to which act of Lord Melville each respectively referred'.[236] The

225 Quoted in Lovat-Fraser (n 209) 239.
226 ibid 235.
227 Fry (n 210) 273–4. The articles are outlined in full in *Trial by Impeachment of Henry Lord Viscount Melville, for High Crimes and Misdeameanors, Before the House of Peers, in Westminster Hall, Between the 29th of April 1806 and the 17th of May 1806* (Longman, Hurst, Rees and Orme 1806) 2–7.
228 Fry (n 207).
229 Lovat-Fraser (n 209) 239–40.
230 Fry (n 210) 267.
231 ibid 272.
232 Lovat-Fraser (n 209) 240.
233 Matheson (n 156) 366.
234 ibid 367.
235 Matheson has commented that 'the line of defence adopted by Melville's counsel may have made a bad impression, since it turned too much on the pure letter of the law and was concentrated on the object of showing that the Commons could not prove Melville's legal guilt' (ibid 368).
236 Fry (n 210) 274.

House of Lords were guided on points of law by a panel composed of judges, to which it made a referral.[237] The speeches of the prosecution managers and the defence make interesting reading, as reference is made to the debate over the procedure that should be employed in the trial, as well as to whether Parliament could choose to apply a different standard than that exercised by the courts. The speech delivered by Samuel Whitbread on 16 May 1806, the 14th day of the trial, is of particular interest given his defence of impeachment as an accountability mechanism and his emphasis on due process and parity with the requirements of the ordinary courts:

> If we view the political history of this country, we see that the mode of trial by impeachment has been employed on various occasions – that sometimes it has been relinquished, at others, *by long delay, it has been brought into disrepute*. We desire, my lords, to vindicate its character.[238]
>
> . . .
>
> My lords, you have heard some complaints respecting the disadvantages the noble defendant suffered under the mode of trial now adopted. If they are such, they are at least of his own seeking. *Lord Melville was to have been prosecuted in a court of law*, where we are told he might challenge his jury, and the late attorney-general was directed to draw up the charge. *This mode was changed by the interposition of a powerful friend*, who *recommended that he should be impeached*, asserting, at the same time, that he was guilty of no crime.[239]
>
> [I]t has been urged before your lordships, that the House of Commons not being governed by the same rules of evidence which prevail in the courts below, the noble defendant has not the same protection which he would receive were he prosecuted under the ordinary forms of law. My lords, the Commons have thought it their duty so far to assert their rights as to declare, *that they are not restricted by the same rules which, for the safety of the subject, are uniformly adopted in the common course of the criminal jurisprudence of this country*. But I beg your lordships distinctly to understand, *that this right* which they most explicitly claim, *they have not on this occasion exercised*; and although the noble defendant would have had no reason to complain if their just immunities had controuled the customary forms of proceedings under the penal code, *yet, in the progress of this prosecution, every part of the proof has been conducted with the same strictness and severity in favour of the accused as is required in the courts below*.[240]

237 ibid 274. The referral concerned the statutory interpretation of the 1786 Act. The judges held that Melville had not committed an offence (Matheson (n 156) 371).

238 *Trial by Impeachment of Henry Lord Viscount Melville* (n 227) 332 (emphasis added).

239 ibid 333 (emphasis added).

240 ibid 342 (emphasis added).

The point Whitbread was making here was that the House of Commons were voluntarily adhering to the evidential standards required by the common law. This is significant, as it was implicitly distancing Whitbread and his fellow managers from the men who had prosecuted Warren Hastings.

Even before the House of Lords voted 'it was apparent that acquittal was likely, for Trotter had taken the whole blame on himself' and the 'managers were not able to present legal proof of illegal conduct on Melville's part.'[241] A contemporary caricaturist, C Knight, published 'Israelites passing through the Red Sea' on 16 May 1806, which depicted Trotter carrying Melville on his shoulders, whilst waves crash around him and a tankard of Whitbread's beer is about to hit him.[242] This has parallels with Gillray's much earlier 'Blood on Thunder fording the Red Sea', which had depicted Hastings being carried by Lord Thurlow through a much calmer sea littered with floating corpses.[243] The Lords acquitted Melville on 12 June 1806.[244]

Lovat-Fraser was of the opinion that the trial was conducted in a fair manner:

> Lord Erskine, the Chancellor, presided over the proceedings in the House of Lords with singular fairness. The Hastings Trial, which had lasted over many years, had brought the process of impeachment into great disrepute, but Erskine took care that no discredit should be thrown upon his conduct of the matter. He insisted that the House should sit, like every other criminal tribunal, *de die in diem*, till the verdict was delivered, and he enforced upon the managers of the House of Commons and on the counsel for Melville the wholesome rules of procedure established for the detection of crime and the protection of innocence in the criminal Courts.[245]

Erskine's insistence on due process mirrored Whitbread's apparent willingness to respect due process and follow the rules of the ordinary courts. This ensured that the trial was significantly shorter than that of Hastings. A contemporary account observed that '[t]he promptitude, impartiality, energy, and talent, with which these proceedings were conducted . . . have rescued the Trial by Impeachment from the disgrace into which it had fallen, and restored it to its former dignity and honor.'[246] It is apparent that the trial was undertaken in accordance with

241 Matheson (n 156) 369.
242 (CS Knight, 15 May 1806).
243 (SW Fores, 1 March 1788).
244 Contemporary caricaturists noted the acquittal. Thomas Rowlandson's 'The Acquittal or Up Setting the Porter Pot' (T Rowlandson, 20 June 1806) shows a disappointed John Bull observing the acquittal, a theme that is shared by Gillray's 'Sketch for a Monument of Disappointed Justice' (H Humphrey, 9 July 1806), which shows Dundas' supporters assisting his acquittal in the Lords.
245 Lovat-Fraser (n 209) 240–1.
246 *Trial by Impeachment of Henry Lord Viscount Melville* (n 227) iv.

many aspects of recognised legal accepted practice, which demonstrated that due process and justice might be safeguarded.

In a recent article, Hutchinson has observed that Melville's acquittal in the Lords was in part owed to his political allies deciding his fate: '[i]t was noted that Melville was acquitted by many of those linked to him; indeed, the acquittal of Melville came as no surprise, as the Lords was packed with ministerial supporters.'[247] Matheson takes a broader view: '[t]hat he had friends among the peers is undoubtedly true, but no more certain than that he had enemies in that House. Moreover some of his friends and former colleagues absented themselves when the verdict was given.'[248] This is an inherent problem with a jury composed of parliamentarians who are known to the accused, as Melville's supporters deliberately stayed away in order to avoid finding him guilty. This may indicate that even some of his allies were not assured of his innocence. Fry was of the opinion that Melville was guilty, as he 'was, of course, guilty all along', but not of the charges made against him, as 'his accusers simply did not know where to look' as there was an 'impenetrable mass of cryptic information'.[249] Indeed Fry was critical of Melville's character and his attitude towards the charges made against him, by not showing 'any hint of shame or guilt', but noted that '[b]y 1806 . . . he was a figure from the past' and previously acceptable behaviour was no longer tolerated in the nineteenth century.[250] Whether in 1806 this claim was correct is something of a moot point, given that Melville had arguably been following contemporary practice, even if explicitly discouraged by legislation, and had ultimately been acquitted of any wrongdoing by the House of Lords.

The significance of the impeachment

The impeachment of Melville enabled the House of Commons to hold a senior minister to account for conduct that was considered criminal. Members of the House of Commons could pursue a senior minister in Pitt's government and do this despite the support Melville enjoyed amongst his allies. As an alternative to impeachment, it is clear that Melville could have been prosecuted in the ordinary courts. However, whether this would have happened if the decision had been taken that impeachment was an inappropriate mechanism to use is a moot point and even if it had been undertaken, it is not clear whether the outcome would have been any different. Melville was viewed by some commentators as having had a lucky escape, and the process of bringing the impeachment and the trial procedure was presented by Whitbread and the Lord Chancellor as fair and in accordance with the standards required by the ordinary courts. Melville's

247 GD Hutchinson, '"The Manager in Distress": Reaction to the Impeachment of Henry Dundas, 1805–7' (2017) 36(2) *Parliamentary History* 198, 203.
248 Matheson (n 156) 371.
249 Fry (n 210) 275.
250 ibid 276.

impeachment and the insistence on due process and fair standards demonstrates the contrast between this and the earlier impeachments in the beginning of the eighteenth century. Nonetheless, the outcome was dependent on how the House of Lords voted, and this political element to the determination of wrongdoing is no longer appropriate and any revised form of impeachment would need to address this.

Conclusion

The four historical case studies have provided a way of informing how impeachment has been understood at different periods of English and British history. The case studies have demonstrated the pivotal role played by impeachment at various stages throughout history, and how it has been used by the House of Commons to hold the executive to account. The case studies have shown how ministers were held to account of a variety of wrongdoings in the 1620s, how impeachment was used to proceed against former ministers at the start of the eighteenth century, how the perceived parliamentary shortcomings in combatting the misgovernment of the East India Company's Indian territory led to the impeachment of its former Governor-General, and how a senior government minister was impeached for criminal conduct relating to the mismanagement of public money. In each of the four case studies, impeachment has been used as an alternative to, or in conjunction with, the other accountability mechanisms. It is possible to see, through contemporary accounts, how impeachment was perceived, especially with the notoriety of Hastings' impeachment and the coverage it received by caricaturists such as James Sayers and James Gillray. Impeachment has been used in instances of significance, in terms of the House of Commons asserting its authority, partisan politics, and genuine concern over the misconduct of colonial officials and the impact that this had on the lives of those they ruled. The significance of impeachment in these four case studies demonstrates the central role played by the House of Commons, and yet also serves as a warning against the dangers of partisan impeachments and offers an opportunity to reimagine how impeachment might operate in the contemporary United Kingdom.

3 Comparative case study I

United States

This chapter draws upon the comparative usage of impeachment and considers the first of two case studies, the United States, which was chosen due to its differences from and similarities to the United Kingdom. This and the other case study will be used to help inform the discussion as to what form the revised procedure of impeachment should take.

Impeachment in a global context

This section considers impeachment in a global context. Ginsburg, Huq, and Landau have recently undertaken considerable research on the comparative use of impeachment around the world. Their research shows the prevalence of impeachment in both presidential and semi-presidential systems. The findings of Ginsburg, Huq, and Landau's research demonstrates this prevalence and the significant number of attempted impeachments since 1990:

> It is very common for democratic constitutions to provide for removal of the head of state under some conditions. As of 2017, 90 percent of presidential and semi-presidential regimes had constitutional rules that laid out a process for removal, either for incompetence, criminal action or some other basis. . . . The ubiquity of constitutional text on impeachment is matched by a similar pervasiveness of attempts to remove presidents. Although attempts are not rare, they are rarely successful. One scholar, Young Hun Kim, notes that some 45 percent of new presidential democracies faced an impeachment attempt in the period 1974–2003, and that nearly a quarter of presidents who served in this period were subjected to an attempt. . . . Supplementing Kim's data, we gathered data on all such attempts between 1990 and 2018, and found at least 210 proposals in 63 countries, against 127 different heads of state.[1]

1 T Ginsburg, A Huq, and D Landau, 'The Uses and Abuses of Presidential Impeachment' (forthcoming publication in *University of Chicago Law Review*) <>https://papers.ssrn.com/sol3/papers.cfm?abstract_id=3461120>, 25.

DOI: 10.4324/9781003269052-4

Therefore, impeachment is very common in presidential systems and semi-presidential systems. Impeachment as a removal mechanism offers a way for the legislature (in the majority of cases) to remove the President from power. Even within parliamentary systems of government, such as Iceland and Denmark, there exist impeachment mechanisms that co-exist with confidence motions.

Illustrative review of high-profile instances of impeachment since 2010

The following section provides an illustrative review of the contemporary use of impeachment around the world, through a consideration of several high-profile impeachments. These short reviews provide context for the two substantial case studies which compose the rest of this chapter. The focus is both presidential and parliamentary systems of government.

Iceland (2010)

In Iceland the former Prime Minister, Geir Haarde, was impeached by the Icelandic parliament in 2010 in relation to his conduct in the 2008 financial crisis.[2] Haarde was convicted by the Landsdomur Court, the body established under the Icelandic Constitution to deal with allegations of ministerial criminal misconduct. Since the establishment of the Landsdomur Court in 2005 it has sat only once, for the trial of Haarde. The court was composed of 15 members, which included parliamentary appointees, constitutional academics, and members of Iceland's Supreme Court. Haarde was convicted on one charge of gross negligence, and the court decided not to impose a punishment.[3] This was because the court held that Haarde was not guilty of bank negligence in relation to the 2008 financial crisis, which, had he been convicted, could have seen Haarde serve a two-year custodial sentence.[4] The decision to impeach Haarde is controversial and raises issues as to how the Icelandic general public view accountability and the impartiality of the court.[5] In response to the decision of the Landsdomur Court, Haarde made an application to the European Court of Human Rights,

2 'Iceland ex-PM Haarde "Partly" Guilty Over 2008 Crisis' *BBC News* (23 April 2012) <>www.bbc.co.uk/news/world-europe-17817174>.

3 The charge related to section 8(c) of the Ministerial Accountability Act and Article 17 of the Icelandic Constitution.

4 R Neate, 'Iceland ex-PM Geir Haarde Cleared of Bank Negligence' *The Guardian* (23 April 2012) <www.theguardian.com/world/2012/apr/23/iceland-geir-haarde-found-guilty>

5 See R Hjalmarsson and I Kovras, 'Should We Prosecute Political Leaders After a Crisis? Lessons from Iceland' *LSE Blog* (6 December 2017) <>https://blogs.lse.ac.uk/europpblog/2017/12/06/should-we-prosecute-political-leaders-after-a-crisis-lessons-from-iceland/>. See also for public opinion in Iceland 'The Court of Impeachment and the Power of Indictment' (Democratic Constitutional Design) <https://stjornarskra.hi.is/en/deliberative-poll/the-court-of-impeachment-and-the-power-of-indictment/>

which held in 2017 that Article 6 of the European Convention on Human Rights, which safeguards the right to a fair trial, and Article 7, no punishment without law, had not been breached.[6]

Paraguay (2012)

Fernando Lugo was the President of Paraguay from 2008 to 2012. In June 2012, he was impeached for 'poor performance of his duties'.[7] Peter Lambert observed:

> There was no mention of corruption, theft, abuse of human rights, violation of the constitution or breach of presidential code. Instead, the charges were based on five counts of 'poor performance' *(mal desempeño de responsabilidades)*, chief among which was that he had been unable to address growing insecurity.[8]

The Paraguayan Chamber of Deputies voted 76 to 1 to impeach the President and in the Senate 39 to 4 voted to remove him from office. According to *The Economist*:

> [H]e was impeached in less than 36 hours, bundled out of office by 39 votes to four in the Senate, and replaced by his deputy and erstwhile ally, Federico Franco. Venezuela and Argentina said it was a coup; but it wasn't quite. The actions of Paraguay's Congress were legal and constitutional. Mr Lugo himself at first accepted his fate. Paraguayans have reacted calmly to it. Nevertheless, the manner in which he was kicked out was not democratic. Above all, he was given no time to organise his defence.[9]

However, despite the shortcomings of the impeachment process, such as the lack of evidence and the time frame, the constitution 'provides no specific criteria for impeachment beyond the stipulation that it can be carried out on the grounds of poor performance of functions by a two-thirds majority'.[10] It has been argued

6 *Haarde v Iceland* (Application no. 66847/12).

7 Section VI: Of the Political Trial [Juicio Político], Article 225: Of the Procedure, outlines how impeachment operates in Paraguay. This is <>www.constituteproject.org/constitution/Paraguay_2011.pdf>. The process requires a two-thirds majority in both the Chamber of Deputies and the Chamber of Senators and even if both chambers vote that a crime has been committed, then this will only remove a President from office. The relevant authorities can then begin criminal proceedings.

8 P Lambert, 'The Lightning Impeachment of Paraguay's President Lugo' *E-International Relations* (9 August 2012) <>www.e-ir.info/2012/08/09/the-lightning-impeachment-of-paraguays-president-lugo/>.

9 'Impeachment, Paraguayan-Style' *The Economist* (30 June 2012) <www.economist.com/node/21557771>. See also L Marsteintredet, M Llanos and D Nolte, 'Paraguay and the Politics of Impeachment' (2013) 24(4) *Journal of Democracy* 110 at 110.

10 See Lambert (n 8).

that the Paraguayan Congress used impeachment 'as a political weapon' to dispose of Lugo, in a manner that was in accordance with the law.[11] The President had attempted to challenge the legality of the impeachment in the Paraguayan Supreme Court on the basis of a lack of due process.[12] The Supreme Court rejected Lugo's appeal 'reasoning that impeachment is a political process under the purview of Congress'.[13]

Brazil (2016)

In 2016, President Dilma Rousseff was impeached by the Lower House of Congress, with 367 members supporting her impeachment and only 137 voting against the impeachment.[14] This satisfied the requirements that two-thirds of members supported the impeachment. Rousseff was convicted by the Senate as the two-thirds requirement was satisfied. The votes in the Senate were 81 voting to convict and only 20 voting to acquit. This meant that the President was removed from office and Michel Temer became President for the remainder of her term. Importantly, the Senate had decided not to prevent Rousseff from holding public office for a period of eight years.[15] What had led to Rousseff's impeachment were allegations that she had frontloaded 'funds for government social programmes and [issued] spending budget decrees without congressional approval ahead of her reelection in 2014. The opposition claimed that these constituted a "crime of responsibility".'[16] This had been common practice by previous Brazilian administrations.

11 Marsteintredet e al. (n 9) 110 at 111. They argued that whilst impeachment is political rather than judicial in process, Lugo's impeachment can be distinguished from others in Latin America where the President was accused of breaking the law: '[i]n comparison, the accusations made against Lugo were clearly political, and it is hard to argue that the president himself had violated any law. This case underlines the political nature of impeachment, which fittingly is called a juicio político (political judgment) in Spanish. The bottom line is that Lugo had lost support from the major parties in Congress, and the opposition used the constitutionally available procedure of impeachment to remove him. The case also demonstrates that presidents need a minimum level of confidence in the legislature to shield themselves against impeachment' (at 117–18).

12 'Paraguay President Fernando Lugo Impeached by Congress' *BBC News* (23 June 2012) <www.bbc.co.uk/news/world-latin-america-18553813>; 'Paraguayan Supreme Court Receives Unconstitutional Appeal on Lugo's Removal' *Merco Press* (12 July 2012) <>http://en.mercopress.com/2012/07/12/paraguayan-supreme-court-receives-unconstitutional-appeal-on-lugo-s-removal>.

13 Marsteintredet et al. (n 9) 114.

14 See 'Brazil President Dilma Rousseff Removed from Office by Senate' *BBC News* (1 September 2016) <www.bbc.co.uk/news/world-latin-america-37237513>.

15 See J Watts, 'Brazil's Dilma Rousseff Impeached by Senate in Crushing Defeat' *The Guardian* (1 September 2016) <www.theguardian.com/world/2016/aug/31/dilma-rousseff-impeached-president-brazilian-senate-michel-temer>.

16 ibid.

South Korea (2016)

In 2016, the President of South Korea, Park Geun-hye, was accused of conspiring with an associate to commit extortion. As President, Park Geun-hye had immunity from prosecution and could not be prosecuted for the criminal offences that she was alleged to have committed.[17] In 2016, the legislature of South Korea, the National Assembly, voted to impeach President Park. However, the decision whether to remove the President from office was undertaken by the South Korean Constitutional Court, which in 2017 ruled that she should be removed from office for violating the law and the South Korean Constitution.[18] Importantly, '[t]he Constitutional Court stressed that it ruled on the legitimacy of the National Assembly's decision to impeach, and not on Park's criminal guilt.'[19] This is an important distinction, as the court was tasked with determining whether the impeachment by the National Assembly could be justified.

Why the case studies were selected: United States and Denmark

The rest of this and the next chapter focuses on the two case studies I undertook: United States and Denmark. This section outlines why I chose these two case studies over other countries that have been considered in the earlier review. The use of impeachment in Iceland offered an opportunity to consider how impeachment was used in a parliamentary system of government. However, whilst the impeachment occurred before the commencement of my PhD studies, the decision of the European Court of Human Rights was not reached until 2017. I decided that I would instead focus on another parliamentary system, Denmark, as my first case study, because there had been the successful use of impeachment in the 1990s and this impeachment had been subsequently considered by the European Court of Human Rights. The impeachment and removal of Rousseff and Park occurred during the course of my PhD studies, and this was one of the reasons why I decided not to select either South Korea or Brazil as a case study. The other reason was that whilst South Korea, Brazil, and Paraguay were presidential systems and would provide interesting case studies, I decided, because of the British influence on the inclusion of impeachment in its constitution, to choose the United States as my second case study. I will explain the rationale and justification for the decision to choose Denmark and the United States as case studies.

17 C Sang-Hun, 'South Korea's Impeachment Process, Explained' *The New York Times* (27 November 2016) <www.nytimes.com/2016/11/27/world/asia/impeaching-south-korea-president.html?smid=tw-share>.

18 C Sang-Hun, 'South Korea Removes President Park Geun-Hye' *The New York Times* (9 March 2017) <www.nytimes.com/2017/03/09/world/asia/park-geun-hye-impeached-south-korea.html>.

19 See H, Lim, 'A Closer Look at the Korean Constitutional Court's Ruling on Park Geun-Hye's Impeachment' *Yale Journal of International Law* (18 May 2017) <>www.yjil.yale.edu/a-closer-look-at-the-korean-constitutional-courts-ruling-on-park-geun-hyes-impeachment/>.

Case study one: United States

The first case study considers the use of impeachment in the United States. The focus here is from a federal perspective, as opposed to considering the impeachment devices that exist at a state level. The case study will briefly consider the understanding and use of impeachment before the enactment of the constitution. It will then outline what is meant by impeachment and how it operates. It will be important to consider who can be impeached and the sanctions available following impeachment. This case study is concerned with the impeachment of the President as head of the executive and whether impeachment can be used against other members of the executive. The United States was selected as a case study due to the influence the British use of impeachment had on the framers of the US Constitution. It was also selected due to the relatively recent impeachment of President Bill Clinton in 1998, an impeachment which was still widely remembered, due to the novelty, at the time, of a presidential impeachment and the subject matter involving extra-marital affairs. Another reason for choosing the United States was the fact that it was a presidential system and impeachment offered the only way to remove a President, whereas in a parliamentary system the Prime Minister could be removed by a vote of no confidence. This would therefore offer an interesting contrast and allow me to draw on considerable academic literature by US scholars.

Impeachment before the drafting of the US Constitution

This section will consider the use and understanding of impeachment of what had been British North America prior to the enactment of the US Constitution. As Hoffer and Hull have explored in their book *Impeachment in America, 1635–1805*, colonial British North America had pre-revolutionary experience of impeachment proceedings in its colonial legislatures.[20] The first 'impeachment' had occurred in 1635 when John Harvey, who was the Governor of Virginia, 'was driven out of the colony and sent to England for judgment' by the Colonial Assembly of Virginia.[21] Following the unilateral Declaration of Independence by the Second Continental Congress in 1776 and the Treaty of Paris in 1783, whereby Great Britain recognised the independence of the 13 former British North American colonies, the newly independent United States debated the best form of government and the suitability of adopting a federal system.[22] It was

20 PC Hoffer and NEH Hull, *Impeachment in America, 1635–1805* (Yale University Press 1984) 8–10.

21 ibid 15.

22 See JP Greene, *Peripheries and Centre: Constitutional Development in the Extended Polities of the British Empire and the United States 1607–1788* (University of Georgia Press 1986), in particular 198–207; CG Fritz, *American Sovereigns: The People and America's Constitutional Tradition Before the Civil War* (Cambridge University Press 2008).

unsurprising that impeachment was included within the federal US Constitution of 1787, which replaced the Articles of Confederation. Potts observes:

> In taking over the impeachment machinery the fathers of 1787 were but doing what they did in constructing almost every other part of the Constitution they adopted, with more or less change, legal principles and governmental devices with which they, as common law lawyers and former British subjects, were familiar.[23]

Reference to how federal impeachment differs from that of British historical practice will be made throughout this case study.

Impeachment in the US Constitution

This next section will consider the incorporation of impeachment in the federal constitution. The provisions to remove a member of the federal executive and judicial branches are outlined in the US Constitution of 1787.[24] This section is concerned with impeachment at a federal level and how impeachment can be used against the President and other members of the executive. The framers of the

23 CS Potts, 'Impeachment as a Remedy' (1926) 12 *St. Louis Law Review* 15, 16. On the influence of English and British use of impeachment see Hoffer and Hull (n 20) 30–4; R Berger, *Impeachment the Constitutional Problems* (Harvard University Press 1973) 1–52; TW Dwight, 'Trial by Impeachment' (1867) 15 *The American Law Register* 257.

24 See *The Constitution of the United States* (Penguin Classics 2017). Impeachment is also found in state constitutions. See for example the New York State Constitution <G:\info\shared\DOSPUBS\DAR\PUBS\CONSTITUTION\Constitution2011.wpd (ny.gov)>. In light of the significance placed on the intention of the framers of the US Constitution when seeking to define impeachment, especially in the case of the Clinton impeachment (1998–9), it is important to appreciate the events of Philadelphia in 1787 and the rationale for including impeachment. See M Farrand, *The Framing of the Constitution of the United States* (Yale University Press 1913), where the author outlines the development of the constitution. For example, a plan known as the Virginia Plan had intended that the President was dependent on the legislature. This was because they would be chosen by the law makers to serve a seven-year term. However, the Convention 'had a decided preference for an independent executive' and that the executive could be removed by impeachment (79). The inclusion of impeachment was controversial. However, the proposal gained the support of the majority (118). It was also decided that the President should be tried by the Senate and not by the Supreme Court (166). For a commentary on the creation of the US Constitution see LW Levy (ed), *Essays on the Making of the Constitution* (2nd edn, OUP 1987), in particular see LW Levy, 'Introduction – The Making of the Constitution, 1776-1789'; JP Roche, 'The Convention as a Case Study for Democratic Politics', especially Part V for a discussion of the Virginia Plan. Impeachment was included within the New York State Constitution. However, it differed as although '[i]mpeachment proceedings could be initiated by the lower house' a special court for the trial of impeachments determined the outcome and it was 'composed of senators, the chancellor, and the judges of the supreme court, or the major part of them' (WP Adams, *The First American Constitutions* (Revised edn, Rowman and Littlefield 2001) 266.

constitution had sought to place safeguards in the use of impeachment. Alexander Hamilton argued that the constitutional arrangements avoided 'the inconvenience of making the same persons both accusers and judges, and guarding against the danger of persecution from the prevalence of a fractious spirit in either of those branches'.[25] Impeachment was established as an integral part of the constitution:

> *Article I*
>
> Section 2
>
> The House of Representatives shall chuse their Speaker and other Officers; and shall have the *sole Power of Impeachment.*
>
> Section 3
>
> . . .
>
> The Senate shall have the *sole Power to try all Impeachments.* When sitting for that Purpose, they shall be on Oath or Affirmation. When the President of the United States is tried the *Chief Justice shall preside*: And no Person shall be convicted without the Concurrence of *two thirds of the Members present.*
>
> Judgment in Cases of Impeachment shall not extend further than to *removal from Office*, and disqualification to hold and enjoy any Office of honor, Trust or Profit under the United States: but the Party convicted *shall nevertheless be liable and subject to Indictment, Trial, Judgment and Punishment, according to Law.*[26]

Therefore, the House of Representatives has the sole power to bring an impeachment and it needs only a bare majority of those members present to do so. This requirement mirrors the powers of the British House of Commons. The sole power of determining whether an impeachable offence has been committed belongs to the Senate. Importantly, the Senate requires a two-thirds majority of all members present to convict. This is different from British practice, as although in Britain the House of Lords determined guilt, it could do so on a bare majority of those members voting. The requirement for a two-thirds majority is an important safeguard that places a restriction on the Senate voting to convict without a clear majority. Such a requirement was important in securing the acquittal of President Andrew Johnson in 1868, President Bill Clinton in 1999, and President Donald Trump in 2020.

Who can be impeached?

This next section will consider who can be impeached by the House of Representatives. Under a literal interpretation of the US Constitution, impeachment

25 *Federalist n.66*, cited in W McKay and CW Johnson, *Parliament and Congress: Representation and Scrutiny in the Twenty-First Century* (OUP 2012) 506.

26 Emphasis added.

is confined to civil officers, which would include members of the executive and judicial branches of government whilst they are in office, but not in the event of their resignation. Impeachment does not apply to military officers or private individuals.[27] This is different from the United Kingdom, where impeachment proceedings have been initiated against royal advisors and ministers, judges, parliamentarians, a Queen Consort,[28] and against private individuals.[29]

Article II of the constitution outlines how impeachment relates to the President:

> Section 2
>
> The President shall . . . have Power to Grant Reprieves and Pardons for Offences against the United States, *except in Cases of Impeachment.*
>
> Section 4
>
> The *President, Vice President and all Civil Officers of the United States,* shall be removed from Office on *Impeachment for and Conviction of, Treason, Bribery, or other high Crimes and Misdemeanors.*[30]

There has been debate about whether the First Lady might fall within the definition of a civil officer for the purposes of Section 4 of Article II.[31] Such a debate originated during the Clinton presidency due to the proactive and influential role undertaken as First Lady by Hillary Clinton.

We shall see ahead that the sanction for being found guilty by the Senate is to be removed from office and possibly also to be disqualified from holding public office again. This raises a number of interesting points. First, if we were to accept that a First Lady or First Gentleman could fall within the definition of a civil office, then how would they be removed from office, and would this be achieved through the abolition of their official role as the President's spouse?

27 McKay and Johnson (n 25) 506.

28 Queen Henrietta Maria, Queen Consort of Charles I. See parliamentary attempts to undermine another Queen Consort, Catherine, wife of Charles II, against the king's wishes: SM Wynne, 'Catherine [Catherine of Braganza, Catarina Henriqueta de Braganca]' in *Oxford Dictionary of National Biography* (OUP 2004). For discussion of why impeachment was not used against Queen Caroline, Queen Consort of George IV see DH Erskine, 'The Trial of Queen Caroline and the Impeachment of President Clinton: Law as a Weapon for Political Reform' (2008) 7 *Washington University Global Studies Law Review* 1, see in particular fn 40.

29 See Chapter 2.

30 Emphasis added.

31 See MJ Broyde and RA Schapiro, 'Impeachment and Accountability: The Case of the First Lady' (1998) 15 *Const. Comment* 479. The authors observed that the Court of Appeals for the District of Columbia Circuit ruled in *Association of American Physicians and Surgeons v. Clinton* 997 F.2d 898 (D.C.Cir. 1993) that the First Lady was a government officer (482). They concluded that from a formal perspective, the First Lady could not be a civil officer, because '[t]he First Spouse is not elected or formally appointed' (495). However, under the functional perspective she could potentially be regarded as a civil officer, due to the nature of her role in acting as a close adviser, confidential agent, and running mate (495–503).

Second, there is debate about whether impeachment could be used to proceed against a former civil officer, even in the event that conduct amounting to high crimes and misdemeanors was subsequently discovered relating to their time in office. In support of the proposition that former civil officers were liable to impeachment, we can point to a number of examples. Proceedings were brought against a former Senator, William Blount of Tennessee in 1799, albeit in that case the impeachment was rejected by the Senate. Blount's case is interesting. Potts argues that the Senate rejected the impeachment brought by the House of Representatives, as Blount was first, not a civil officer as he had been a Senator, and second, he was no longer a Senator. For Potts the key reason was the first: '[t]he arguments clearly show that the first contention was the one mainly relied upon, and the Senate's action has always been regarded as having established the fact that members of Congress are not impeachable.'[32] Therefore, what motivated the Senate was the fact that Blount was a member of the legislature and outside of the scope of Article II.

Another example is from 1876, when the Secretary of State for War, William W Belknap, was impeached by the House of Representatives and he resigned prior to the proceedings reaching the Senate. However, despite Belknap's resignation the Senate in this instance proceeded to trial.[33] Broyde and Schapiro observed that '[s]cholars today generally agree that in principle former officials are subject to impeachment.'[34] Writing in 1926, Potts observed the long-running debate

32 See Potts (n 23) 17 for a discussion on why members of Congress cannot be impeached.

33 See J Isenbergh, 'Impeachment and Presidential Immunity from Judicial Process' (1999) 18(53) *Yale Law and Policy Review* 53, 96–9 for a discussion of whether impeachment can extend to former civil officers. Isenbergh rejected the concern raised by Akhil Amar ('If You Convict, You Must Evict' *Legal Times* [8 February 1999]) that impeachment proceedings could be brought against private individuals: 'impeachment simply is not a practical, or even conceivable, weapon against private persons, except in the most extraordinary or exotic circumstances. . . . [However] Impeachment of private persons is not absolutely alien to American Practice. . . . Therefore, the point that Amar advances as though a devastating counterexample against my theory of impeachment turns out to be more damaging to the conventional view' (97–8). Isenbergh had considered the examples of former Senator Blount and Secretary of State for War Belknap, whilst drawing upon the English tradition which did permit the impeachment of private persons, such as Warren Hastings, whose impeachment occurred after his resignation as Governor-General of Bengal, but for activities undertaken when in office. Turley observed that 'the *only* impeachment discussed in the Constitutional Convention was the impeachment of the Governor General of the East India Company colony, Warren Hastings, for his abuses in India. Hastings, however, had already resigned when the House of Commons impeached him' (emphasis added), J Turley, 'Congress as Grand Jury: The Role of the House of Representatives in the Impeachment of an American President' (1998–1999) 68(3) *Geo. Wash. L. Rev.* 735, 780. Isenbergh points out that Hastings was impeached 'for corrupt and oppressive conduct in India *beyond the reach* of local law' (emphasis added) (fn 204, 97). This is interesting as it could perhaps permit the impeachment of a civil officer who had exercised power in US-controlled territory during a period of occupation (i.e. Iraq or Afghanistan), and they could be impeached for acts committed during their tenure.

34 Broyde and Schapiro (n 31) 490. See also Potts (n 23).

about whether former civil officers were liable to impeachment and cited John Quincy Adams' support of impeaching a former Secretary of State in 1846,[35] as well the Senate's approach to accepting jurisdiction to try Secretary Belknap in 1876.[36] The decision of the House of Representatives to impeach Donald Trump in 2021, despite his leaving office within a short period of time, shows that a former civil officer could be tried by the Senate even though their term of office has expired, or indeed that would have been the case had Trump resigned the presidency.

This second point, whether a former civil officer could be impeached, is important as it shows that the scope of impeachment is not fettered by the expiry of a term, resignation, or in the case of members of the cabinet, dismissal by the President. By way of comparison, it had always been British practice that impeachment could be used against those who currently hold or who have held office.[37]

Finally, it is important to note the number of impeachments that have occurred. Since 1787, there have been over 60 instances of impeachment proceedings being initiated in Congress, of which only 18 have led to impeachment.[38] Examples of the actual impeachments include three Presidents, a Secretary of State for War, federal judges, and a Senator.[39] The majority of those impeached have been federal judges, including Justice Samuel Chase of the Supreme Court in 1805.[40] The last judge to be removed by way of impeachment was Thomas Porteous Jr. of the Federal District Court in Louisiana in 2010.[41]

35 Potts (n 23) 19.

36 ibid 20.

37 For example, impeachment had been used as a political weapon as part of the dispute between the Whigs and Tories. George I's Whig ministers had used impeachment to proceed against leading Tories who had served as ministers during Queen Anne's reign. The impeachments related to their time in office and occurred after they were no longer in government (see PDG Thomas, *The House of Commons in the Eighteenth Century* (Gregg Revivals 1992) 36. For details on the political situation in 1714 and the rise of the Whigs see JH Plumb, *The Growth of Political Stability in England 1675–1725* (Macmillan 1967) 159–89.

38 For a complete list and the Senate's verdict in each case see <www.senate.gov/artandhistory/history/common/briefing/Senate_Impeachment_Role.htm>.

39 See McKay and Johnson (n 25) 507.

40 MS Hurwitz, 'The Impeachment of Federal District Judge Samuel B. Kent' (2009) 30(2) *The Justice System Journal* 223. Hurwitz observed: 'thirteen federal judges have faced an impeachment trial, nine of whom were found guilty by the Senate or resigned from the bench before final action in the Senate. Justice Samuel Chase, who was acquitted by the Senate, is the only Supreme Court justice to have been impeached by the House' (223). It should be noted that unlike the United Kingdom, where a senior judge can be removed by a resolution of both Houses of Parliament under the Act of Settlement 1701, in the United States, the only device to remove judges is impeachment.

41 J Steinhauer, 'Senate, for Just the 8th Time, Votes to Oust a Federal Judge' *The New York Times* (8 December 2010).

The scope of an impeachable offence

This next section is concerned with the scope of an impeachable offence. In order to achieve this it will be necessary to consider academic opinion and engage with the debate over the interpretative role in the original meaning of the constitution.

Article II of the constitution defines an impeachable offence as treason, bribery, or other high crimes and misdemeanours. The meaning of what constitutes an impeachable offence has proved controversial, with uncertainty and disagreement amongst academics and scholars about the precise meaning of the term high crimes and misdemeanours. Opinion is divided between a more flexible interpretation to suit the object of the current political climate and the agenda of the current composition of the House of Representatives and House Judicial Committee, and a strict adherence to the intentions of the original framers of the US Constitution.[42] In determining whether there are grounds for impeachment, there will inevitably be a debate on whether the House of Representatives is constricted by the original intent of the framers. Katyal observes that '[a]lthough there are arguments for and against the use of original intent, many of those arguments depend on who is doing the interpreting.'[43] This is telling, as when applied to the arguments relating to the legitimacy of the proceedings against President Clinton, '[t]he Democrats argued that "high crimes and misdemeanors" had a very narrow meaning at the founding of the Constitution, and the Republicans responded by arguing that they should not be hemmed in by a two-century-old

42 See JH Dougherty, 'Inherent Limitations Upon Impeachment' (1913–1914) 23 *Yale Law Journal* 60, 70. Dougherty was critical of the broad approach taken by Lawrence in an article published at the time of the Johnson impeachment: '[t]hose who seek to expand the power of impeachment by surrounding it with such an atmosphere of awe, deal only in generalities, never cite a case; their only reliance is upon the words which have been inherited from the English practice, to wit, "high crimes and misdemeanors." These words, it may be acknowledged, invest the impeachment court with "an awful discretion"; but nevertheless they designate a circumscribed area of jurisdiction, however extensive it may be' (70). See W Lawrence, 'The Law of Impeachment' (1867) 15(11) *The American Law Register* 641. Lawrence, who was a member of the House of Representatives, had argued that impeachment for 'high crimes and misdemeanors' was not limited to indictable offences as recognised by statute or case law: '[i]t is absurd to say that impeachment is here a mode of procedure for the punishment of crime, when the Constitution declares its object to be removal from and disqualification to hold office, and that "the party convicted shall nevertheless be liable and subject to indictment, trial, judgment, and punishment, according to law," for his crimes' (644). Lawrence supported his interpretation based upon English usage of impeachment as 'the authorities are abundant to show that the phrase "high crimes and misdemeanors," as used in the British and our Constitution, are not limited to crimes defined by statute or as recognised at common law' (647). To provide further justification for this interpretation, Lawrence had given an example of the absurdity of a President being able to commit acts such as violating the laws of Canada or Mexico without having committed a criminal offence within US federal law, and therefore not being liable for impeachment (662).

43 NK Katyal, 'Impeachment as Congressional Constitutional Interpretation' (2000) 63 *Law and Contemporary Problems* 169, 191.

interpretation of a living document.'[44] It is unsurprising that in the four cases of presidential impeachment that there has been controversy over the scope, or rather lack of definition of its limits, or that those seeking to remove a President from office will argue against adopting either a narrow interpretation of the framers' intent, or to avoid being bound by originalism.[45]

In an article published at the time of the Clinton impeachment, Presser considers the intention of the framers:

> The Framers considered impeachment to be a vital device intended to guarantee that the President and other federal officials would act with integrity. Indeed, it was a device designed to ensure that the President and other federal officials would do what they were supposed to do, because they would know that they would face removal if they did not. . . . [46] The *Federalist No. 64*, one of the few numbers written by John Jay, who was to become the first Chief Justice of the United States, provides one very clear indication of what the Framers intended with regard to impeachment. . . . Jay made plain that when a President fails to live up to the requirement of trust, honor, and virtue that is necessary to meet his treaty-making and other executive responsibilities – if, in short, he is not an honorable or virtuous person who will perform his duties in the interest of the people – impeachment is available to remove him.[47]

Presser was clear that *The Federalist* was to be taken as showing what had been meant by impeachment and that this interpretation had been endorsed by Presidents Jefferson and Madison.[48] Such an interpretation is very broad and does not require a specific criminal offence to have been committed. This is a useful reminder of the scope of impeachment as envisaged by the framers and demonstrates that the scope of an impeachable offence, whilst drawing upon British practice, was intended to be both broad and available to cover situations where

44 ibid 169.

45 See for example the view of the House Managers during the impeachment of Andrew Johnson: '[i]t is said if the impeachable crimes are not defined by law the power of impeachment will be undefined and dangerous. The power to determine impeachable crimes by the Senate is no more undefined than the power of the common law courts to determine common-law crimes. Impeachment is regulated by principles as well defined and permanently settled as the fundamental and eternal doctrines of right reason, and justice pervading the parliamentary jurisprudence of civilized nations, and, like the common law, it has emerged from primeval errors and adapted itself to an advanced civilization' (per William Lawrence, 40th Congress, 1868), cited in Katyal (n 43) 174. Lawrence was the author of 'The Law of Impeachment' (n 42).

46 SB Presser, 'Would George Washington Have Wanted Bill Clinton Impeached?' (1999) 67 *Geo. Wash. L. Rev.* 666, 667.

47 ibid 668–9.

48 ibid.

the office holder's conduct fell below the standards, not necessarily of a legal nature, of the times.

In terms of what should be an impeachable offence, it was decided not to include maladministration as a grounds for removal, and instead to use high crimes and misdemeanours.[49] Presser argued that 'the only evidence on the definition of impeachable offenses we have from the debates at the 1787 Constitutional Convention in Philadelphia appears to suggest that more than mere maladministration, something approaching "great and dangerous offences," or an "[a]ttempt to subvert the Constitution" is required.'[50] He was clear that a distinction had to be drawn 'between mere "maladministration" and the betrayals of the Constitution.'[51] Thus, partisan use of impeachment went contrary to what had been intended.[52] According to Presser:

> At the time the Framers inserted the phrase 'high Crimes and Misdemeanors' into the Constitution, they had a wealth of English experience with those words on which to draw, and it appears clear that the Framers intended and understood that the phrase 'high Crimes and Misdemeanors' was to be interpreted according to the meaning it was given by English common law.[53]

Presser made reference to Raoul Berger's[54] analysis of English impeachments, which demonstrated that the grounds related to criminality in connection to office, or general unfitness to hold office.[55] Presser noted:

> The English cases lend further support to the notion derived from *The Federalist* and the text of the Constitution that impeachable offenses, 'high Crimes and Misdemeanors' if you will, are acts that are inconsistent with the obligations and duties of office, that involve putting personal or partisan concerns ahead of the interests of the people, and that demonstrate the unfitness of the man to the office.[56]

Such an interpretation based on the framers' intentions (which is originalism) had been criticised by Levinson:

> I find at least two things astonishing about most of these discussions. The first is the assumption that we must necessarily comply with the wishes of

49 ibid 670–1.
50 ibid 671.
51 ibid.
52 ibid 672.
53 ibid 673.
54 See Berger (n 23).
55 Presser (n 46) 673–4.
56 ibid 674.

> the Founding generation in regard to presidential tenure in office and the standards for impeachment. Why would anyone believe this? To put it mildly, the Framers were living in a political and intellectual world radically different from our own. As Ackerman himself demonstrates in his current work on the election of 1800, the Framers rather fantastically envisioned a polity free of parties, in which the President would indeed be the best, i.e., most virtuous, man, chosen by electoral colleges of virtuous local notables.[57]

Levinson was clear as to the shortcomings in adopting an originalist approach, as put simply the framers' understanding of how the US Constitution would operate no longer bears any semblance to how it actually functioned.[58] The necessity, or otherwise, of following an originalist interpretation of the US Constitution is a very moot point and whilst it divides scholars, the view presented by Levinson has considerable merit. It makes sense, from an evolutionary position, to see the scope of impeachment as something to be determined at a given time by the House of Representatives. Congressman Gerald Ford was of the opinion that high crimes and misdemeanours meant

> whatever a majority of the House of Representatives considers to be at a given moment in history; conviction results from whatever offense or offenses two-thirds of the other body considers to be sufficiently serious to require removal of the accused from office.[59]

This is an attractive position as it reflects the reality of the workings of politics and how the scope of an impeachable offence might be determined, without necessarily being bound by arguments over the framers' meaning. This can be justified by the fact that impeachment is limited to removal from office or disqualification, and the existence of the two-thirds majority requirement in the Senate.

It is important to note that the debate over the meaning and scope of impeachment is not new, in the sense that in 1867, Lawrence[60] had sought to argue that impeachment was broader than indictable offences, whereas in 1926, Potts[61] had been critical of adopting such a broad approach. It is clear that in the event of any presidential impeachment, the meaning of what conduct amounts to high crimes and misdemeanours will remain a moot point, and it is arguable that, as in the impeachment of President Clinton, the House of Representatives will not be tied

57 S Levinson, 'Transitions' (1999) *Yale Law Journal* 2215, 2233.

58 See SM Griffin, *American Constitutionalism: From Theory to Politics* (Princeton University Press 1996), in particular 182–8 for the different types of originalist interpretation of the US Constitution and how these are used as one method in judicial interpretation of the law.

59 CONG. REC. H3113–14 (daily ed. 15 April 1970) (statement of Representative Gerald R Ford).

60 Lawrence (n 42).

61 Potts (n 23).

to a definition. This reflects reality and as just stated, the broad approach, with reference to specific indictable offences, is to be preferred as reflects the purpose of impeachment, to remove individuals deemed through their conduct to be unsuited to civil office, which does not require that such conduct must fall within a specific criminal offence.

Michael J Gerhardt argues that the framers intended impeachment to cover conduct that would amount to a political crime, without needing to be an actual crime, and provides a lucid account of what is meant by impeachment.[62] He observed that the drafters had deliberately 'narrowed the range of impeachable offenses for public officeholders to "Treason, Bribery, or other high Crimes and Misdemeanors", although the English Parliament always had refused to constrain its jurisdiction over impeachments by restrictively defining impeachable offenses.'[63] Despite restricting the range of offences, the US Constitution differed from Britain, as unlike the British model there was a clear separation between criminal proceedings and impeachment proceedings, although the US model did not define high crimes and misdemeanours.[64] The refusal to define would permit the House of Representatives to proceed in the future 'on a case-by-case basis'.[65] The problem is that these previous instances of impeachment, the precedents, are capable of different interpretations, to support or to argue against impeachment, such as in the case of how the Democrats and Republicans differed over how to interpret the impeachments of Chief Justice Samuel Chase and President Andrew Johnson.[66]

Another interesting point to consider in determining the scope of an impeachable offence was the focus on political crimes as opposed to all actual criminal offences. It was clear that impeachment proceedings were intended to cover political crimes that were committed against the federal state, which provides guidance on the framers' view: '[a]lthough the concept "political crimes" uses the term "crimes," the phrase did not necessarily include all indictable offenses. Nor were all indictable offenses considered "political crimes".'[67] This drew upon the British understanding of high crimes and misdemeanours and '[t]he delegates at the Constitutional Convention were intimately familiar with impeachment in colonial America, which like impeachment in England, had basically been a political proceeding.'[68] Interestingly, a President could commit a criminal offence and this offence would not be grounds for impeachment.[69]

62 MJ Gerhardt, 'The Lessons of Impeachment History' (1999) *Faculty Publications* Paper 603.
63 ibid 605.
64 ibid 605–6.
65 ibid 616.
66 See Katyal (n 43) 182–3 for a discussion on the role of precedent and how it was used during the Clinton impeachment.
67 Gerhardt (n 62).
68 ibid 610–11.
69 ibid 615.

However, a contrary view is that impeachment is both a judicial and a criminal process, with impeachable offences being 'common law offenses, not limited to statutory crimes', as 'all courts of criminal jurisdiction ultimately have the same purpose – protection of the public. Impeachment lies for serious misconduct against which the representatives and senators, acting responsibly as grand jurors and judges, feel a duty to protect the nation.'[70] However, this presumes that a political body will act *responsibly* and in the public, and *not partisan*, interest in first determining whether to support the accusations and second whether the offence has occurred. Whilst impeachments for relatively insignificant federal judges might engender such an approach, it is doubtful that a high-profile presidential impeachment would be regarded as not being tainted by political and partisan considerations. As Theodore W Dwight observed when cautioning against political impeachments: '[i]t is the weakness of a *political* tribunal that, whether justly or not, it labors under the imputation of being moulded by faction.'[71] From Dwight's commentary it is apparent that he did not believe that impeachment could be used as a non-partisan device.[72] Hence the importance of having the safeguards of requiring a two-thirds majority of Senators to convict and having the Chief Justice preside over the trial.

This contrary view would place the scope of impeachment within a legal, rather than a purely political, framework. Whilst there are advantages in restricting impeachment to specific indictable offences and limiting the broad scope of what could amount to be impeachable offence, this arguably does not reflect the purpose of impeachment within the US Constitution. This raises the interesting question as to whether a revised form of impeachment in the United Kingdom should have such a broad scope or whether it would be expedient to limit this within a statutory framework. The answer to this question would depend on considerations as to the normative purpose of impeachment within a UK setting. Therefore, whilst the broad approach adopted within the US Constitution is a tenable interpretation of how it should work in the United States, it would not be appropriate to follow this approach in the United Kingdom. The rationale for this conclusion will be addressed in Chapter 9.

The trial process

In terms of the trial in the Senate, the Chief Justice of the US Supreme Court would preside in cases of presidential or vice-presidential impeachments, otherwise it would normally be the Vice President in his capacity as the President

70 'The Scope of the Power to Impeach' (1975) 84(6) *The Yale Law Journal* 1316, 1335–6.
71 Dwight (n 23) 283.
72 See ibid 258 for a description of the English precedents as 'excitements of the most heated party contests'. See also Dwight's warning: 'the process of impeachment often greatly disappoints those who resort to it. . . . It has been noticed that many of those who have employed this means to ruin their enemies have themselves . . . been the victims of similar proceedings' (Dwight (n 23) 282).

of the Senate.[73] Where the Chief Justice presides, as in the case of William H Rehnquist during the trial of President Clinton, or John Roberts during the trial of President Trump, the role of the Chief Justice is limited to attempting to oversee the trial and he cannot determine the outcome, even if he believed that there was no case to answer, or that the Senators were not abiding to the terms of the oath relating to how they would act impartially. The trial takes place in the Senate, which is a political body, although it is expected to take on a judicial role to determine guilt and senators swear an oath to be impartial as jurors.[74] It is important to note that the Senate became a directly elected body only as a result of the Seventeenth Amendment in 1913 and was relevant to why the framers had originally given the role to the Senate.

The sanction for being convicted by the Senate

The power of impeachment carries no other sanction than an automatic removal from office and a possible disqualification from holding future office. However, it is possible for a person to be impeached and later hold office, such as Alcee Hastings, who was removed from his position as a Federal District Judge in the Southern District of Florida and subsequently elected to the House of Representatives.[75] This is its primary function, and therefore a resignation, such as Nixon in 1974 from the presidency and Samuel B. Kent in 2009 from the federal bench,[76] had achieved what was intended by commencing impeachment proceedings.[77] Hurwitz has observed that most of those who are to be impeached resign, trying to 'avoid the stigma of being one of the few federal judges to have been

73 Note that this offends the theory of the separation of powers, JK Goldstein, 'Constitutional Change, Originalism, and the Vice Presidency' (2013) 16(2) *Journal of Constitutional Law* 369.

74 SP Fino, 'Impeachment Trial Senators Swear an Oath Aimed at Guarding "Against Malice, Falsehood, and Evasion"' *The Conversation* (18 January 2020) <https://theconversation.com/impeachment-trial-senators-swear-an-oath-aimed-at-guarding-against-malice-falsehood-and-evasion-130120>.

75 See D Johnston, 'Hastings Ousted as Senate Vote Convicts Judge' *The New York Times* (21 October 1989). In Hastings' case he had been acquitted by a criminal court of the charges that were used in the impeachment: 'Mr. Specter, a former Philadelphia District Attorney, and Mr. Bingaman, a former Attorney General in New Mexico, both said the evidence failed to convince them of Judge Hastings's guilt. Mr. Specter said he was particularly concerned about the case because it was the first time that impeachment proceedings had been brought against an official who had been tried by a jury and acquitted. Both said they had reached their decisions after extensive review of the evidence.' Alcee Hastings is the Congressman for Florida's 20th Congressional District <https://alceehastings.house.gov>.

76 Kent was a judge in the Federal District Court. See Hurwitz (n 40). Kent had pleaded guilty to obstruction of justice and had received a custodial sentence, although he had not resigned as a judge and would have been entitled to draw a salary during his time in prison (223–4). Kent resigned after the House Judiciary Committee and the House of Representatives both voted to impeach. He resigned before he could be removed by the Senate (224).

77 McKay and Johnson (n 25) 596.

impeached, a strategy employed by President Richard Nixon but not President Clinton'.[78] It should be emphasised that resignation prior to trial has not always prevented the impeachment from proceeding to the trial.[79] Therefore, it may well have been possible for the House of Representatives to have impeached Nixon despite his resignation, although it is questionable whether the Senate would have proceeded with the trial.

This was different from the scope of impeachment in the United Kingdom,[80] which could result in a range of sanctions[81] and was not confined to removing a person from office; see for example the impeachment and trial of Warren Hastings[82] from 1787 to 1795 and Dr Henry Sacheverell[83] in 1710 where Hastings had already resigned and Sacheverell was being impeached for a sermon that he had delivered as a minister of religion. If convicted by the Senate there is scope for further sanction, as the former President loses immunity upon automatically being removed from office[84] and may be tried before the ordinary courts for any criminal acts which he has committed.[85] Black is clear that the Supreme Court was never intended to have the jurisdiction to judicially review the removal of a President, as in 1787 it was determined to have the impeachment trial in the Senate rather than before the Supreme Court and

> [s]o far as I can find, not one syllable pronounced or written in or around the time of the adoption of the Constitution gives the faintest color to the supposition that the Supreme Court was expected to have anything to do with impeachments, or the trial thereof, or appeals thereon.[86]

Indeed, Black remarked about the lack of evidence of this being considered and the impracticality and unconstitutionality of the Supreme Court seeking to reinstate

78 Hurwitz (n 40) 225.

79 See Senator William Blount of Tennessee in 1799 and Secretary of State for War William W Belknap in 1876.

80 Impeachment was used in the English Parliament until 1707, but not in the Scottish Parliament.

81 The sanctions are explored in Hoffer and Hull (n 20) 3. Impeachment could result in the death penalty, the forfeiture of land, or a significant financial penalty.

82 See PJ Marshall, *The Impeachment of Warren Hastings* (OUP 1965).

83 See generally M Knights (ed), *Faction Displayed: Reconsidering the Impeachment of Dr Henry Sacheverell: Parliamentary History* (Wiley-Blackwell 2012). Sacheverell was a Church of England clergyman who was impeached for undermining the Glorious Revolution of 1688, by virtue of his sermon, *The Perils of False Brethen* (M Knights, 'Introduction: The View from 1710' in M Knights (ed), *Faction Displayed: Reconsidering the Impeachment of Dr Henry Sacheverell: Parliamentary History* (Wiley-Blackwell 2012) 3).

84 The President enjoys immunity from criminal prosecution but not from civil suit. See *Clinton v Jones* 520 US 681 (1997).

85 See Isenbergh (n 33). Isenbergh is of the view that if the President is acquitted, then this should be a bar from a future prosecution in the criminal courts when he is no longer in office.

86 CL Black, *Impeachment: A Handbook* (Yale University Press 1974) 59.

a President.[87] If the court did have the power in cases of impeachment, then moving beyond Black's example of the reinstated President, the Supreme Court could review the removal of any of its own members and reinstate accordingly.

Finally, the President cannot grant a pardon in the event of impeachment. However, a President can issue a pardon where someone has been impeached and this is followed (or indeed preceded) by a custodial sentence being imposed.[88] In the United Kingdom, the monarch cannot pardon in the event of impeachment, although she may pardon any punishment conferred by the House of Lords.[89]

Presidential impeachments

This next section will consider the impeachments of President Clinton in 1998, President Trump in 2019 and 2021, and the attempt to impeach President Nixon in 1974.

The attempt to impeach Richard Nixon and his subsequent resignation

The first impeachment to be considered is the attempt in 1974 to impeach President Richard Nixon. President Nixon was accused of committing criminal offences in connection with the Watergate scandal. It is important to note that Nixon was never impeached and the process was terminated as a result of his resignation in August 1974. The Watergate scandal led the House Judiciary Committee to begin impeachment proceedings against Nixon on the basis that he obstructed the investigation of Watergate and the unlawful conduct of his supporters. Mark Nevin observes the role of Nixon's supporters within the Republican Party in attempting to protect the President from being forced to resign

87 ibid 61.

88 Alternatively, an outgoing President could seek a pardon by his successor. For example, Nixon was pardoned by his successor to prevent future criminal prosecution. It might be possible for the President to pardon himself and other civil officers within his administration (see Isenbergh (n 33) 56), fn 9 who explored the possibility that if a President was indicted in office, then he could pardon himself: '[o]n the specific question of indictment of a President in office, there is the further technical problem that the President's power of pardon could undo it'. On 5 August 1974, President Nixon was advised by the US Department of Justice that he was unable to pardon himself: MC Lawton, Acting Assistant Attorney General, Office of Legal Counsel, 'Presidential or Legislative Pardon of the President' (5 August 1974) <www.justice.gov/sites/default/files/olc/opinions/1974/08/31/op-olc-supp-v001-p0370_0.pdf>.

89 See the Act of Settlement 1701 which states: '[t]hat no Pardon under the Great Seal of England be pleadable to an Impeachment by the Commons in Parliament.' This prevents the monarch from preventing the Lords from trying the accused, although it does not prevent a pardon upon conviction. An example of how a monarch had attempted to pardon someone who the House of Commons sought to impeach was Charles II, who pardoned the Earl of Danby after articles of impeachment had been submitted to the House of Lords. This led Sir Francis Winnington to comment: '[a]n impeachment is of no purpose when a pardon shall stop our mouths' (*Howell's State Trials* (London, 1809–1826) 775, quoted by Berger (n 23) 45.

and from being impeached.[90] However, this support eroded over time due to the political realities of having an election with Nixon in office and the damage that this would do to Republican House and Senate candidates.[91]

Despite the support of loyalists, Republican Congressman were starting to support the impeachment: '[o]nce they got a good look at all the evidence against Nixon, however, some House Republicans felt the evidence of the president's guilt was "positively overwhelming" and voted to impeach him.'[92] The proceedings were of a bipartisan nature and supported by members from both parties. According to Frank O. Bowman,

> Peter Rodino, a New Jersey congressman . . . cautiously but firmly steered the House Judiciary Committee to a bipartisan consensus on procedure and finally, after long and careful debate, to a strongly bipartisan vote on articles of impeachment against Richard Nixon.[93]

The Washington Post reported that '[t]he bipartisan support for the article adopted last night makes impeachment by the House seem more than likely. The majority included three conservative Southern Democrats and three conservative Republicans.'[94] According to Gerhardt, the House of Representatives was under pressure from the public to vote to impeach Nixon.[95] The committee had voted to approve three articles of impeachment.[96] What proved crucial to shoring up the bipartisan support of Nixon's impeachment was the fact that the Supreme Court had ordered the President to release tapes that confirmed his involvement with Watergate. This led leading Republicans, including Barry Goldwater, to stop supporting Nixon and to tell the President that unless he resigned, then he would be impeached and convicted:

> Resignation was never mentioned, but the three [Republican] leaders let Nixon know that he had almost no support left in either the House or the Senate. Goldwater told Nixon he doubted he would get more than fifteen votes to acquit in the Senate, and Rhodes told the president the situation was even worse in the House, with maybe only ten representatives voting against impeachment.[97]

90 M Nevin, 'Nixon Loyalists, Barry Goldwater and Republican Support for President Nixon During Watergate' (2017) 27(3) *Journal of Policy History* 403.
91 ibid 418–19.
92 ibid 420.
93 FO Bowman III, 'Falling Out of Love with America: The Clinton Impeachment and the Madisonian Constitution' (2001) 60(5) *Maryland Law Review* 5, 10.
94 R Lyons and W Chapman, 'Judiciary Committee Approves Article to Impeach President Nixon, 27 to 11' *The Washington Post* (28 July 1974).
95 MJ Gerhardt, *The Federal Impeachment Process: A Constitutional and Historical Analysis* (2nd edn, University of Chicago Press 2000) 32.
96 ibid 27.
97 Nevin (n 90) 422.

The withdrawal of support from fellow Republicans led Nixon to resign the day after his meeting with Goldwater. Nixon acknowledged in his resignation speech that he had lost the confidence of Congress.[98] Therefore, had Nixon not resigned, it is arguable that he would have been impeached and, based on the nature of his conduct, may have been removed from office by the Senate. This was because he had clearly lost the support of his own loyalists within the Republican Party and knew that a majority of Republicans would support the impeachment in the House of Representatives and vote to convict. Nixon's resignation demonstrates that the threat of impeachment, so long as members of the President's own party are willing to act in a bipartisan manner, could force a President to resign rather than being removed from office by the Senate. It must be observed that the circumstances regarding Watergate were unique, and the decision of leading Republicans to remove their support from the President was a result of the times and popular opinion. However, there is still some debate over whether Nixon could have survived an impeachment and been acquitted. Journalists had predicted that the House of Representatives 'would overwhelming approve at least the first two articles of impeachment' and that the two-thirds majority in the Senate would also be satisfied. On the other hand, John Dean, who wished to have Nixon removed, had later speculated that 'Nixon might very well have eked out a Johnsonian escape in the Senate.'[99] It is doubtful that this would have happened given the circumstances of the case and the mood of the mainstream party, even if Nixon retained support amongst his loyalists.[100]

The impeachment of William Jefferson Clinton, 1998–1999

William Jefferson Clinton became President in January 1993 and during his second term in office he became only the second President to be impeached. It is necessary to set out a brief factual account of the events that led to the impeachment. The starting point is the dissolution of the Whitewater Development Corp in 1992, in which William Clinton and his wife, Hillary, lost in excess of $40,000. As a result of the scandal surrounding Whitewater, in 1994 the US Attorney General appointed an independent counsel to conduct an investigation.[101] Within six months, Ken Starr, the former Solicitor General under President George HW Bush, was appointed as the new independent counsel investigating the allegations

98 DE Kyvig, *The Age of Impeachment: American Constitutional Culture since 1960* (University Press of Kansas 2008) 177.
99 ibid 176.
100 Nevin (n 90) 423–4.
101 P Barkham, 'Clinton Impeachment Timeline' *The Guardian* (18 November 1998) <www.theguardian.com/world/1998/nov/18/clinton.usa>. For further details on the timeline relating to Whitewater and the subsequent investigation see 'Time Line' (Washingtonpost.com, 1998) <www.washingtonpost.com/wp-srv/politics/special/whitewater/timeline.htm>.

relating to Whitewater.[102] The investigation led to a trial and conviction of the Clintons' business partners for fraud.[103] During this time Monica Lewinsky had joined the White House in 1995 as an intern and during 1995–6 had an 18-month sexual relationship with President Clinton.[104] Starr's investigation continued and in January 1998, Linda Tripp, who had been secretly recording her phone calls with Monica Lewinsky, provided the investigation with 20 hours of material. This led to Starr being given permission by the US Attorney General to investigate the allegations that Clinton and Lewinsky had a sexual relationship.[105] As a result of the Supreme Court's decision in *Clinton v Jones*,[106] Paula Jones was able to bring a civil suit against President Clinton for alleged sexual harassment that had occurred when he was Governor of Arkansas.[107] As part of the litigation the President was compelled to testify under oath and when questioned about Lewinsky, he denied that they had had an affair. In January 1998, he told journalists that he had not had sex with Lewinsky.[108] In August 1998, Clinton testified before a grand jury and admitted inappropriate conduct, but he denied lying under oath during his testimony in the *Clinton v Jones*[109] litigation.[110]

On 5 October 1998, the House Judiciary Committee voted to commence an inquiry into whether the President should be impeached.[111] The articles of impeachment were 'pushed through' the committee on 'a straight party-line vote'.[112] This was in contrast to the bipartisan nature of the committee in approving the articles of impeachment against Nixon.[113] Subsequently, on 8 October, the House of Representatives voted to support the impeachment proceedings. The inquiry was supported by testimony from Ken Starr and the evidence that he had accumulated during the course of his investigation. At the time of impeachment, the House of Representatives was composed of 227 Republican, 207 Democratic Representatives, and one independent member.[114] Four articles of impeachment were drawn up and debated by the House of Representatives. However, only two received the bare majority needed (228 for and 206 against, and 221 for and 212 against, respectively) to proceed to the Senate for the actual impeachment trial. It is clear that party membership was the significant factor in why the House of Representatives voted to impeach Clinton. The articles of impeachment that were voted for by the House of Representatives were as follows:

102 Barkham (n 101).
103 ibid.
104 ibid.
105 ibid.
106 *Clinton v Jones* 520 US 681 (1997).
107 Barkham (n 101).
108 ibid.
109 *Clinton v Jones* 520 US 681 (1997).
110 Barkham (n 101).
111 ibid.
112 Bowman (n 93) 10.
113 ibid.
114 This was the 105th Congress.

Article I

> [The President] has willfully corrupted and manipulated the judicial process of the United States for his personal gain and exoneration, impeding the administration of justice. . . [as he under oath] willfully provided perjurious, false and misleading testimony to the grand jury concerning one or more of the following: (1) the nature and details of his relationship with a subordinate Government employee; (2) prior perjurious, false and misleading testimony he gave in a Federal civil rights action brought against him; (3) prior false and misleading statements he allowed his attorney to make to a Federal judge in that civil rights action; and (4) his corrupt efforts to influence the testimony of witnesses and to impede the discovery of evidence in that civil rights action.

Article II

> [The President] has prevented, obstructed, and impeded the administration of justice, and has to that end engaged personally, and through his subordinates and agents, in a course of conduct or scheme designed to delay, impede, cover up, and conceal the existence of evidence and testimony related to a Federal civil rights action brought against him in a duly instituted judicial proceeding.[115]

It is important to note that although the 105th Congress remained in office until 3 January 1999, and Clinton was impeached on 19 December 1998, the House of Representatives was a 'lame duck Congress',[116] as elections had taken place on 3 November 1998, albeit electing a 106th Congress. The House of Representatives in the 106th Congress had a broadly similar composition to the 105th Congress, with 223 Republican, 211 Democratic Congressmen, and one independent member. As had been the case in British practice, an election does not affect the validity of the impeachment and the trial subsequently took place in the Senate.

The trial itself took place before the Senate and was presided over by William H Rehnquist, the Chief Justice of the US Supreme Court.[117] Rehnquist's role was to act as the presiding judge and the Senators would serve as the jury:

> [F]or the most part, having found himself adrift in a process he could do little to steer, the Chief Justice went with the flow.

115 'Impeachment of President William Jefferson Clinton: Constitutional Provisions; Rules of Procedure and Practice in the Senate when sitting on Impeachment Trials; Articles of Impeachment Against President William Jefferson Clinton; President Clinton's Answer; and Replication of the House of Representatives' (US Senate, 106th Congress, Document 106–2, 13 January 1999) <www.gpo.gov/fdsys/pkg/CDOC-106sdoc2/pdf/CDOC-106sdoc2.pdf>, 15–18.

116 See B Ackerman, *The Case Against Lameduck Impeachment* (Seven Stories Press 1999).

117 The rules and the procedure governing the trial before the Senate and the power of the Senate during the course of the trial are available here <www.gpo.gov/fdsys/pkg/CDOC-106sdoc2/pdf/CDOC-106sdoc2.pdf>.

> And by the time the trial ended early this afternoon with President Clinton's acquittal, the nation's ranking jurist was drily tossing off one-liners to the 100 erstwhile jurors sitting before him, and gamely allowing himself to be used as a prop in a let's-put-this-behind-us display of bipartisanship.[118]

The Senate was obligated under the constitution to render impartial justice. The oath was important, as it

> immediately distinguishes the Senate role from that of the House, since the Constitution gives the House the power to impeach, or indict, a public official, and reserves for the Senate the neutral role of determining whether those allegations are true and what should be done about them.[119]

As has been previously observed:

> An impeachment is an accusation followed by a trial, on which the Constitution itself imposes safeguards of a judicial character. In impeachment proceedings the representatives and senators do not have the unfettered discretion of legislators; they are participants in a process largely governed by its own common law and history.[120]

The composition of the Senate at the time of the trial was 55 Republican and 45 Democratic Senators. Clinton was subsequently acquitted by the Senate on both articles as the two-thirds majority needed to convict could not be met (Article I, 55 Senators supporting Clinton and 45 voting to convict; and Article II, with 50 voting to acquit and 50 voting to convict).

THE CONTROVERSIAL NATURE OF THE CLINTON IMPEACHMENT

The impeachment of Clinton is controversial for many reasons; *inter alia*, the partisan nature of the proceedings before the House and the Senate,[121] the uncertainty over whether he had actually committed an impeachable offence,[122] whether his conduct amounted to criminal conduct as understood by the ordinary law, and whether the impeachment was disproportionate.[123]

118 RW Stevenson, 'The President's Acquittal: The Chief Justice; Rehnquist Goes with the Senate Flow, "Wiser, but Not a Sadder Man"' *The New York Times* (13 February 1999).

119 J Biskupic, 'Rehnquist to Transform Senate into Jury' *The Washington Post* (7 January 1999).

120 'The Scope of the Power to Impeach' (n 75) 1335.

121 KA Popp, 'The Impeachment of President Clinton: An Ugly Mix of Three Powerful Forces' (2002) 63(1)-(2) *Law and Contemporary Problems* 223 at 223.

122 ibid 227. The author observed: 'one can reasonably conclude that the President did not commit impeachable offenses.'

123 Isenbergh (n 33) 54. See Bowman, 'Falling out of Love' (n 93) 9: 'Bill Clinton's offenses, poorly as they reflect on him as a human being, were substantively trivial and constitutionally insignificant.'

The academic reaction to the impeachment on these matters does not find general consensus. Isenbergh has observed that '[t]he impeachment . . . was dismissed by a good number in the academic mainstream as beyond the pale of legitimacy. Some of this reflected – transparently on occasion – a prevalence of ideological sympathy with the President in academic circles.'[124] According to Karen A Popp, who had been an Associate Counsel to President Clinton, 'The impeachment itself, which did not occur until eleven months after the story was first reported, however, would not have occurred at all but for the three forces indicated above – the independent counsel, the House Republicans, and the media.'[125] It must be noted that impeachment was not intended as a partisan device to proceed against political enemies in the absence of conduct that was properly at the time regarded as amounting to impeachable conduct. Gerhardt is clear on this point:

> [C]ongressional practices reflect the judgment that the Constitution envisions that impeachment should not be used to punish or to retaliate against impeachable officials, such as the President and federal judges, because of their opinions, policy differences, or innocent errors of judgment. Nor should impeachment be used for largely partisan purposes; hence, some senators refused to convict Associate Justice Samuel Chase or President Andrew Johnson for fear that if either were removed, future presidents or judges from the senators' party likely would be punished in the impeachment process just by virtue of their party affiliation. Rather, impeachment generally should be deployed against impeachable officials for having engaged in some misconduct that has caused serious injury to the Republic or to the constitutional system.[126]

Richard K Neumann has argued that impeachment was used from the 1960s onwards by the Republican Party as a political weapon to discredit its political opponents and to rein in the judiciary, or to create seats on the Supreme Court that the President could fill. Neumann's argument is scathing of the misuse of impeachment:

> After the failed impeachment of President Andrew Johnson in 1868, a long period of largely non-partisan and bipartisanship in impeachments ensued. But since 1968, some elements in the Republican Party have been willing to use impeachment as a partisan weapon; to inflict political damage on their opponents and as part of a campaign to control the Supreme Court and the lower federal courts.[127]

124 Isenbergh (n 33) 54.
125 Popp (n 121) 224.
126 Gerhardt (n 62) 624–5.
127 RK Neumann, 'The Revival of Impeachment as a Partisan Political Weapon' (2006–2007) 34(2) *Hastings Const. L.Q.* 162.

This willingness to use impeachment, especially from 1995 to 2007 when the Republicans had a 'razor-thin' majority in Congress, demonstrated 'Party insecurity' and insecurity 'about their ability to hold on to [power]'.[128]

The political attacks by the Republican Party on the federal judiciary, who were seen as opposed to the beliefs of the party, is evidenced by Nixon's second campaign for the presidency when he 'made complaints about the Warren Court one of the centerpieces' of his campaign.[129] Impeachment was considered against Warren's proposed successor, Associate Justice Abe Fortas, and also Associate Justice Douglas, by 'the mainstream of the Republican Party', which resulted in Fortas resigning before he could be impeached.[130] Although Douglas was not impeached, the threat of impeachment was influential in how Douglas approached *Roe v Wade*,[131] which was a significant decision relating to a woman's right to choose whether she terminated a pregnancy. According to Kyvig, the threat of impeachment had an effect on Douglas' role as a judge, as this meant that 'his bold constitutional views would be muted' and the new Chief Justice prevented Douglas from writing the court's majority judgment.[132]

There have also been concerns that the impeachment proceedings in the House of Representatives might not be fair or that the decision to impeach would be influenced by external pressures, as had been the case with Nixon and Clinton. Gerhardt has observed that the need for a Senate trial had always been regarded as a safeguard against the House's 'intemperate action'.[133] Furthermore, Gerhardt has argued:

> The House has rarely, if ever, and the Senate has never successfully committed a serious or extreme abuse of its impeachment authority . . . all efforts to use the impeachment process for partisan ends . . . have failed.[134]

Indeed, there was a real concern that impeachment could be abused if it was used to remove an individual without 'clear proof of the commission of an impeachable offence', as this could lead to future impeachments that were purely of partisan nature. This concern had previously proved influential in the Senate's acquittal of Chief Justice Chase in 1805 and President Johnson in 1868.[135] This argument is important and needs to be balanced against the concern that there *have been* inappropriate impeachments, as in the case of Clinton, where it is arguable that

128 ibid 166–7.
129 Kyvig (n 98) 61.
130 ibid 63. According to Kyvig, Fortas had engaged in 'highly compensated extrajudicial work [that] tested the bounds of the relevant canons of judicial ethics', even if his conduct 'presented a prima facie case of unethical conduct' 83.
131 410 US 113 (1973).
132 Kyvig (n 98) 110–11.
133 Gerhardt (n 95) 32.
134 ibid 55.
135 ibid 55–6.

the President's conduct, even if there is debate over whether, first, it was criminal, and second, whether it amounted to an impeachable offence, was motivated by political expediency and could discredit the use of impeachment, regardless of the outcome in the Senate.

The fear that impeachment could be used as a partisan weapon had been a factor in the acquittal of Chief Justice Chase in 1805 and has led some academics to discredit the motivations of those Republicans who sought to impeach President Johnson in 1867 and 1868. This was not a concern removed from the minds of the men who had framed the constitution. On 15 February 1798, Thomas Jefferson had written to James Madison, and had observed:

> I see nothing in the mode of proceeding by impeachment but the most formidable weapon for the purposes of dominant faction that ever was contrived. It would be the most effectual one of getting rid of any man whom they consider as dangerous to their views, and I do not know that we could count on one third on an emergency. It depends then on the H. of Representatives, who are the impeachers: & there the majorities are of 1. 2. or 3 only & these sometimes one way & sometimes another: in a question of pure party they have the majority, & we do not know what circumstances may turn up to increase that majority temporarily if not permanently. I know of no solid purpose of punishment which the courts of law are not equal to and history shows that in England impeachment has been an engine more of passion than of justice.[136]

In England there had always been a fear that opportunist impeachment would result in retaliation. Commenting on the use of impeachments in the early eighteenth century, Plumb had observed that '[i]mpeachments . . . could boomerang.'[137] A similar point had been made in 1867 by Dwight, based on his reading of impeachments in the seventeenth and eighteenth centuries.[138]

Because of how both Houses of Congress and the President are elected, the political composition of each branch will vary, and therefore there might be a danger that if the necessary requirements are met – a bare majority in the House of Representatives and a two-thirds majority in the Senate – a President could be removed from office by way of impeachment, despite having been elected by a majority of the Electoral College. The United States does not have a parliamentary system and therefore the political composition of both Houses is not sufficient for Congress to remove the President and thus treat impeachment as a vote of no confidence. The controversy over whether Clinton's alleged conduct fell within the definition of 'high crimes and misdemeanors' is problematic, as

136 Cited by Dougherty (n 42) 71. The original letter is <https://founders.archives.gov/documents/Madison/01-17-02-0057>.
137 Plumb (n 37) 160.
138 See Dwight (n 23) 258 and specifically fn 75.

despite the acceptance by the Senate in acquitting Chief Justice Chase in 1805 and President Andrew Johnson in 1868 that there needed to have been an indictable offence committed, such an interpretation was not universally accepted at the time of Clinton's impeachment. This was a charge made by the Clintons' White House Press Secretary: '[b]ecause of politics, the House majority party has impeached the president because they could do it, because they had the power to do it and without making an effective case for it.'[139]

Turley is clear that the House adopts a lower standard (than the Senate) when impeaching as it is the Senate that will determine the merits of the charges. Turley argued that whilst he was not suggesting that 'the House should always gravitate to impeach but rather, where there is credible evidence supporting articles of impeachment, the House should not confuse its insular institutional role with that of the Senate.'[140] This is because '[s]imilar to a grand jury, the House does not rule on the ultimate merits of impeachment allegations, a function given exclusively to the Senate . . . Rather, articles of impeachment are a type of constitutional indictment.'[141]

Therefore, could the Republicans have achieved the removal of Clinton from the presidency without the proceedings playing out in Congress? Clearly the only method under the constitution to actually remove a President against his will is impeachment. However, the threat of impeachment and the damage done to his reputation amongst his political allies could have compelled Clinton to resign. This could have occurred where first, Clinton wished to avoid a Senate trial and possible criminal sanctions[142] from the ordinary courts in the event that he was removed from office (as in the case of Richard Nixon) and seek a Presidential Pardon from his successor, Vice President Albert (Al) Gore; or second, where Clinton would resign to spare his party, family, and administration the trauma of the impeachment process and to help the chances of his then Vice President in the 2000 General Election.[143] Ackerman opposed Clinton's resignation in such

139 'White House Weighs Impeachment Trial Strategy' *CNN* (21 December 1998) <>http://edition.cnn.com/ALLPOLITICS/stories/1998/12/21/impeachment.folo/>.

140 Turley (n 33) 781–2.

141 ibid 775.

142 This presupposes that Clinton's conduct was criminal and would have attracted the attention of prosecutors.

143 However, it would be wrong to presume that the impeachment had damaged Clinton's popularity with the electorate. Despite being impeached, Clinton left office in January 2001 with very high popular approval ratings and his Vice President, Al Gore, narrowly lost the 2000 General Election, despite winning the popular vote, due to the decision of the US Supreme Court, *Bush v Gore* 531 US 98 (2000), which prevented a re-count in parts of Florida. It was reported that Gore considered the Clinton impeachment to have been a factor in his defeat: 'Mr Gore "forcefully" blamed the former president for his loss, saying that the Monica Lewinsky sex scandal and the low esteem in which voters held Mr Clinton had proved serious obstacles to his campaign', B Fenton 'Gore blamed Clinton for his defeat in election' *The Telegraph* (8 February 2001).

circumstances as drawing the US system closer to the parliamentary system.[144] Ackerman had argued that '[i]f a man can be driven from office for lying about his sexual misadventures, why should he not also be driven from office for something like making a disastrous decision on a fundamental matter of public policy?'[145]

The first impeachment of President Donald J Trump

THE LEAD-UP TO IMPEACHMENT: THE PRESIDENTIAL ELECTION OF 2016

The 2016 presidential election had resulted in the respective charge that the two candidates were unsuitable for office. The Democratic candidate, Hillary Rodham Clinton was accused of being 'crooked Hillary'[146] and would be 'locked up'[147] by her opponent, the Republican candidate, Donald J Trump. The allegations against Clinton were linked to her use of a private email account whilst serving as Secretary of State under President Barack Obama. Donald Trump was accused of being racist and of mistreating women, especially with the release of the infamous *Access Hollywood* recording.[148] The second presidential debate between the two candidates saw Trump invite women to attend the debate who had alleged sexual assault or rape against Clinton's husband, Bill Clinton.[149] During the campaign, Clinton's opponents had mooted impeachment if she were to become President.[150] Equally, Trump's

144 B Ackerman, 'What Ken Starr Neglected to Tell Us' *The New York Times* (14 September 1998), cited in Levinson (n 57) 2234.

145 ibid.

146 An example of this is 'Crooked Hillary Clinton and her team "were extremely careless in their handling of very sensitive, highly classified information." Not fit!' (Donald J Trump, Twitter, 6 July 2016).

147 Donald Trump during the campaign had called for the prosecution of Hillary Clinton: '"[s]he has to go to jail," he said at a Pennsylvania rally', see A Zurcher, 'US Election 2016: Presidential Race Goes Down the Drain' *BBC News* (15 October 2016) <www.bbc.co.uk/news/election-us-2016-37548004>. However, his support for such a prosecution did not survive his victory: '[b]ut instead of joining his supporters in the calls to prosecute her, the former reality star told the crowd in Grand Rapids, Michigan: "That plays great before the election . . . nah, we don't care." The Republican ruled out prosecuting Ms Clinton in the days after the election, saying it was "no longer something he felt so strongly about" and he did not want to hurt the family.' C Mortimer, 'Donald Trump Says Pledge to Jail Hillary Clinton Played "Great Before the Election" but Now "We Don't Care"' *The Independent* (10 December 2016).

148 D Victor, '"Access Hollywood" Reminds Trump: "The Tape Is Very Real"' *The New York Times* (28 November 2017).

149 L Stack, 'Donald Trump Featured Paula Jones and 2 Other Women Who Accused Bill Clinton of Sexual Assault' *The New York Times* (9 October 2016).

150 See H Gold, 'Clinton: Threats to Impeach Me Are "Ridiculous"' *Politico* (23 October 2014) <www.politico.com/story/2015/10/hillary-clinton-responds-impeachment-threat-215129>; A Phillips, 'A House Republican Already Wants to Impeach Hillary Clinton' *The Washington Post* (9 September 2016) <www.politico.com/story/2015/10/hillary-clinton-responds-impeachment-threat-215129>.

conduct and the sexual accusations against him led to calls for him to be investigated.[151] As a result of Trump's election there have been calls to impeach Trump and this has generated considerable political, popular media, and academic commentary. Trump was investigated by Special Counsel Robert Mueller, whose report, delivered in 2019, concluded that no offences had been committed.[152] When viewed holistically, the most recent US presidential elections have demonstrated that impeachment has been used as a threat to rival candidates, however likely, or unlikely, to succeed, and then by the defeated candidate against the winner.

The language used during the election and in US politics generally, the broad accusations of illegality, the reduction of the press to 'fake news', the investigations into alleged criminal conduct in the Trump campaign and transition team, and the attacks still made against Hillary Clinton do not present an attractive image of presidential politics in the United States.

If the Mueller report did not result in Trump's impeachment, it was the President's subsequent dealings with the Ukrainian President that provided the Democrat-dominated House of Representatives with the grounds for impeaching him.

A CALL FOR IMPEACHMENT

In the case of Trump there had been an attempt by legal academics and political scientists to bring his conduct within the scope of an impeachable offence.[153] Trump was not unique as his predecessors had previously faced calls for their impeachment.[154] There is significant debate as to the scope and definition of high crimes and misdemeanours and scholars have looked to the British tradition of impeachment to gauge the framers' intentions. Most notably this was undertaken in the 1970s by Raoul Berger[155] and more recently by Frank Bowman.[156]

151 See J Ducharme, 'Hillary Clinton: "Very Credible" Sexual Assault Allegations Against Donald Trump Should Be Investigated' *Time* (18 November 2017) <>http://time.com/5030586/hillary-clinton-donald-trump-sexual-assault/>; C Mindock, 'Donald Trump's Sexual Assault Allegations: The Full List of Women Who Have Accused the President' *The Independent* (5 December 2017).

152 See RS Mueller, III, Report on the Investigation into Russian Interference in the 2016 Presidential Election, Volume I, March 2019 <www.justice.gov/storage/report.pdf>.

153 L Tribe and J Matz, *To End a Presidency: The Power of Impeachment* (Basic Books 2018); AJ Lichtman, *The Case for Impeachment* (William Collins 2017).

154 See for example A McCarthy, *Faithless Execution: Building the Political Case for Obama's Impeachment* (Encounter Books 2014); D Kucinich, *The 35 Articles of Impeachment and the Case for Prosecuting George W Bush* (Feral House 2008).

155 Berger (n 23).

156 FO Bowman III, *High Crimes and Misdemeanors: A History of Impeachment for the Age of Trump* (Cambridge University Press 2019).

THE 2019 IMPEACHMENT

Trump was impeached by the House of Representatives in December 2019. In many ways, it had looked inevitable since 2018, when the Democrats gained a majority in the House of Representatives, that Trump would be impeached, subject to a sufficient charge being found on which to impeach him. Indeed, the Democrats' leader in the House, Speaker Nancy Pelosi, was criticised for not impeaching Trump earlier. Pelosi had defended her decision not to support the calls for an earlier impeachment, remarking,

> we will proceed when we have what we need to proceed. Not one day sooner . . . Everybody has the liberty and luxury to espouse their own position and to criticize me for trying to go down the path in the most determined, positive way.[157]

Trump was impeached on two articles. The first related to the abuse of power and the second related to obstruction of Congress.[158] In the first article, Trump was accused of abusing his power and having 'solicited the interference of a foreign government, Ukraine, in the 2020 United States Presidential election'. Trump had sought to put pressure on Ukraine by withholding funding for military assistance in exchange for an announcement that his political rival, Joe Biden, the former Vice President, would be investigated for corruption, and that Ukraine was behind the foreign interference into the 2016 election. In the second article, Trump was accused of obstructing Congress from exercising its sole power of impeachment, as Trump had ordered his executive agencies not to comply with the House of Representatives' subpoenas, therefore preventing an effective investigation into his conduct. Article Two was clear:

> Through these actions, President Trump sought to arrogate to himself the right to determine the propriety, scope, and nature of an impeachment inquiry into his own conduct, as well as the unilateral prerogative to deny any and all information to the House of Representatives in the exercise of its 'sole power of Impeachment'.

On 18 December 2019, with few exceptions, the House of Representatives voted along party lines to impeach Trump. The first article was approved by 230

157 D Obeidallah, 'Nancy Pelosi Was Right About Trump's Impeachment and the Democrats Were Wrong' *NBC News* (20 December 2019) <www.nbcnews.com/think/opinion/nancy-pelosi-was-right-about-trump-s-impeachment-democrats-were-ncna1105401>.

158 The full text of the Articles of Impeachment can be found here <https://judiciary.house.gov/sites/democrats.judiciary.house.gov/files/documents/articles%20of%20impeachment.pdf>.

votes to 197 and the second article by 229 to 198. *The New York Times*' view of the impeachment was apt:

> Acquittal in the Republican-controlled chamber may be likely, but the proceeding is certain to further aggravate the political and cultural fault lines in the country that Mr. Trump's presidency has brought into dramatic relief. Regardless of the outcome, the impeachment votes in the House put an indelible stain on Mr. Trump's presidency that cannot be wiped from the public consciousness with a barrage of tweets or an angry tirade in front of thousands of his cheering supporters at a campaign rally.[159]

A few days before the House voted, the Democrat leader in the Senate, Charles E Schumer, had written to the majority leader, Mitch McConnell, expressing his concern that the trial in the Republican controlled Senate must be fair: '[t]he trial must be one that not only hears all the evidence and adjudicates the case fairly; it must also pass the fairness test with the American people.'[160] Schumer had called for the use of subpoenas to gather documents and to summon witnesses to give evidence. This was rejected by McConnell, who stated clearly: 'I am not an impartial juror. . . . This is a political process. . . . I expect we will have a largely partisan outcome in the Senate. I'm not impartial about this at all.'[161] That same day President Trump described the impeachment proceedings as a 'partisan . . . crusade' which was 'an unprecedented and unconstitutional abuse of power by Democrat Lawmakers'.[162]

There was significant controversy surrounding the type of trial that Trump would receive in the Senate. Pelosi had delayed sending the articles of impeachment to the Senate, hoping to put pressure on McConnell to allow witnesses to give evidence, as had happened during the Clinton impeachment. *The New York Times* in its editorial of 19 December 2019 took the position that 'President Trump Deserves a Real Trial' and that '[r]efusing to take their impeach responsibilities seriously promises to stain the Senate and the Republican Party.'[163]

159 N Fandos and MD Shear, 'Trump Impeached for Abuse of Power and Obstruction of Congress' *The New York Times* (18 December 2019) <www.nytimes.com/2019/12/18/us/politics/trump-impeached.html?action=click&module=RelatedLinks&pgtype=Article>.

160 'Charles E Schumer to Mitch McConnell' (15 December 2019) <www.democrats.senate.gov/imo/media/doc/Impeachment%20Letter%20To%20Leader%20McConnell.pdf>.

161 'McConnell: "I Am Not an Impartial Juror"' *The Guardian* (17 December 2019) <www.theguardian.com/us-news/live/2019/dec/17/trump-news-today-live-impeachment-democrats-republicans?page=with:block-5df930038f087e8308e5fee2#block-5df930038f087e8308e5fee2>.

162 'President Trump to Nancy Pelosi' (17 December 2019) <www.whitehouse.gov/wp-content/uploads/2019/12/Letter-from-President-Trump-final.pdf>.

163 'President Trump Deserves a Real Trial' *The New York Times* (19 December 2019) <www.nytimes.com/2019/12/19/opinion/donald-trump-impeachment.html?action=click&module=Opinion&pgtype=Homepage>

The decision of McConnell not to allow new evidence or witnesses to be called was unsuccessfully challenged during the course of the trial. Of significance would have been the potential testimony of the former National Security Advisor, John Bolton, relating to Trump's dealings with Ukraine.

The trial took place before Chief Justice Roberts who presided over the proceedings.[164] The Senate determined its own procedures for the trial by a majority vote, which meant that the Republicans could determine the format of the trial. Trump's allies were keen to criticise the impeachment as partisan. Ken Starr observed: '[i]n the world's longest-standing constitutional republic . . . instead of a once-in-a-century phenomenon, which it had been, presidential impeachment has become a weapon to be wielded against one's political opponent.'[165] The Senate voted not to hear from witnesses. *The New York Times* editorial of 31 January carried the headline 'A Dishonorable Senate'. The editorial observed:

> How could senators cast such a consequential vote – how could they call what they were doing a trial – without hearing from the people with the most direct knowledge of the actions that led to impeachment? Every impeachment trial in American history had included witnesses. . . . Given the seriousness of the charges against Mr. Trump, it's hard to envision anything that this president could do that would require Republican senators to vote for his removal.[166]

Trump's acquittal by the US Senate on 5 February 2020 was hardly surprising given the requirement of a two-thirds majority and the fact that the Democrats were in the minority.[167] The vote, with the exception of the Republican Mitt Romney, was on party lines. The next question that needs to be addressed is: what will be the consequences of the Trump impeachment and the President's inevitable acquittal? Congressman Ted Lieu was clear about the significance of the impeachment: '[w]hether Donald Trump leaves in one month, one year or

164 T McCarthy, 'John Roberts: Justice Once Labelled a "Disaster" by Trump to Oversee Impeachment Trial' *The Guardian* (3 January 2020) <www.theguardian.com/us-news/2020/jan/03/trump-impeachment-john-roberts-chief-justice-trial?CMP>.

165 D Mastrangelo, 'Ken Starr: Impeach Has Become a "Weapon to Be Wielded Against One's Political Opponent"' *Washington Examiner* (27 January 2020) <www.washingtonexaminer.com/news/ken-starr-impeachment-has-become-a-weapon-to-be-wielded-against-ones-political-opponent>.

166 'A Dishonourable Senate: Republican Legislators Abdicated Their Duty by Refusing to Seek to the Truth' *The New York Times* (31 January 2020) <www.nytimes.com/2020/01/31/opinion/republicans-impeachment-congress.html?action=click&module=Opinion&pgtype=Homepage>.

167 N Fandos, 'Trump Acquitted of Two Impeachment Charges in Near Party-Line Vote' *The New York Times* (5 February 2020) <www.nytimes.com/2020/02/05/us/politics/trump-acquitted-impeachment.html?action=click&module=Spotlight&pgtype=Homepage>.

five years, this impeachment is permanent. . . . It will follow him around for the rest of his life, and history books will record it.'[168]

It must be emphasised that whichever candidate had won the 2016 presidential election they would have been threatened with impeachment. It is not inconceivable that if Donald Trump had lost in 2016, that he, with an eye to running again in 2020, would have campaigned for Hillary Clinton's impeachment. Until 2018 the Republicans had a majority in the House of Representatives, and this could have provided the impetus for Clinton's impeachment. However, the question remains whether, as a consequence of Trump's first impeachment (notwithstanding the extraordinary circumstances surrounding the Trump presidency and the specific allegations contained within the articles of impeachment), the increased polarisation of politics will mean that successive presidents will routinely face being impeached.[169]

The second impeachment of President Trump

Trump's second impeachment, in 2021, managed to gain the support of ten House Republicans. This increased bipartisan support is unsurprising, especially in light of what Trump was impeached for – the incitement of an insurrection against the US government. However, what was perhaps surprising was that fewer Republicans supported the impeachment or abstained from voting. Trump's impeachment was presented as a way to remove Trump from office and to disqualify him from holding future office, in light of the perceived risks of Trump remaining in power. The second Trump impeachment was the first against a lame-duck President, that is, a President who is serving out his term before the President-Elect, Joseph Biden, was sworn in within a matter of a week. The Senate trial was the first impeachment of a former President and this is significant, as the Senate's agreement to hold the trial resolved the uncertainty over whether a former civil officer could be impeached. The Democrat managers had argued that the impeachment of Secretary Belknap was clear precedent for impeachment in these circumstances. On 26 January 2021, the Senate voted 55–45 in support of the argument that a former civil officer could be tried by the Senate.[170]

Whilst Nixon's resignation was secured by the threat of impeachment, it appears that the fact that Trump was no longer in office did not diminish his political opponents' support for impeachment. Perhaps the chief factors in securing his

168 Fandos and Shear (n 159).

169 This was a point addressed by Carl Hulse, 'In a Polarised Era, Will Impeachment Become a "New Normal"?' *The New York Times* (12 December 2019) <www.nytimes.com/2019/12/12/us/impeachment-democrats-republicans.html>.

170 D Smith, 'Boost for Trump as 45 Republican Senators Vote to Dismiss Impeachment' *The Guardian* (26 January 2021) <www.theguardian.com/us-news/2021/jan/26/trump-impeachment-republicans-senate-vote-to-dismiss>; D Smith, 'The Crucial Differences in Trump's Second Impeachment Trial' *The Guardian* (7 February 2021) <www.theguardian.com/us-news/2021/feb/07/trump-senate-impeachment-trial>.

second impeachment was to condemn Trump's actions in support of the insurrection in January 2021 and to attempt to secure his disqualification from holding future public office. Therefore, it is not sufficient that the President is no longer in office, rather there is a need to seek disqualification.

Trump's second impeachment trial was presided over by Patrick J Leahy, a Democrat Senator and the Senate President Pro Tempore. The Chief Justice of the Supreme Court was not presiding as Trump was no longer the President.[171] Senator Leahy's role did not preclude him from voting and prior to the trial he declared: '[w]hen I preside over the impeachment trial of former President Donald Trump, I will not waver from my constitutional and sworn obligations to administer the trial with fairness, in accordance with the Constitution and the laws.'[172] Trump was acquitted by the Senate, as the prosecution failed to persuade two-thirds of Senators to convict Trump. Reaction to Trump's acquittal was mixed. Representative Jamie Raskin declared on Twitter:

> In the most bipartisan presidential impeachment vote in the history of the country, a powerful majority of both houses of Congress found that the former President incited violent insurrection against the Union & the Congress. History will record his terrible constitutional crime.[173]

A counter-view was advanced by Victoria Bekiempis in *The Guardian*:

> The impeachment process and trial in the Senate will lose its power of deterrence, as politics – not any judgment of law or right or wrong – is what actually informs its decisions. Therefore, Trump's strong political power among Republicans was actually the deciding factor in the trial, not any legal argument or burden of proof of wrongdoing. That is not likely to instill a fear of impeachment for future presidents. In fact, it is likely to encourage strong-arm behaviour.[174]

In light of the seven Republican Senators who voted to convict Trump, it is fair to say that Raskin's positive assessment has some grounding, even if the reality was that Trump was acquitted despite a bipartisan effort to convict. The view from Bekiempis in *The Guardian* reflects the problem of requiring a two-thirds

171 N Fandos, 'Senator Patrick Leahy, the Longest-Serving Democrat, Will Preside Over Trump's Impeachment Trial' *The New York Times* (24 January 2021) <www.nytimes.com/2021/01/25/us/politics/patrick-leahy-trump-impeachment.html>.

172 ibid.

173 See *Twitter* (14 February 2021) <https://twitter.com/RepRaskin/status/1360764565060005889?s=03>.

174 V Bekiempis, 'Trump's Acquittal Shows Paltry Punch of Impeachment Process' *The Guardian* (14 February 2021) <www.theguardian.com/us-news/2021/feb/14/trump-impeachment-acquittal-process-politics>.

majority to convict, which may have once been a constitutional safeguard, but due to political considerations there is unlikely to be a conviction.

Conclusion

It is necessary to consider what impeachment in the United States can demonstrate in terms of how a revised form of impeachment might operate in the United Kingdom. It is apparent that there was a dominant political motivation in impeaching Presidents Johnson, Clinton, and Trump in 2019. However, the attempted impeachment of President Nixon and the circumstances of President Trump's second impeachment in 2021 demonstrate that impeachment can serve a purpose in relation to wrong conduct that offends the constitution and undermines democracy. It is necessary to accept the shortcomings of impeachment in the United States. President Woodrow Wilson was critical, noting that

> [i]ndignation so great as to overgrow party interest may secure a conviction: nothing less can. Indeed, judging by our past experiences, impeachment may be said to be little more than an empty menace. The House of Representatives is a tardy grand jury and the Senate an uncertain court.[175]

The former British Ambassador to the United States, Viscount Bryce, described impeachment as 'the heaviest piece of artillery in the congressional arsenal, but because it is so heavy it is unfit for ordinary use'.[176] These criticisms are sound and reflect the perceived problems with impeachment. It can be said that the legal side to the impeachment process has been hollowed out over time, with the Senate trial never really reflecting the intentions of the framers. This was clear in the approach taken by the Senate during the first Trump impeachment in 2019. However, impeachment, as demonstrated by President Nixon and President Trump in 2021, proves a powerful tool that, if used at an appropriate time, can prove effective and may gain enough bipartisan support to succeed. Therefore, it could be concluded that, despite the risks of politically motivated impeachments which can be safeguarded against by the need for a two-thirds majority to convict in the Senate, impeachment offers an important safeguard for exceptional circumstances.

175 W Wilson, *Congressional Government: A Study in American Politics* (2nd edn, Houghton, Mifflin and Company 1885) 276.

176 J Bryce, *The American Commonwealth*, Volume I (Liberty Fund 1995) 190.

4 Comparative case study II

Denmark

This chapter will consider Denmark as a case study for the use of impeachment. It will begin by comparing the UK and Danish Constitutions, before considering how impeachment operates in Denmark. There will then be a review of the impeachment of Erik Ninn-Hansen, the Minister of Justice, who was impeached in 1993 and Ninn-Hansen's subsequent application to the European Court of Human Rights.

Why Denmark was chosen as a case study

Denmark was chosen as a case study for a number of reasons. The first reason was because the Danish Constitution contains a provision for impeachment. Despite the development of a parliamentary system of government and the ability of the Folketing, which is the Danish Parliament, to remove a government by holding a vote of no confidence, impeachment has been used as recently as 1993. The fact that ministerial decisions can attract a criminal penalty of up to two years or a fine is of special significance given the fact that Denmark is a member of the Council of Europe and the European Union, which imposes safeguards against any procedure that is contrary to the rule of law or human rights. The chapter will look at the impeachment of Erik Ninn-Hansen, the Minister of Justice, who in 1993 was impeached for violating section 5(1) of Act no. 117 of 15 April 1964,[1] as a result of disregarding his ministerial duties under the Aliens Act.[2] This impeachment was subject to an application to the European Court of Human Rights.[3] In an admissibility decision in 1999 the Court held that there had been no violation of Article 6 of the European Convention on Human Rights (ECHR). The decision will be explored ahead. Finally there was the impeachment of the former Immigration Minister Inger Støjberg in 2021.

The second reason why Denmark was chosen as a case study was because it is a constitutional monarchy with a parliamentary system of government.[4] The third

1 In Danish the Act is lov nr. 117 af 15. april 1964 om ministres ansvarlighed.

2 In Danish the Act is Udlændingeloven.

3 *Erik Ninn-Hansen v Denmark* (Application no. 28972/95, May 1999).

4 A significant difference between the Danish parliamentary system and the United Kingdom's is the dominance of coalition governments in the former. See E Damgaard and P Svensson, 'Who Governs? Parties and Policies in Denmark' (1989) 17 *European Journal of Political*

DOI: 10.4324/9781003269052-5

reason was because the Danish Constitution was heavily influenced by the 'English' constitution and therefore has a legislature (albeit one which, following the enactment of the 1953 Constitution, is unicameral),[5] cabinet government, and a constitutional monarchy.[6] The Danish Constitution contains mechanisms to hold ministers to account and these are similar in part to those that exist within the constitution of the United Kingdom.[7] The influence of the English Constitution on the creation of the June Constitution of 1849 and its subsequent revision by the June Constitution of 1866 was important in shaping Danish views of constitutionalism.[8] As a result of its tradition of royal absolutism, Denmark had no constitutional tradition and was not attracted to the models offered by the French or the German States' Constitutions. The bicameral legislature created by the 1849 Constitution, with two chambers, the Folketing and the Landsting, was not based on the equivalent chambers in the United Kingdom.[9] The Landsting was not modelled on the House of Lords due to a reluctance to create a division between different classes in society and did not have eligibility requirements. However, following the defeat of Denmark in the Prusso-Danish War of 1864, the Danish Constitution was revised in 1866 and the landed elite achieved the imposition of eligibility requirements to serve in the Landsting.[10]

As a result of the Folketing in 1901 achieving the right from the king to force a government from power by holding a vote of no confidence, Denmark has a parliamentary system of government. However, the Danish style of parliamentarianism

---

Research 731. This trend in the prevalence of coalition government has continued, see C Green-Pedersen and PB Moretensen, 'Who Sets the Agenda and Who Responds to it in the Danish Parliament? A New Model of Issue Competition and Agenda-Setting' (2010) 49 *European Journal of Political Research* 257. This coalition style of government is useful to understanding Danish politics during the time that 'Tamilgate' occurred.

5 Since the abolition of the Landstinget in 1953 Denmark has had a unicameral Parliament. The Danish system contains a number of checks-and-balances mechanisms to allow members of the Folketing to hold the government to account. Mads Qvortrup has observed that it 'is unique among single chamber parliaments as it is the only legislature in western Europe which allows a minority of its members to demand referendums on bills proposed by the government' (M Qvortrup, 'Checks and Balances in a Unicameral Parliament: The Case of the Danish Minority Referendum' (2000) 6(3) *The Journal of Legislative Studies* 15, 16.

6 See N Clemmensen, *Denmark's Constitution 150 Years: England and the Danish Constitution of 5 June 1849* (Royal Danish Ministry of Foreign Affairs 1999) for a discussion on the influence of the English Constitution on the drafters of the Danish Constitution.

7 These mechanisms will be discussed ahead. Of particular relevance of ministerial responsibility to Parliament and the ability of the Folketing, the Danish Parliament, to remove a government by holding a vote of no confidence.

8 The need for a constitution was created by a number of factors. These are outlined in Clemmensen (n 6). These factors include the tension between Denmark and its German Duchies of Schleswig-Holstein and the question over the nature of the constitution, the impact of the 1848 revolutions in France and Prussia, and the recognition on the part of the monarchy that reform was needed. See in particular 6–18.

9 See Clemmensen (n 6) 19–22. The British model was far too aristocratic and did not suit the Danish tradition or the mood of the times.

10 ibid 30–1.

is different from that of the United Kingdom.[11] A key difference is the rarity of majority governments in Denmark. Clemmensen has observed:

> Majority governments are actually rare in Denmark, but even in such cases the government will generally enter into negotiation with the opposition. In other words, it is not a case of Cabinet responsibility in the British sense with its principle of confrontation between government and opposition . . . the *Folketing* debates rarely compel much interest – not even among the members. The decisions are made elsewhere and not rendered visible in verbal brawls as in the British Parliament or the French National Assembly.[12]

Another difference is that the Folketing shares legal sovereignty with the Danish Supreme Court, as the Supreme Court held in *Tvind*[13] that an Act of the Folketing was unconstitutional.[14]

The fourth reason why Denmark was selected as a case study was because Denmark has been a Contracting State to the ECHR since 3 September 1953.[15] This means that Denmark must comply with the ECHR. Individuals who allege that their Convention Rights have been violated have a right to bring a case to the European Court of Human Rights. As is the case with the United Kingdom, Denmark is a dualist state and required domestic legislation in the form of the 1992 Act of the European Convention on Human Rights[16] to incorporate the ECHR into domestic law.[17]

It is interesting to observe that as was the case with the United Kingdom, Denmark was concerned with the constitutional implications of incorporating the ECHR into domestic law, as the Act was based on an assumption that there was a 'clear condition that the preservation of the constitutional status quo ex ante should be maintained'.[18] Which meant that it was Parliament and not the courts which was responsible 'for keeping Danish law in accordance with the convention and the

11 ibid 31–3. The right of the Folketing to hold a vote of no confidence and the obligation of the government to resign was codified by the 1953 Constitution.

12 ibid 32–3.

13 19 February 1999 (I 295/1998).

14 See JA Jensen, 'Denmark: The 150th Anniversary of the Danish Constitution and a Landmark Decision of the Supreme Court' (1999) 5(4) *European Public Law* 492, 496–9; JA Jensen, 'Constitutional Chronicle – Denmark: The Separation of Power with Special Regard to the Role of the Judiciary' (2000) 12(1) *European Review of Public Law* 149.

15 'Human Rights in Danish Law' (The Danish Institute for Human Rights) <www.humanrights.dk/about-us/human-rights-in-denmark/human-rights-in-danish-law>.

16 In Danish the Act is entitled Lov in Den europæiske Menneskerettighedskonvention.

17 The Act incorporated the ECHR into Danish law on 29 April 1992. The Act eventually came into force on 1 July 1992. See D Sloss, 'Domestic Application of Treaties' (2011) *Santa Clara Law Digital Commons* <>http://digitalcommons.law.scu.edu/facpubs/635/>; 'Human Rights in Danish Law' (The Danish Institute for Human Rights) <www.humanrights.dk/about-us/human-rights-in-denmark/human-rights-in-danish-law>.

18 J Elo Rytter and M Wind, 'In Need of Juristocracy? The Silence of Denmark in the Development of European Legal Norms' (2011) 9(2) *International Journal of Constitutional Law* 470, 479.

dynamic case law of Strasbourg' and that 'the courts may apply a presumption to the effect that Danish law is in accordance with the convention.'[19] This means that

> the courts should generally refrain from autonomous interpretations of the convention; in particular, an Act of Parliament should only be set aside by Danish courts if the act's incompatibility with the convention follows with *sufficient certainty* from Strasbourg case law.[20]

In Denmark, an Act can be set aside by the courts, whereas in the United Kingdom, it may, as a last resort, be declared by a senior court to incompatible with the convention and remain good law.[21] Another difference is the courts approach to Strasbourg's jurisprudence.[22]

The status of the ECHR is the same as in the United Kingdom as it can be repealed by primary legislation; consequentially, Jorgen Albak Jensen has observed that '[i]n an international context Denmark generally considers itself as a leading country when it comes to the protection of human rights. However, this position – imagined or real, has not been secured by constitutional principles.'[23] Nevertheless, unlike the UK Constitution, the Danish Constitution does contain a list of rights, although these rights are not entrenched and can be repealed by an Act of Parliament.[24]

19 ibid 479.

20 ibid 480.

21 The power to make such a declaration is found in section 4 of the Human Rights Act 1998 See *Ghaidan v Godin-Mendoza* [2004] UKHL 30, per Lord Steyn [42] and [46].

22 Jensen, 'Denmark: The 150th Anniversary of the Danish Constitution' (n 14) 493. This is an interesting point and is also true of the United Kingdom, given its role in drafting the ECHR. A reason for this similarity towards the constitutional status of rights perhaps can be seen from the influence of the English Constitution on the framers of the Danish Constitution of 1849 and their distrust of French revolutionary constitutionalism. Clemmensen has written that in Denmark '[t]here was a strong preference for referring to the Declaration of Rights rather than the French Declaration of the Rights of Man, the down-to-earth English "my home is my castle" rather than the high-flown principles. If they must be high-flown, at least they had to be English, such as the Habeas Corpus Act.' (Clemmensen (n 6) 24).

23 This appears to be classically English in its view of the protection of civil liberties as protected through the ordinary law of the land, as opposed to a constitutional declaration of rights. The Danish position had very similar echoes to AV Dicey's view: '[t]he *Habeas Corpus* Acts have . . . done for liberty of Englishmen more than could have been achieved by any declaration of rights' (*Introduction to the Study of the Law of the Constitution* (Liberty Classics 1982) 134). This was a view shared by some twentieth-century politicians including John Major. For example see I Leigh and R Masterman, *Making Rights Real: The Human Rights Act in Its First Decade* (Hart Publishing 2008) 9: 'the Rt Hon John Major MP is reported to have said with Diceyan confidence, "we have no need of a Bill of Rights because we have freedom."'

24 According to Rytter and Wind, 'Danish courts have – reluctantly and, certainly, very carefully – started to use ECHR case law when interpreting human rights law.' (Rytter and Wind (n 18) 471).

Jensen, 'Denmark: The 150th Anniversary of the Danish Constitution' (n 14) 493. Jensen viewed the protection of human rights within Denmark as unsatisfactory and not adequate when compared with rights properly protected by a constitution.

The fifth reason for the selection of Denmark as a case study was that, since 1 January 1973, Denmark has been a member of the European Union and therefore has to abide by the obligations for members. These obligations extend to the protection of democracy, human rights, and the rule of law.[25] Any perceived erosion of these obligations will lead to action by the European Commission, as in the case of Poland.[26] It must be noted that the United Kingdom is no longer a member of the European Union.

Finally, as a result of the aforementioned factors, Denmark was chosen as a case study because it demonstrated how impeachment could co-exist in a parliamentary system of government alongside other parliamentary mechanisms of ministerial accountability, which are similar to those currently used within the United Kingdom. This co-existence and actual usage of impeachment, rather than a perception that it is obsolete, due to the other mechanisms which are available, is of particular interest given the fact that Denmark seeks to respect the separation of powers and the rights protected in the ECHR. Therefore, as a case study, Denmark presents an opportunity to provide guidance on overcoming the potential problems with using impeachment within the United Kingdom, which include issues relating to the current methods of ministerial accountability, the right to a fair trial under Article 6 of the ECHR and the liberties and rights protected by the common law, and the separation of power between the political (here the legislative) and judicial functions of the state. This presents an opportunity to look at a legal-cum-constitutional transplant, by transferring certain aspects of the Danish use and procedure of impeachment into the United Kingdom's constitutional system. In terms of a transplant, this would be of considerable interest, given the influence of the 'English' Constitution on the drafters of the Danish Constitution of 1849.

Responsibility and accountability of the executive

Demark is a constitutional monarchy. The Danish Constitution is outlined in the Constitutional Act of Denmark. The Constitutional Act was introduced on 5 June 1953 and replaced the previous constitution of 1849. The previous constitution was influenced by the constitution of the United Kingdom of Great Britain and Ireland and there are still many similarities between the two constitutional monarchies. Under section 12 of the Constitutional Act, the supreme authority is vested in the King of Denmark, the current monarch being Queen Margrethe II, although it is stipulated that ministers exercise this on the monarch's behalf.[27]

25 See Article 2 of the Treaty on European Union.

26 See 'European Commission acts to preserve the rule of law in Poland' (European Commission, 25 July 2017) <http://europa.eu/rapid/press-release_IP-17-2161_en.htm>.

27 In the United Kingdom, there is a constitutional convention that the government shall act on behalf of the monarch. See W Bagehot, *The English Constitution* (5th edn, Kegan Paul, Trench and Co 1888) on the three rights of the monarch. Bagehot observed that '[t]he Queen is only at the head of the dignified part of the constitution. The prime minister is at

Section 13 states that the monarch enjoys legal immunity and cannot be held to account for her actions. This is the same position as in the United Kingdom where Her Majesty the Queen enjoys the legal prerogative of immunity from prosecution. The monarch's personal immunity remains the case despite the introduction of the Crown Proceedings Act 1947. However, ministers are responsible 'for the conduct of government'. The monarch has the power to appoint and dismiss ministers,[28] although the ministers are also responsible to the Folketing for decisions taken by their ministry,[29] which has the power to pass a vote of confidence and the ministers are obliged in the event of losing the vote to leave office at once, although the Prime Minister is expected to remain in place until a new government has been formed.[30] The Danish government exercises prerogative powers and a minister 'can decide any matter within their portfolio, unless a statute explicitly specifies otherwise'.[31]

The impeachment of ministers in Denmark

There have been five instances of ministerial impeachments since the first Danish Constitution was adopted in 1849.[32] These occurred in 1856, twice in 1877, 1910, and 1993.[33] The only convictions occurred in 1910 and 1993, and these particular impeachment proceedings will be considered ahead.

Scope of an impeachable offence

Section 16 of the Constitutional Act concerns the impeachment of ministers. The grounds for impeachment is 'maladministration of office'.[34] Therefore, whilst

the head of the efficient part. The Crown is according to the saying, the "fountain of honour;" but the Treasury is the spring of business' 48.

28 Section 14 of the Constitutional Act.

29 This is similar to individual ministerial responsibility in the United Kingdom.

30 Section 15 of the Constitutional Act. In the United Kingdom, a vote of no confidence in the House of Commons requires the government to resign (see section 2 of the Fixed-term Parliaments Act 2011).

31 J Gronnegaard Christensen, 'Delegation and Administrative Organization: An Overview of Danish Regulatory Administration 1950–2000' (Department of Political Science, University of Aarhus) 9. This is similar to the Ram Doctrine, see A Lester and M Weait, 'The Use of Ministerial Powers Without Parliamentary Authority: The Ram Doctrine' (2003) (Autumn) *Public Law* 415. See also the debate on the appropriateness of the Ram Doctrine between Lord Lester of Herne Hill and Baroness Scotland of Asthal (HL Deb 25 February 2003, vol 645, cols 12–13).

32 JA Jensen, 'Political Accountability in Denmark' in L Verhey, H Broeksteeg and I Van den Driessche (eds), *Political Accountability in Europe: Which Way Forward: A Traditional Concept of Parliamentary Democracy in a EU Context* (Europa Law Publishing 2008) 67.

33 H Skovgaard-Petersen, 'Legal and Political Accountability in Denmark – an Overview' (received 3 October 2017). I am extremely grateful to Henrik Skovgaard-Petersen, Head of Section, Constitutional Law and Human Rights Division, The Danish Ministry of Justice for kindly drafting guidance on the operation of impeachment in Denmark.

34 The framers of the 1787 US Constitution were clear that impeachment required something more serious than maladministration. See SB Presser, 'Would George Washington Have Wanted Bill Clinton Impeached?' (1999) 67 *Geo. Wash. L. Rev.* 666–71.

impeachment would appear to be restricted to failures in office and is not as wide as 'high crimes and misdemeanours',[35] which has been used in the United Kingdom and the United States, it actually includes breaches of the criminal law. The impeachment can be initiated either by the Folketing or the monarch, although in the case of the monarch, it would be the Danish government that now exercised this power. This offers two alternative methods for removing a minister from office.[36] Unlike a vote of confidence, the impeachment mechanism contained in section 16 implicitly requires there to be evidence of 'maladministration of office', and this will need to be determined by the Court of Impeachment. According to Henrik Skovgaard-Petersen:

> [The responsibility of ministers] is fleshed out in the Ministerial Responsibility Act of May 15, 1964. It follows from section 1 of the Act that ministerial responsibility in the sense of section 13 of the Constitutional Act *arises only from maladministration of office*. Criminal offences that have no connection with the minister's role as member of the Cabinet *cannot be a valid ground* for impeachment.
>
> . . .
>
> The most significant provision fleshing out the responsibility of ministers for maladministration of office is section 5 of the Ministerial Responsibility Act. Under section 5(1), a minister is liable to criminal responsibility if, *intentionally or as a result of gross negligence*, he is in breach of the duties incumbent on him under the Constitutional Act or other legislation or which flow from the nature of his office. Under section 5(2), section 5(1) shall apply if a minister *provides Parliament with incorrect or misleading information* or if he *conceals from Parliament information which is of significance for Parliament's assessment of the matter in hand.*[37]

The scope of the impeachment model in Denmark is to permit the criminal sanction of decisions taken by ministers (or in exceptional circumstances other individuals) which are deemed to fall within the meaning of 'maladministration'. The statutory guidance under section 5 of the Ministerial Responsibility Act 1964 is clear that the minister's conduct must be intentional or grossly negligent, which prevents carefully considered decision-making from falling outside of the ambit of the criminal law.

Therefore, in Denmark, a minister who acts in a grossly negligent manner when taking a decision which results in a major policy failure could be impeached, whereas in the United Kingdom, such a minister could be dismissed by the Prime Minister or face a vote of confidence by the House of Commons. In Denmark, a minister who misleads or conceals information from the Folketing

35 Within the British context this has included corruption, abuse of position, and treason.
36 Sections 14 and 15 of the Constitutional Act.
37 Skovgaard-Petersen (n 33).

can be impeached, whereas in the United Kingdom, whilst this is a breach of the Ministerial Code,[38] the ultimate sanction could be dismissal or resignation. Finally, a minister who breaches the law whilst acting in an official capacity could be impeached in Denmark, whereas in the United Kingdom, this would result in the department being held responsible: an example of this would be a minister in Denmark who ignored a court order and would risk a custodial sentence and a fine, whereas in the United Kingdom, a minister can order their officials to ignore a court order and avoid criminal sanction.[39] It must be observed the UK Parliament *could still* impeach a minister for ignoring a court order or for lying to Parliament, and these may well be two appropriate instances where impeachment provides a remedy where the ordinary courts cannot provide a sanction that is sufficiently proportionate or the matter is non-justiciable, and the consequences of the ministerial misconduct are sufficiently serious to be regarded as a breach of the constitution[40] and even resignation is not regarded as a sufficient remedy.

In both Denmark and the United Kingdom, impeachment would not be applicable where a minister's conduct related to acts beyond the scope of their office, such as drink driving, fraud, domestic violence, or perverting the course of justice.[41]

The co-existence of impeachment and votes of no confidence raises a number of points. First, how many times has a minister or an entire government been removed from office by a vote of no confidence?[42] The use of votes of no confidence against an entire cabinet 'is a very rare occurrence', and no individual minister has been removed by way of a vote of no confidence, although, 'a minister likely to face a vote of no confidence by Parliament will either resign or

38 *Ministerial Code* [1.2]. See for example the resignation of Leon Brittan on 24 January 1986 for misleading the House of Commons and John Profumo on 5 June 1963 for lying to the House of Commons. See O Gay and T Powell, 'Individual Ministerial Responsibility – Issues and Examples' (House of Commons Library, Research Paper 04/31, 5 April 2004).

39 See for example a minster ignoring a court order and being found in contempt of court. In *M v Home Office* [1994] 1 AC 377 whereby the Home Secretary was held in contempt of court, however, this was in a corporate and not a personal capacity and the Home Office was fined. For academic commentary see C Forsyth, 'Leading Administrative Law Cases: M v Home Office [1994] 1 AC 377' (*Cambridge University Legal Studies Research Paper Series*, Paper No. 50/2016, September 2016). For more recent examples see M Beckford, 'Theresa May Accused of Unacceptable and Regrettable Behaviour by Judge' *The Telegraph* (20 June 2012); D Taylor, 'Home Secretary Ignores Court Order and Sends Asylum Seeker to Kabul' *The Guardian* (14 September 2017).

40 Sir Richard Scott concluded that ministers had breached the constitution as a result of their behaviour (V Bogdanor, 'Scott Report' (1996) 74 *Public Administration* 593, 610–11).

41 For example see ahead for a discussion of the Alberti frauds, where Peter Albert Alberti, a former Danish minister, was not impeached for committing fraud, as he had committed the offences prior to becoming a minister, whereas Viscount Melville was impeached in the United Kingdom in 1806 as a result of alleged financial misconduct in connection to has handling of departmental money.

42 See Jensen (n 32) 66, fn 3.

be dismissed by the Prime Minister.'[43] The second point is to ask whether this range of options are regarded as complementing one another. For example, if impeachment had not been contained in section 16 of the Constitutional Act then the question is whether the Folketing would have relied upon section 15 of the Constitutional Act to remove a minister from office. Of importance for this book, in the United Kingdom, the House of Commons does have the power to remove a minister or a government via a vote of no confidence.[44]

Sentences and pardons

In Denmark, ministers are tried by the Court of Impeachment which has the power to impose custodial sentences on ministers and therefore the outcome of the impeachment may see the accused deprived of their liberty or the imposition of a fine. This is different from the United States, whereby in the case of a presidential impeachment, the most serious sanction that the Senate can impose is to remove the President from office. However, it must be observed that in the United States, a federal impeachment does not prevent subsequent criminal sanctions. Section 24 of the Constitutional Act provides that the monarch is able to pardon a minister for a sentence that has been passed by the Court of Impeachment. In practice, the power to pardon is undertaken by the Minister of Justice. However, this use of the prerogative is not unfettered, as the guidance to the Act makes clear:

> The Minister only pardons people if there are special personal circumstances in favour of a pardon. These could be illness, age or family circumstances, for instance. In practice, most pardons are granted before people have begun to serve their sentences. . . . The *Government cannot pardon* a Minister sentenced by the Court of Impeachment on its own initiative. The Government *must propose a motion in Parliament* and try to gain a majority for it.[45]

Therefore, the Folketing is required to give its consent to the granting of a pardon. This restricts the ability of a minister to be pardoned by his colleagues. The operation of pardons in cases of impeachment is different from the United Kingdom, whereby a pardon can be granted only once a person had been convicted after the impeachment trial in the House of Lords and does not require the approval of Parliament.[46]

43 Skovgaard-Petersen (n 33).
44 The last time a government was removed by way of a vote of no confidence was that of James Callaghan in 1979.
45 'My Constitutional Act with Explanations' (The Danish Parliament) <www.thedanishparliament.dk/Publications/My_Constitutional_Act_with_explanations/Chapter%203.aspx>.
46 See the Act of Settlement 1701.

The procedure and operation of the Court of Impeachment

Part VI of the Constitutional Act is solely concerned with the procedure and operation of the Court of Impeachment. The Court of Impeachment was first established by the 1849 Constitution. Since its creation the Court of Impeachment has tried five cases. Section 59 outlines the composition of the Court of Impeachment. The members are divided into two groups, the 'senior ordinary members of the highest court of justice of the Realm' and the 'members elected for six years by the Folketing according to proportional representation'.[47] The Court of Impeachment must consist of an equal number of each group, with a limit of 15 per group.[48] No member of the Folketing can be a member of the Court of Impeachment.[49] This requirement is important as this distinguishes the role of the Folketing and the Court of Impeachment in the entire process, with the former determining whether an impeachment should proceed and the latter to act as judge.

The Court of Impeachment has a president who is elected by the members of the Court.[50] Section 60(1) states that '[t]he Court of Impeachment shall try such actions as may be brought by the King or the Folketing against Ministers.' However, the Court of Impeachment is not just limited to the impeachment of ministers.[51] Non-ministers can be tried by the Court of Impeachment, but only if (a) they are accused of crimes which the king 'may deem to be particularly dangerous to the State' under subsection 2, (b) the king decides that subsection 2 applies,[52] and (c) the Folketing gives its consent.[53] Importantly, the '[r]ules on the Court of Impeachment shall be provided by statute' and this will provide certainty as to the operation of the impeachment proceedings and trial. The Impeachment Act 1954[54] provides guidance on how the Court will operate. Section 2(5) provides that the members of the Court retain their positions for the course of the proceedings, even if the length of their term should have expired. The Act provides the Court with the power *inter alia* to compel a defendant to attend.[55]

47 Section 59(1).

48 ibid. 'The composition is based on the assumption that the special cases which fall under the Court's competence ought to be decided by a group of judges which comprises not only persons trained in law but also persons with special knowledge of political matters.' ('Preparatory Report on the application of Article 6, paragraph 1, of the ECHR by the courts of Denmark' (Cour de Cassation) <www.courdecassation.fr/venements_23/colloques_4/2000_2038/on_the_9441.html>.

49 ibid. This approach differs from the United Kingdom and the United States, as in both countries it is members of the House of Lords or the Senate who act as the jury and determine guilt.

50 Section 59(2).

51 This is the case with impeachment in the United Kingdom but not in the United States, where impeachment is limited to civil officers.

52 This would be on the advice of the monarch's ministers.

53 Section 60(2).

54 In Danish it is *Rigsretsloven*.

55 Section 33 of the Impeachment Act 1954.

The regulation of judicial misconduct

Arguably, unless a judge falls within the scope of section 60(2) and is considered 'particularly dangerous to the State', they cannot be impeached.[56] Section 64 is concerned with the dismissal of judges and states that '[j]udges shall not be dismissed except by judgement.' The function of disciplining judges is undertaken by the Special Court of Revision (Den Saerlige Klageret).[57]

The impeachment of Ninn-Hansen in 1993

This section will consider the impeachment of Erik Ninn-Hansen who was the Danish Minister of Justice from 1982 to 1989. Ninn-Hansen was involved in a controversy concerning applications for family reunification from Tamil refugees who had fled Sri Lanka. The issue was that Ninn-Hansen had attempted to fetter Danish Law, the Aliens Act, by holding up visa applications for family members of Tamil refugees from Sri Lanka. Danish law permitted family members to enter Denmark in order to be reunited with their family who had reached Denmark.

The impeachment of Ninn-Hansen is significant for a number of reasons: first, as Jensen observed, the fact that post-1910, 'most constitutional commentators believed that the Impeachment Court would never be used again, as the parliamentary principle would "take care" of incompetent ministers', which meant that impeachment was viewed similarly to the way it was in the United Kingdom, to have fallen into disuse and at best to be a historical relic, and second, that it had been assumed that impeachment had been superseded by the ability of Parliament to hold ministers to account.[58] This is the same as in the United Kingdom, where ministerial responsibility to the House of Commons is said to have superseded the need for parliamentary impeachment.[59] It can be seen that impeachment was not regarded as a relic when the Folketing decided to begin impeachment proceedings against Ninn-Hansen.

56 '[Judges] Cannot Be Dismissed but Can Be Impeached for Negligence or Criminal Acts' ('Denmark Human Rights Practices, 1994' (US Department of State, February 1995) <http://dosfan.lib.uic.edu/ERC/democracy/1994_hrp_report/94hrp_report_eur/Denmark.html>).

57 The Ombudsman established by the Constitution of 1953 does not have jurisdiction to consider complaints made against members of the judiciary. See S Anderson, 'Judicial Accountability: Scandinavia, California and the U.S.A.' (1980) 28(3) *The American Journal of Comparative Law* 393, 396.

58 Jensen, 'The 150th Anniversary of the Danish Constitution' (n 14) 495. See also Jensen (n 32) 67, where he discussed the use 'of a binding vote of no-confidence' as having replaced the use of the Court of Impeachment.

59 See Chapter 8.

Immigration as an issue in Danish domestic politics

It is important to consider how immigration was an important issue in Danish politics at the time of 'Tamilgate'. Christoffer Green-Pedersen and Pontus Odmalm have written on the political attitude towards immigration that existed in Denmark in the 1980s and 1990s.[60] Green-Pedersen and Odmalm have contrasted Denmark's and Sweden's policies towards immigration and observed that '[t]he more restrictionist position of the Danish centre-right parties has been central to turning immigration into a highly salient and contested policy issue which has also contributed to significant policy changes.'[61] This was in part due to the electoral popularity of the Danish centre-right, such as the success enjoyed by the Liberals and Conservatives.[62] They note that '[w]ith the exception of a few shorter periods, the bourgeois bloc in Denmark has controlled the majority in the Danish parliament.'[63] As a consequence of Danish changes to economic migration policy in the 1970s, which meant that labour migration was prevented, the chief source of immigration has been those seeking asylum and those seeking family reunification.[64] Family reunification became politically controversial in the 1980s. It was in this context that the decision by the Minister of Justice to fetter the law relating to family reunification can be seen. Family reunification, a part of the more liberal immigration reforms that had been introduced in the 1980s, was clearly unpopular with right-wing politicians and Ninn-Hansen had publicly stated that they were a risk to Danish nationality.[65] It was unsurprising that 'Tamilgate' would prove to be so politically contentious.

Furthermore, the issue of how the government and the Folketing responded to the issue of immigration is important to understand the role of coalition governments in Denmark. Importantly, whilst 'Denmark has often had a Social Democratic government. . . [it has] almost always [had] a bourgeois parliamentary majority.'[66] This bourgeois majority represented the right-wing parties in the Folketing. The question of immigration in Denmark only became 'a growing campaign issue in the 1990s.[67] In the 2001 Danish election, it was one of the central, if not *the* central, campaign issues.'[68] The impact that immigration had on

60 C Green-Pedersen and P Odmalm, 'Going Different Ways? Right-Wing Parties and the Immigrant Issue in Denmark and Sweden' (2008) 15(3) *Journal of European Public Policy* 367. It is also useful to see immigration and the national response particularly to the issue of asylum seekers in a European context. See GP Freeman, 'Migration Policy and Politics in the Receiving States' (1992) 26(4) *The International Migration Review* 1144.
61 Green-Pedersen and Odmalm (n 60) 368.
62 ibid.
63 ibid 369.
64 ibid 370.
65 ibid 371.
66 C Green-Pedersen and J Krogstrup, 'Immigration as a Political Issue in Denmark and Sweden' 47 (2008) *European Journal of Political Research* 610, 615.
67 Although the family reunification policy had proved controversial in the 1980s.
68 ibid 619.

politics at the time that the 'Tamilgate' scandal occurred may not have been of such prominence as in 2001, but it was nonetheless problematic for the Danish coalition government which took office in 1982. This was because the government required the support of the Social Liberals and the Progress Party in the Folketing and whilst

> [t]he government's main focus was to revive the Danish economy and get a stable bourgeois majority behind economic policy . . . all non-economic issues were very problematic from the centre-right governments because they highlighted bourgeois disunity and often activated a nongovernmental majority in government.[69]

The reform of the immigration law in 1983 was opposed only by the Progress Party and led to an increase in asylum seekers. Consequentially, increased immigration to Denmark 'put the administration of the new law under pressure. Furthermore, the years 1984, 1985, and 1986 saw intensified mass media coverage with a critical angle on refugees and immigration.'[70] Ninn-Hansen supported reforming the law to combat increased immigration and this resulted in immigration no longer being such a political issue in Denmark.[71] Prior to the resignation of the Danish government in 1993, it was the Progress Party that campaigned against immigration and only when in opposition did the Liberals and Conservatives focus on immigration as a political issue.[72] This proved to be successful, as the Liberals were able to form a government after the 2001 elections.[73]

The Tamilgate Scandal and the role of the Ombudsman

The controversy concerning the illegal policy of delaying visas to Tamil refugees from Sri Lanka became known as the 'Tamilgate Scandal' in Denmark. The use of the word 'gate' to refer to the scandal drew parallels with the Watergate scandal in the United States and clearly emphasised the importance of the alleged misconduct in Danish popular and political culture. The Parliamentary Ombudsman undertook an investigation and the report 'received considerable public attention and resulted in public criticism of the Government's refugee policy'.[74]

Parliamentarians had responded to the Ombudsman's report by asking the Danish government to establish a Court of Inquiry, so that Ninn-Hansen's conduct could be investigated.[75] However, whilst Ninn-Hansen 'had no objections . . .

69 ibid 621.
70 ibid.
71 ibid 621–2.
72 Green-Pedersen and Krogstrup (n 66) 622.
73 ibid 624.
74 *Ninn-Hansen v Denmark* (1999) (Application no. 28972/95); (1999) 28 EHRR CD96.
75 ibid.

the Government resisted and such a proposal was not adopted.'[76]After a television programme 'in which [Ninn-Hansen's] conduct and the discharge of his official duties were severely criticised' and the public debate which ensued, the government agreed to establish a Court of Inquiry to investigate the government's policy and Ninn-Hansen's conduct in connection with the Tamil refugee family reunification applications.[77] This entailed a change to the Administration of Justice Act 1990 (section 21a) to permit such a Court of Inquiry to be established.[78] The Court of Inquiry that was established in 1990 was led by a judge of the Danish Supreme Court and was assisted by a lawyer who acted as an interrogator to represent the public interest.[79] The proceedings were held in camera until December 1990 and thereafter the Court of Inquiry undertook the investigation in the open.[80] When he appeared before the Court of Inquiry, Ninn-Hansen was offered the right to legal assistance, which he refused; he was given access 'to the written material which formed the basis of the interview' and 'he was informed that he had the right to remain silent and that, in case he chose to give testimony, this would not be under oath.'[81]

The Court of Inquiry was clear that it 'is not going to pronounce a judgment – which would presuppose the legal arguments from counsel – but issue a report – *i.e* . a recommendation to others – with regard to the issues which have been examined during the investigation.'[82] The procedure adopted by the Court of Inquiry was inquisitorial, rather than adversarial in nature.[83] The judge presiding over the Court of Inquiry observed that

> [i]f anybody wishes to make written submissions to the court it cannot at the outset be expected that the court will take the initiative to arrange an adversarial procedure, requesting replies, rebuttal and counter-rebuttal from everybody who has made statements.[84]

Rather, anyone giving testimony was allowed 'to raise questions and to suggest that further evidence be produced'.[85] The procedure adopted by the Court of Inquiry appeared to be fair to all those who gave evidence before it.

The report was published in January 1993 and made '*inter alia*, serious criticism of [Ninn-Hansen's] discharge of his official duties in his capacity as Minister of Justice in respect of the handling of the Tamil refugees' family reunification

76 ibid.
77 ibid.
78 ibid 3.
79 ibid.
80 ibid 3–4.
81 ibid 3.
82 *Ninn-Hansen v Denmark* (n 74).
83 ibid.
84 ibid.
85 ibid.

cases'.[86] Ninn-Hansen was held to have adopted a policy of delaying visas for the families of Tamil refugees, which was illegal and in contravention of Danish law.[87] The report also criticised the Prime Minister and led to the resignation of the Danish government.[88] The report concluded that the Danish Prime Minister knew about Ninn-Hansen's conduct in delaying the family reunifications of Tamil refugees and had attempted to cover up this illegal policy. As a consequence of this the Prime Minister had given Parliament and the Parliamentary Justice Committee 'deliberately misleading information'.[89] According to the *Independent*, 'The core question was how much did Mr Schluter [the Prime Minister] know about the affair? Was he deliberately withholding information when he proclaimed before parliament in April 1989 that 'nothing has been swept under the carpet.'[90] The Court of Inquiry's report concluded that the Prime Minister's speech to Parliament in 1989 was 'directly untrue'.[91] The Prime Minister denied that he had misled Parliament, and in his resignation speech, he stated:

> I have heard the criticisms and it is still my opinion that I have not deprived the parliament of important information. But the judge (heading the inquiry) charactised (sic) my relationship with the parliament in such a way that it would not be right for me to continue as Prime Minister.[92]

The impeachment of Ninn-Hansen

The Danish Parliament was able to respond to the Court of Inquiry's report by impeaching the former minister. The indictment was that Ninn-Hansen had violated section 5(1) of Act no. 117 of 15 April 1964, which imposed obligations on how ministers were to perform their duties whilst in office: '[a]ccording to this provision a minister is liable to punishment if he wilfully or by gross negligence disregards the duties which fall on him under the Constitution, or under other laws, or due to the nature of his office.'[93] He was also indicted for 'having disregarded his duties under the Aliens Act (Udlændingeloven) to the extent that a number of aliens could not obtain a family reunification although they had, under the Act, a right thereto'.[94]

86 ibid 5.
87 S Lambert, '"Tamilgate" Revelations Force Danish PM's Resignation' *The Independent* (15 January 1993).
88 *Ninn-Hansen v Denmark* (n 74) 5.
89 Lambert (n 87).
90 ibid.
91 ibid.
92 ibid.
93 *Ninn-Hansen v Denmark* (n 74) 99.
94 ibid 5.

There is no equivalent of this statutory requirement in English law. Indeed, the closest is the Ministerial Code[95] which contains the non-legal duties of ministers, including their responsibility to Parliament and the requirement to uphold the Seven Principles of Public Life.[96] With regard to the laws that apply to a minister as part of her official duties, a minister could face liability if she committed a criminal offence (such as bribery pursuant to the Bribery Act 2010, or misconduct in public office), but she is personally protected from sanction in the event of contempt of court.[97]

The Folketing appointed prosecutors, which is similar to the manager system used in the United Kingdom and the United States. The Court of Impeachment relied upon the transcripts of the Court of Inquiry after holding by a majority of 21 to 3 that these would assist the court and not replace the evidence adduced before the court.[98] On 22 June 1995, a majority of the Court of Impeachment held that Ninn-Hansen had violated his duties under the 1964 Act and sentenced him to a four-month custodial sentence, which was suspended.[99] The judgment of the Court of Impeachment could not be appealed.[100] Ninn-Hansen made an application to the European Court of Human Rights on 6 December 1990. His complaint was that he had not received a fair trial for the purposes of Article 6 of the ECHR in 'the determination of the criminal charges against him':

a) the proceedings in the Court of Inquiry did not comply with the requirements of fairness and were to some extent held in camera, and that these proceedings and their outcome made a proper evaluation of evidence in the Court of Impeachment impossible;
b) the Court of Impeachment was not an independent and impartial tribunal;
c) the Court of Impeachment refused the applicant permission to hear two witnesses in support of his claim to dismiss the case;
d) the Court of Impeachment allowed the use of the transcripts from the Court of Inquiry;
e) the Court of Impeachment decided to continue the proceedings despite the applicant's state of health;
f) the case was not determined within a reasonable time.[101]

The European Court of Human Rights rejected the applicant's submission regarding the Court of Inquiry and the impact on the subsequent impeachment

95 Ministerial Code, Cabinet Office, January 2018.
96 These had first been identified by Lord Nolan, see Standards in Public Life: First Report of the Committee on Standards in Public Life (Volume 1), May 1995, Cm 2850-I.
97 *M v Home Office* [1994] 1 AC 377.
98 *Ninn-Hansen v Denmark* (n 74) 9.
99 ibid 12.
100 ibid.
101 ibid 16–17.

trial.[102] The argument that the Court of Impeachment's composition breached Article 6 was also rejected. The fact that Parliament appointed lay judges did not mean that the appointees were biased and there were sufficient safeguards in place:

> The Court recalls, furthermore, that Article 6 § 1 of the Convention requires independence not only from the executive and the parties but also from the legislator, i.e. Parliament. . . . However, *mere appointment* by Parliament cannot be seen to cast doubt on the independence or impartiality of the court. The applicant has not alleged that any of the judges in question actually took instructions or actually was biased. Although political sympathies *may play part* [sic] in the process of appointment of lay judges to the Court of Impeachment the Court does not consider that this alone gives legitimate doubts as to their independence and impartiality.[103]

The lay judges were there to provide political knowledge and they never outnumbered the judicial members of the Court of Impeachment.[104] The Court also rejected the submission that the Supreme Court judges sitting on the Court of Impeachment were not impartial as some of the judges had heard the applicant's appeals from the Court of Inquiry. The applicant had not argued that the judges were personally biased against him. The Court applied an objective standard to determine impartiality:

> Having regard to the scope and nature of the decisions made by the Supreme Court, concerning fixing of time-limits for submission of observations to the Court of Inquiry and the extent to which witnesses before the Court of Inquiry could have access to testimonies of other witnesses, the Court finds that the applicant's fear that the Supreme Court judges involved in these pre-trial decisions lacked impartiality cannot be regarded as objectively justified. Nor can the fact that the professional judges participating in the Court of Impeachment were colleagues of the judge who had presided over the Court of Inquiry and the fact that the Court of Inquiry held its sessions in the offices of the Supreme Court lead to the conclusion that the applicant's fear that the judges lacked impartiality and independence was objectively justified.[105]

The Court also rejected the argument that 'the media had entertained a consistent and negative press campaign against him which had in fact determined his guilt prior to the trial and had influenced the participating judges.'[106] The

102 ibid 18–19.
103 ibid 20 (emphasis added).
104 ibid 19–20.
105 ibid 21.
106 ibid 22.

Court of Impeachment's refusal to hear two witnesses and its use of the Court of Inquiry's transcripts did not amount to a violation of Article 6 of the ECHR.[107] Neither did the fact that the Court of Impeachment continued with the proceedings whilst the applicant was unwell amount to a breach of Article 6 of the ECHR.[108] Finally, the Court dismissed his argument that he had not been tried within a reasonable period of time.[109]

It is important to note that use of impeachment is understood by the actors within the Danish Constitution as being restricted to criminal offences. Jensen commented that as a consequence of the establishment of the parliamentary principle, 'there is general agreement that the Impeachment Court will only take action when a minister is suspected of actual criminal offences, as happened in the *Tamil* case.'[110] Jensen has observed that in Denmark there has been debate on 'three connected issues: the size of the Court, the need for non-judicial members of the Court, and the need for a special Impeachment Court at all'.[111] The participation of the lay members was prompted by the remit of the Impeachment Court to consider political conduct, which today has been superseded by the parliamentary principle.[112] Jensen observed:

> The weight of the opinion therefore seems to be that a future Impeachment Court should consist only of legally qualified judges. If this point of view is accepted, there is no longer any need for a Special Impeachment Court, and it would seem natural to use the ordinary court system for impeachment cases.[113]

Furthermore, Jensen had also raised the issue of judicial workload, with the Impeachment Court putting the Supreme Court under additional pressure given the number of judges required to serve on the court.[114]

What does the Danish model of impeachment mean for the United Kingdom?

This section will consider the significance of the Ninn-Hansen impeachment in Denmark on how a revised form of impeachment could be used again in the United Kingdom. Chapter 9 will consider how impeachment might operate in the United Kingdom and consideration will be made to ensure that this complies with the ECHR, the rule of law, and the common law principles of natural justice.

107 ibid 22–3.
108 ibid 24–5.
109 ibid 26–7.
110 Jensen, 'The 150th Anniversary of the Danish Constitution' (n 14) 495.
111 ibid.
112 ibid.
113 ibid 496.
114 ibid.

Therefore, it will be expedient to briefly explore how the Danish use of impeachment will have significance for any UK use of impeachment.

First, in the case of Ninn-Hansen the accusation was made by the Folketing and based on the findings of the Ombudsman and the Court of Inquiry. Therefore, prior to the decision to impeach, there had been two extensive investigations into Ninn-Hansen's conduct and the impeachment could not be regarded as a majority in the Folketing misusing this mechanism. It is important to observe that there is no requirement to have either type of inquiry before holding a vote on impeachment. However, by having had both inquiries before impeaching Ninn-Hansen it demonstrated that impeachment could be regarded as an appropriate consequence of the two previous negative findings. In other jurisdictions impeachment may involve determinations by parliamentary committees or judicial bodies. For example, in the United States, it is the House Judiciary Committee that will determine whether there are grounds for impeachment, and if it is satisfied that an impeachable offence has been committed then it is at this stage that the House of Representatives will vote on the articles of impeachment. In the United Kingdom, any impeachment could potentially take place after a select committee report, a public inquiry, or a report by the Parliamentary and Health Service Ombudsman and could compliment these existing accountability and responsibility mechanisms. However, as it stands the House of Commons may impeach without such preliminary investigations.

Second, in Denmark, the trial was presided over by both lay members and judges. There was a clear distinction between the Parliament's having voted to impeach and then appointing prosecutors, and the members of the Court of Impeachment who determined guilt. This separation of personnel, and the fact that the lay members, albeit political appointees, are not influenced by the will of parliamentarians, led the European Court of Human Rights to conclude that there had been no violation of Article 6 of the ECHR.[115] In the case of the United Kingdom, the procedure for impeachment would need to be reconsidered. As a consequence of the House of Lords Act 1999 and the Constitutional Reform Act 2005, the House of Lords has been transformed, no longer having a judicial function and the only 'judicial members' being retired senior judges. Historically, the Lord Chancellor in his capacity as the Lord High Steward would have played an important role in presiding over the trial and determining the procedure that would be used. However, as a result of the Constitutional Reform Act 2005 the Lord Chancellor is no longer the Speaker of the House of Lords and indeed, since the appointment of Jack Straw in 2007, all Lord Chancellors have been members of the House of Commons, although a member of the House of Lords could still be appointed to this role. Neither is there a requirement that the Lord Chancellor be a lawyer.

The Danish model of impeachment, which retains the role of the Folketing, but relies on a Court of Impeachment, could provide an example of how the

115 See *Ninn-Hansen v Denmark* (n 74).

rights under Article 6 of the ECHR and the common law could be protected. If the Danish model were wholly, or partially adopted, this would amount to a constitutional transplant and would require careful consideration. Such a consideration will be undertaken in Chapter 9. It is unlikely that the United Kingdom's exit from the European Union will have any impact on its commitment to remain a member of the Council of Europe.

Part Two

UK Constitution and accountability

5 Executive accountability in the United Kingdom

The purpose of this chapter is to provide the context within which to consider the meaning of accountability, the UK model of parliamentary government and the importance of ministerial responsibility to Parliament, and the existing political accountability mechanisms that already operate in the United Kingdom. This review of the literature will then inform Chapter 6 and Chapter 7, where the issue of accountability within the UK Constitution, and whether impeachment could serve a role in buttressing existing accountability mechanisms, will be addressed. This chapter will offer a review of the academic literature and consider the nature of accountability. Accountability is a vast area with an ever-increasing amount of literature. Therefore, this chapter cannot attempt to provide a broad account of accountability. Instead, what will be offered is an account of how ministers are held to account for conduct that is contrary to accepted constitutional norms or perceived to be misconduct.

What do we mean by accountability?

We will now consider the existing academic debate surrounding the meaning, definition, and value of accountability. It is necessary to consider what is meant by accountability within the UK Constitution. Day and Klein observed that '[p]olitical accountability begins when individuals are given responsibility for carrying out tasks on behalf of their fellow citizens'[1] and

> [t]he problems of political accountability in modern societies, and the ambiguities of the concept in today's environment, stem precisely from the fact that while our ideas were born in relatively simple societies, they have developed in societies which have become increasingly complex over the centuries.[2]

The complexities of modern governance and the perhaps simple need to ensure that those exercising power are held to account by those entrusting them to

1 P Day and R Klein, *Accountabilities: Five Public Services* (Tavistock Publications 1978) 6.
2 ibid 7.

DOI: 10.4324/9781003269052-7

exercise this power and representing the citizens are at odds. This is in the sense that accountability is extremely complex and will interpreted differently, as what is desired by accountability (and also importantly, whether in a given moment, accountability is effective) will depend on the circumstances and who you ask. Accountability is subjective, as whilst it is possible to identify some core tenets of accountability that could perhaps be universally agreed upon within the United Kingdom (e.g. that ministers must be accountable to Parliament, and that Members of Parliament are accountable to their constituents), what this accountability requires is disputed or sometimes the legitimacy of a form of accountability can be challenged (one example is judicial review of politically sensitive decisions, such as whether to advise the monarch to prorogue Parliament).

The term accountability has taken on a broad meaning. According to Tony Wright, the former parliamentarian:

> [t]here are daily demands for someone or something to be 'held to account'. The routine response to a whole range of political issues is a call for 'more accountability'. . . . So pervasive has the language of accountability become – and so synonymous it now is with every desirable attribute of democracy and good government – that the concept is in danger of losing all critical meaning.[3]

This presents a problem, as to whether the increased use of accountability and the need to counter every shortcoming in how the actors within the constitution operate requires more or better accountability. Wright's view is supported by Richard Mulgan:

> A word which a few decades or so ago was used only rarely and with relatively restricted meaning . . . now crops up everywhere performing all manner of analytical and rhetorical tasks and carrying most of the major burdens of democratic 'governance.'[4]

This reflects the development of accountability theories in the 1960s and 1970s and how accountability has become a go-to phrase or term in modern usage. As a term, accountability has its historical origins in the eleventh century and its roots were in accounting and bookkeeping.[5] This need for those entrusted with power and resources to account to others for their conduct, to be accountable to somebody more powerful than themselves, to be compelled to explain, to apologise for errors, and accept the consequences, are arguably essential ingredients of accountability.

3 T Wright, 'The Politics of Accountability' in M Elliot and D Feldman (eds), *The Cambridge Companion to Public Law* (Cambridge University Press 2015) 96.

4 R Mulgan, ' "Accountability": An Ever-Expanding Concept' (2000) 78(3) *Public Administration* 555.

5 M Bovens, R Goodin and T Schillemans, 'Public Accountability' in M Bovens, R Goodin and T Schillemans (eds), *The Oxford Handbook of Public Accountability* (OUP 2016) 2–3.

However, is accountability devoid of meaning or now just a catch-all term that is too slippery for a clear definition? Mark Bovens has observed that '[i]n contemporary political and scholarly discourse "accountability" often serves as a conceptual umbrella that covers various other distinct concepts, such as transparency, equity, democracy, efficiency, responsiveness, responsibility and integrity.'[6] If we accept Bovens' observation and acknowledge that accountability is an umbrella term and that when we use the word accountability, we are often seeking more than one or two things, it calls into question whether this seemingly catch-all approach is a problem and does it render accountability nothing more than a hollow slogan. There is certainly a need to be conscious that we must be clear about the normative importance of accountability within a given relationship and context. Here the focus is on the accountability of ministers for their decisions and is concerned with proper use of ministerial powers and the integrity of the constitution and the willingness to conform to accepted constitutional norms. Therefore, we are looking at the accountability of ministers to Parliament, seen through the relationship of ministers to the House of Commons. It is important to be aware that whilst too little accountability in any given situation may be detrimental, too much accountability can be intrusive, counter-productive, and corrosive to the efficient operation of the functions to be carried out by an actor within the constitution. Matthew Flinders has warned of the dangers of too much accountability, and these are valid concerns as any argument for 'increased' accountability must reflect upon whether this is needed, or whether it can be better achieved by an existing or alternative mechanism.[7]

It is important to consider how accountability can be understood as a term. The nature of accountability was considered by Guerin, McCrae, and Shepheard in a discussion paper for the *Institute for Government*:

> At heart, accountability is about a relationship – between those responsible for something and those who have a role in passing judgement on how well that responsibility was discharged. The relationship can take various forms:
>
> - Oversight: the relationship involves one side overseeing the other through direct reporting lines for performance.
> - Regulation: the relationship involves one side regulating the other through the setting and enforcement of rules about how certain things should be done.
> - Inspection: the relationship involves one side inspecting the other through assessments of how well responsibilities have been discharged.
> - Scrutiny: the relationship involves one side scrutinising the other through the ability to question and report on what has happened.[8]

6 M Bovens, 'Analysing and Assessing Accountability: A Conceptual Framework' (2007) 13(4) *European Law Journal* 447, 449.

7 M Flinders, 'Daring to Be a Daniel' (2011) 43(5) *Administration and Society* 595.

8 B Guerin, J McCrae and M Shepheard, 'Accountability in Modern Government: What Are the Issues?' (A Discussion Paper, Institute for Government, April 2018) <www.

This account is helpful as both the theory of accountability generally and this book are concerned with relationships. The focus of this book is the relationship between the House of Commons and senior ministers. A useful approach when thinking about accountability is that of the editors of the *Oxford Handbook of Public Accountability*, where they pose five questions for thinking about accountability: (i) who, (ii) to whom, (iii) for what, (iv) which standards, and (v) why. Within the context of the executive's accountability to the House of Commons in the United Kingdom, questions (i) and (ii) are concerned with the relationship between the executive and the legislature. This relationship is based on the legitimacy of the exercise of executive powers by the government and the need for these powers to be carried out in a democracy, not directly by the monarch, but by parliamentarians on her behalf. It is possible to talk about this as delegation of the business of government from the House of Commons to the government; however, there is a risk of oversimplifying the fact that actual delegation in law is from the monarch to her government.

In terms of the delegation of power, Strom considered delegation and accountability in parliamentary democracies and used the agent and principal model. According to Strom the principal who delegates the power to the agent deserves an honest agent. The ability to ensure that the agent is honest will depend on the willingness and ability of the principal (and accountability mechanism/forum) to enforce this. Strom identified a chain of delegation: (i) from voters to Parliament, (ii) Parliament to Prime Minister and government, (iii) Prime Minister to ministers, and (iv) ministers to civil servants. These according to Strom were the four types of delegation in a parliamentary democracy. Here the focus is on (ii) which is the delegation from Parliament to the government and the need for senior members of the government to be accountable to the House of Commons. Strom also looked at oversight to prevent abuse by an agent and observed that there were four ways that a principal can do this: (i) contract design, (ii) screening and selection, (iii) monitoring and reporting, and (iv) institution checks. Strom observed that both (iii) and (iv) are post-event measures. Strom argued that parliamentary government was weaker on post-event accountability. This was because of the shortcomings of a confidence vote, dominance of government (because of the fusion between the executive and legislature), and the non-use of impeachment. Whilst interesting, Strom's observations were not specific to the United Kingdom and were based on how parliamentary systems of government work in a general sense.

UK model of Parliament government

A central feature of the UK Constitution is that governments (the Prime Minister and ministers) are held personally and directly to account by Parliament. The use of language is important: do we mean that ministers are responsible to

---

instituteforgovernment.org.uk/sites/default/files/publications/IfG%20accountability%20discussion%20paper%20april%202018.pdf 7>.

Parliament, accountable to Parliament, or held to account by parliamentarians? The Supreme Court's decision in *R (on the application of Miller) v Prime Minister (No. 2)*[9] recognised the importance of parliamentary accountability when it restricted the ability to prorogue Parliament using the prerogative, justifying the restriction based on parliamentary sovereignty and parliamentary accountability. Ever since the resignation of Sir Robert Walpole in 1742 it can be seen that a government owes its position to the confidence of the House of Commons, and therefore the ability to govern the country is dependent on having the support of a sufficient number of Members of Parliament. The debate over the importance of ministerial responsibility to Parliament, the rise of political parties, the perceived erosion of the convention of individual ministerial responsibility, and the resulting parliamentary decline thesis is extremely important in understanding the role of parliamentarians in ensuring that the government respects the House of Commons, explains its decisions, accounts for failures, enters into a meaningful dialogue, and potentially permits individual ministers to apologise or ultimately resign from office. Therefore, the lynchpin of ministerial accountability within the political constitution is ministerial responsibility (both individually and collectively) to Parliament. The prominence of ministerial responsibility and the expectations placed upon it as an accountability mechanism are a product of constitutional and political history. Flinders has considered the change in the nineteenth century concerning ministerial responsibility to Parliament, arguing that the convention of ministerial responsibility was suited to a time before the modern state.[10] In terms of the ability of Parliament to control the executive, he observed that whilst '[t]he mid-nineteenth century can be interpreted as the zenith', the changing point was the reforms brought about by the Second Reform Act 1867.[11] The effectiveness of ministerial responsibility was tested during the course of the twentieth century.[12]

Today the terms responsibility and accountability are used to suggest that responsibility is required to ensure accountability. However, the terms overlap and may mean the same things to commentators and actors with the constitution. This raises the question as to whether they can be distinguished. Arguably, it is not possible to distinguish between responsibility and accountability. This was the view of the Public Service Committee:

> It is not possible absolutely to distinguish an area in which a minister is personally responsible, and liable to take blame, from one in which he is constitutionally accountable. Ministerial responsibility is not composed of two

9 [2019] UKSC 41.

10 M Flinders, 'Shifting the Balance? Parliament, the Executive and the British Constitution' (2002) 50 *Political Studies* 23, 24.

11 ibid 25.

12 For a consideration of ministerial responsibility see chapter 4 'The Doctrine of Ministerial Responsibility' in G Marshall (ed), *Constitution Conventions: The Rules and Forms of Political Accountability* (OUP 1984).

> elements which have a clear break between the two. Ministers have an obligation to Parliament which consists in ensuring that Government explains its actions. Ministers also have an obligation to respond to criticisms made in Parliament in a way that seems likely to satisfy it – which may include, if necessary, resignation.[13]

During a debate on the Second Report from the Public Service Committee,[14] Giles Radice MP emphasised the committee's rejection of the distinction between accountability and responsibility:

> With respect to definition, the Committee rejected the distinction that Sir Robin Butler attempted to draw when he came before the Scott inquiry between accountability and responsibility – in other words, that Ministers are always accountable to Parliament for the work of their Department but are not necessarily responsible for everything that happens in those Departments. We point out that it is not possible to distinguish clearly an area in which a Minister is personally responsible, and liable to take blame, from one in which he or she is merely constitutionally accountable. That is why we concluded: Ministerial responsibility is not composed of two elements with a clear break between the two. Ministers have an obligation to Parliament which consists in ensuring that government explains its actions. Ministers also have an obligation to respond to criticism made in Parliament in a way that seems likely to satisfy it – which may include, if necessary, resignation. However, as a Committee we are not obsessed, except in one respect to which I shall return, with the question of resignation. In fact, we tended to agree with my right hon. Friend the Member for Bethnal Green and Stepney (Mr. Shore) that Parliament undervalues accountability, and that proper and vigorous scrutiny in accountability may be more important to Parliament's ability to correct error than forcing resignations.[15]

This position rejecting the feasibility of such a distinction is a sound one and reflects the realities of government and its relationship with Parliament, and the overlapping purposes that we expect from accountability and responsibility. What is important, in Radice's view, is that the emphasis is on correcting errors and not resignation. Resignation is a nuclear option in many ways, as in the long-term enhanced ministerial accountability may be improved by greater scrutiny which surely serves as a greater deterrent than an occasional resignation.

13 Public Service Committee, *Ministerial Accountability and Responsibility*, Second Report (1995–96, HC 313), [21].

14 ibid.

15 HC Deb 12 February 1997 vol 290 col 274.

The difficulty in attempting such a distinction has not always been universally shared. According to Cripps,

> The [Conservative] government in its response to the Public Service Committee attempted to distinguish between ministerial responsibility and ministerial accountability. It suggested that responsibility implies an element of personal credit or blameworthiness for an outcome, whereas accountability involves the constitutional duty of ministers to account to Parliament for their departments.[16]

This meant that the minister might not be responsible, as blame could lie elsewhere, but could be accountable.[17] Cripps noted that 'there is a degree of sophistry about such a distinction and it is not easy to draw in practice.'[18] Blackburn and Kennon observed:

> Accountability and responsibility are often distinguished in the context of a minister's professional work, in order to emphasise on the one hand, the extent to which a minister can be called to account for his department's work and is required to answer in Parliament ('ministerial accountability'); and on the other hand, those areas of departmental business for which the minister is responsible in the sense of being personally involved and by inference blameworthy if blunders are made ('ministerial responsibility'). . . . These distinctions are regularly propagated in theory but their application in practice may become confused, especially in respect of the larger or more politically sensitive areas of government work.[19]

It is clear that any distinction may be artificial and arguably obscures the analysis. The literature has shown a variety of views and the relative interchangeability of the key terms.

A lack of accountability: the unfettered executive?

We will now consider the literature surrounding concerns that there is a lack of executive accountability, which is due to perceived criticisms of ministerial responsibility to Parliament and the parliamentary decline thesis.

16 Y Cripps, 'The Consequence of Disclosure in the Public Interest' in C Forsyth and I Hare (eds), *The Golden Metwand and the Crooked Cord: Essays in Honour of Sir William Wade QC* (OUP 1998) 305.

17 ibid 306.

18 ibid.

19 R Blackburn and A Kennon, *Griffith & Ryle on Parliament: Functions, Practice and Procedures* (2nd edn, Sweet & Maxwell 2003) 45.

The literature on accountability

In terms of the perception that there is a lack of adequate accountability, Dunleavy et al. noted that '[i]n the twentieth century several generations of commentators have lamented the declining accountability of the executive to the Commons, and at no time more persistently and plausibly than during Margaret Thatcher's last years in office.'[20] One academic commentator has observed that

> [w]hile there is currently much concern regarding the ability of Parliament to scrutinise the executive, the issues raised are not particularly new. They are variants of long-standing concerns, which predate the Thatcher years and reflect, among other things, the lack of a codified constitution and the nature of a public sector without statutory authority.[21]

Furthermore, Guerin, McCrae, and Shepheard were critical of the failure to hold those responsible to account:

> Even when ministers are clearly responsible for policies they have pursued in the light of warnings, they are not held to account by the Prime Minister or by Parliament. There are numerous examples of ministers staying on after overseeing failures in their department, where the failure is clearly attributable to the minister themselves.[22]

Guerin and colleagues considered the reasons for why accountability was weak:

> There are three factors underpinning the weak accountability that is perpetuating failure. They are: fundamental gaps in accountability in Whitehall; a failure of accountability beyond Whitehall to keep pace with an increasingly complex public sector landscape; and a pervading culture of blame.[23]

Interestingly they noted that '[w]hile accountability certainly involves apportioning blame when something goes wrong, it should also foster an environment that leads to improvement. This is what the public cares most about – preventing failures recurring, rather than simple retribution.'[24]

The literature on the Scott inquiry serves a useful role in highlighting late twentieth-century concerns over inadequate accountability, which was a result of the shortcomings of ministerial responsibility. In terms of enforcing ministerial

20 P Dunleavy, GW Jones, J Burnham, R Elgie and P Fysh, 'Leaders, Politics and Institutional Change: The Decline of Prime Ministerial Accountability to the House of Commons, 1868–1990' (1993) 23(3) *British Journal of Political Science* 267, 268.

21 M Flinders, *The Politics of Accountability in the Modern State* (Ashgate 2001) 42.

22 Guerin et al. (n 8) 10.

23 ibid 5.

24 ibid 6.

responsibility, Vernon Bogdanor (within the context of the Scott Report) was critical of the lack of consequences for acting in an improper manner:

> The fact that constitutionally improper things can occur without anyone, whether minister or civil servant, paying the penalty, casts some doubt, surely, as to whether concepts such as ministerial accountability and responsibility remain genuine conventions of the constitution or fictions designed to obscure the way in which our system of government actually works.[25]

In another article commenting on the Scott Report, Bogdanor observed:

> The fundamental problem is that the principle of ministerial accountability imposes obligations upon ministers which are owed to Parliament, but under modern conditions of party government Parliament finds it difficult to ensure that these are actually fulfilled.[26]
>
> . . .
>
> The crucial problem is that Parliament lacks mechanisms which can be brought into play when ministers seek to evade the rules of accountability. In theory, Parliament can seek the resignation of the minister concerned, but, under modern conditions of party discipline, that will hardly ever be successful.[27]

Bogdanor's concerns are valid and illustrate the problem facing the constitution and the inadequacy of ministerial responsibility, where the government has sufficient support in the House of Commons and is willing to disobey accepted constitutional norms.

In his book on the Scott Report, Adam Tomkins observed:

> The single most important weakness of Britain's constitutional structures which the Scott story identified was the present inability of the parliamentary constitution to act as a sufficiently powerful check on executive power. That inability is caused not as much by any systemic failing as it is by a political unwillingness on the part of those who matter: namely, parliamentarians. The problem is not so much that the executive dominates Parliament. Rather, it is that political parties dominate members of Parliament.[28]

The problem was the unwillingness of Members of Parliament to hold the executive to account. How true this is today will depend on circumstances and personalities, and it is clear that political accountability requires the House of Commons to be proactive in holding the executive to account. Tomkins was critical of the accountability of

25 V Bogdanor, 'The Scott Report' (1996) 74 *Public Administration* 593, 611.
26 V Bogdanor, 'Ministerial Accountability' (1997) 50(1) *Parliamentary Affairs* 71, 78.
27 ibid 79.
28 A Tomkins, *The Constitution After Scott: Government Unwrapped* (OUP 1998) 269–70.

ministers within the constitution: '[t]he great strength of the parliamentary constitution is that it recognise the essential truth that ministers will try to do anything which they think they can politically get away with.'[29] This reflects the wider issue, as raised by Tompkins, of an unwillingness by parliamentarians to engage with real accountability.

The parliamentary decline thesis

This next section will consider the arguments that Parliament is in decline as a result of executive dominance since the creation of the modern political party. It will be necessary to consider the views of leading political scientists in order to test the strength of the argument that Parliament is in decline. Writing in 2000, Philip Norton[30] was concerned about the imbalance between Parliament and the government.[31] There was never 'any "golden age" of Parliament'.[32] However, there were 'a number of reasons for Parliament's inability to scrutinise the government effectively'.[33] One cause was the role of political parties which 'limits the capacity of MPs to call government to account'.[34] Norton was writing in the context of his chairmanship of the Commission to Strengthen Parliament and his analysis was at a time when the current government enjoyed a very large majority in the House of Commons. These concerns were not atypical of the 2000s and would lead to reforms to the House of Commons and the operation of select committees. In 2019, Philip Norton considered the argument whether Parliament was in decline.[35] He observed that '[t]he perception of decline developed towards the end of the nineteenth century and was pervasive throughout the twentieth.'[36] This perception, according to Norton, was 'arguably overstated'.[37] The counter-argument considered by Norton was that 'Parliament is demonstrating a new assertiveness in its relationship to the executive', the background to this being 'significant changes in the twenty-first century' such as 'constitutional change . . . structural and procedural change . . . and political change'.[38] The significance of the Select Committee on Reform of the House of Commons' *Rebuilding the House* report[39] resulted in important reforms to the House of Commons.[40]

29 ibid 271.
30 Professor the Lord Norton of Lough.
31 P Norton, 'Reforming Parliament in the United Kingdom: The Report of the Commission to Strengthen Parliament' (2000) 6(3) *The Journal of Legislative Studies* 1.
32 ibid 4.
33 ibid.
34 ibid.
35 P Norton, 'Parliament: The Best of Times, the Worst of Times' in J Jowell and C O'Cinneide (eds), *The Changing Constitution* (9th edn, OUP 2019).
36 ibid 158.
37 ibid 159.
38 ibid 163–4.
39 Select Committee on Reform of the House of Commons, *Rebuilding the House*, First Report of Session 2008–09, HC 1117.
40 Norton (n 35) 170.

Norton considered the argument that legislative scrutiny by the House of Commons was 'weak, if not the weakest, part of parliamentary scrutiny' and noted the reforms that have occurred since the 2000s.[41] In his conclusion Norton argued that Parliament's relationship with the executive has improved. Importantly, he commented: '[i]n facing the government, Parliament is now stronger than at any time since the developments of mass-membership political parties in the 1860s. It has a capacity to fulfil its functions to an extent that was previously lacking.'[42] Norton is clear that the situation is not ideal.[43]

Matthew Flinders argued that 'Parliament matters. Despite long-standing concerns regarding the balance of power between the executive and parliament it has always remained the primary institution of the British polity.'[44] He is clear that the executive 'does take parliament seriously'.[45] However, there were then concerns about executive dominance of the relationship.[46] Matthew Flinders and Alexandra Kelso reviewed the parliamentary decline thesis and how accurate a way this was to describe the executive's relationship with Parliament.[47] They concluded that '[n]arratives of parliamentary decline may have dominated popular and scholarly discourse throughout the twentieth century but maybe the time has come to "think again" in a more precise, empirically grounded but theoretically informed manner.'[48]

In 2010, Peter Riddell considered the merits of the parliamentary decline thesis and held that the view 'is a gross over-simplification'. He argued that 'the declinists are wrong in their view of both the past and the present. Debates were better attended 40 or 50 years ago but back-benchers had much less influence.' Riddell considered the research by Philip Norton and Philip Cowley that demonstrated the increase in rebellions amongst backbench Members of Parliament and observed the importance of an assertive House of Lords and the establishment of departmental select committees in 1979. He concludes by noting that '[m]ost MPs are more active, both in their constituencies and at Westminster, than they have ever been.'[49]

In 2013, Anthony King and Sir Ivor Crewe offered a scathing critique of executive accountability:

> The folklore of the British constitution demands that government ministers, especially cabinet ministers, are responsible for whatever goes on in their department, that they are accountable to parliament both for their own

41 ibid 173–4.
42 ibid 185.
43 ibid.
44 Flinders (n 10) 38.
45 ibid.
46 ibid 38–40.
47 M Flinders and A Kelso, 'Mind the Gap: Political Analysis, Public Expectations and the Parliamentary Decline Theory' (2011) 13 *BJPIR* 249.
48 ibid 265.
49 P Riddell, 'In Defence of Politicians: In Spite of Themselves' (2010) 63(3) *Parliamentary Affairs* 545, 549.

> actions and for the actions of their officials and that, if either they or their officials have been seriously at fault they should resign. . . . All that was – and still is – almost pure fantasy. Most ministers who make mistakes . . . do not resign and are most unlikely to be sacked. . . . The doctrine known solemnly as the convention of 'individual ministerial responsibility' has been a myth for well over a hundred years.[50]

Furthermore, King and Crewe viewed Parliament as being on the periphery:

> Anyone who investigates government blunders is bound to be made aware . . . that parliament as an institution occasionally barks, frequently nips at its master's heels but very seldom bites. . . . As a legislative assembly, the parliament of the United Kingdom is, much of the time, either peripheral or totally irrelevant. It might as well not exist.[51]

This view was countered by Meg Russell and Philip Cowley:

> This may be in line with the conventional 'parliamentary decline thesis' and comparative views of Westminster, but is inconsistent with the empirical evidence. The data that we have presented make clear that the British parliament has significant influence, at all stages of the policy process.[52]

This willingness, especially prevalent in those supportive of a legal constitution, to accept the parliamentary decline thesis, was countered in 2011 by Jonathan Sumption QC:

> Far from increasing inexorably over the past generation, as Lord Steyn suggested, the degree of ministerial control over the House of Commons has if anything declined in recent years. . . . Studies of Parliamentary behaviour . . . show that today's MPs are far more fractious than their predecessors. The House of Commons was in fact at its most docile and compliant in the face of the whips in the 1950s and early 1960s. . . . The accountability of ministers to Parliament has clearly varied in its intensity and has always been imperfect. But it is wrong to dismiss it as nominal or insignificant, or as falling below some earlier ideal, or as warranting in itself a higher degree of accountability to the Courts.[53]

50 A King and I Crewe, *The Blunders of Our Governments* (Oneworld 2013) 347.

51 ibid 361.

52 M Russell and P Cowley, 'The Policy Power of the Westminster Parliament: The "Parliamentary State" and the Empirical Evidence' (2015) 29(1) *Governance: An International Journal of Policy, Administration and Institutions* 121, 132.

53 J Sumption, 'Judicial and Political Decision-Making: The Uncertain Boundary' (2011) *The FA Mann Lecture* 17.

This was in response to Lord Steyn's criticism of the executive dominance of the House of Commons in *R (on the application of Jackson) v Attorney-General*.[54] Sumption was attempting to demonstrate that some observers were far too quick to presume executive dominance.

I would argue that the central issue in understanding the relationship (and the perceived balance of power) between Parliament and the executive is the form of parliamentary government that exists in the United Kingdom. Whilst I would agree that the effectiveness of ministerial responsibility to Parliament was reduced by the development of the modern political party, this should not mean that Parliament is ineffective in holding the executive to account. I would disagree with the fatalism inherent to the parliamentary decline thesis and whilst acknowledging the shortcomings of parliamentary accountability, I would argue that Parliament has shown itself throughout the course of the Brexit proceedings to be proactive and willing at times to seize the initiative from the executive. I would also argue that the role of Parliament in holding the executive to account would benefit from being strengthened, to enable it to deal with instances of extreme unconstitutional conduct by the executive. Whether impeachment could improve political accountability will be addressed in Chapter 7.

54 [2005] UKHL 56, [71].

6 The existing political accountability mechanisms

This chapter critically reviews how the existing accountability mechanisms operate and how impeachment might buttress these mechanisms in achieving greater political accountability of the executive, both in terms of compliance with accepted constitutional norms and the proper exercise of ministerial power. The focus here is how the executive is held to account by mechanisms that are political, rather than legal, in nature, and are concerned with the integrity of the constitution and the proper use of ministerial powers. Chapter 6 will help inform the discussions throughout this book and will provide the basis for the proposal to reform impeachment in Chapter 9.

This chapter is divided into two parts. Part one will begin clarifying the key elements of the constitutions in which a modernised process of impeachment would be operating. Part two is concerned with the accountability of the executive and how impeachment could cooperate along the existing political accountability mechanisms.

The nature of the United Kingdom's system of government

Part one considers the nature of the United Kingdom's system of government and the importance of responsible government. It will look at how the constitution is defined and its key principles and features. It is not intended to be exhaustive given the breadth of the subject matter and is provided as a grounding for the arguments contained within this book. It is a clarification of the key elements of the constitution, and this will help to provide context for how a modernised form of impeachment would operate.

Unwritten or uncodified constitution

The United Kingdom possesses an uncodified constitution, one that is a product of historical evolution and which has enabled the development of a parliamentary democracy and the retention of a monarchy within the framework of accepted constitutional constraints. Unlike the majority of other countries, the UK Constitution is uncodified as it is not written down in one document, and therefore is

DOI: 10.4324/9781003269052-8

characterised as unwritten.[1] It is important to clarify that, first, even the US constitutional system is not entirely written or codified in one document; for example, there exist constitutional conventions or the jurisprudence of the Supreme Court, and, second, that an increasing amount of the sources that compromise the UK Constitution, such as legislation of constitutional importance and key codes defining how the constitution operates, are written in nature. Some academics and judges have argued that the United Kingdom cannot be said to possess a constitution, as what it does have is a system of government, rather than a formal constitution.[2] However, this view can be criticised for relying on an artificial definition to exclude the realities of the United Kingdom's constitutional system of government.

The three branches of government

Within the UK Constitution there exist at a national level three branches of government. The first branch is the legislature that is responsible for making law, scrutinising the executive's use of powers conferred on it by the legislature and holding the executive to account through a variety of mechanisms.[3] In the United Kingdom, the legislature is Parliament, which is composed of the House of Commons, the House of Lords, and the Queen in Parliament. The second branch is the executive that is responsible for governing the country, enforcing the laws enacted by the legislature, and with responsibility for foreign policy and defence. In the United Kingdom, the executive can be divided between the dignified function of the monarch, who exercises her prerogative powers under the advice of her ministers, and the efficient, that is the real, exercise of power by the Prime Minister and the cabinet. The third branch is the judiciary that is responsible for adjudicating on legal disputes and determining that those accused of criminal offences receive a fair trial. The United Kingdom consists of three distinct jurisdictions and has a Supreme Court that, with some exceptions, is the highest appeal court.[4]

It is important to note that the UK Constitution has never conformed to the classic doctrine of the separation of powers, as outlined by Montesquieu and within 50 years explicitly rejected in the House of Commons as ever having

1 The other countries that possess an unwritten constitution are New Zealand and Israel.

2 See the discussion of the 'big C' and 'little c' constitutions in chapter 3, 'Britain's Traditional Constitution' in A King (ed), *The British Constitution* (OUP 2007); Lord Neuberger, 'UK Supreme Court Decisions on Private and Commercial Law: The Role of Public Policy and Public Interest' (Centre for Commercial Law Studies Conference 2015, 4 December 2015); FF Ridley, 'There Is No British Constitution: A Dangerous Case of the Emperor's Clothes' (1988) *Parliamentary Affairs* 340.

3 Philip Norton observed that the legislatures' 'core defining role . . . is not to *make* law but rather to *give assent* to it.' *Parliament in British Politics* (2nd edn, Palgrave 2013) 7.

4 The exception is Scotland, where only certain types of appeal can be heard by the Supreme Court.

applied to Great Britain.[5] Nonetheless, the overlaps which exist within the United Kingdom's system of government have been somewhat reduced by the Constitutional Reform Act 2005, which reformed the office of the Lord Chancellor and replaced the Appellate Committee of the House of Lords with a Supreme Court. The separation of powers is best understood as an ideal, rather than as an actual construct of the constitution.

In the United Kingdom, the legislative and executive branches of government can be regarded as fused. This means that all members of the government must, according to the requirements of constitutional convention, be members of either House of Parliament.[6] Such a requirement is a product of constitutional history and the transfer of the control of executive power from the monarch to Parliament as a consequence of the Glorious Revolution. Walter Bagehot in his book *The English Constitution* observed that this fusion was 'the efficient secret' of the constitution.[7] However, this has led to concern over the executive's dominance of the House of Commons. Lord Hailsham warned against an 'elective dictatorship',[8] echoing previous concerns raised by Sir Leslie Scarman in his Hamlyn Lecture.[9] As recently as 2005, Lord Steyn began his judgment in *R (on the application of Jackson) v Attorney-General*[10] warning about the executive's (then Tony Blair's Labour government) dominance of the House of Commons.[11] The critics of this perceived actual, or inherent, risk of executive dominance proposed a solution through the legal constitution. This was rejected by Griffiths in his seminal work, 'The Political Constitution'.[12] Concerns over perceived executive dominance of the House of Commons, based on the presumption that a majority equates to a guaranteed block of support, feeds into the parliamentary decline thesis and can be treated with some degree of caution.

Constitutional monarchy

The United Kingdom is a constitutional monarchy, with the powers of the monarch having been greatly reduced over the course of constitutional developments in the seventeenth and eighteenth centuries. The powers of the state are the powers of the Crown, and the government is conducted by parliamentarians on

5 See the debate in 1806 over the appointment of the Lord Chief Justice, Lord Ellenbourgh to serve in cabinet. See FTH Fletcher, *Montesquieu and English Politics (1750–1800)* (Porcupine Press 1980) 137 for an interesting account of the debate.

6 Please note that this requirement is a political one, as opposed to being required by law. For example, Field Marshal Smuts was a member of the War Cabinet during the Second World War, despite not being a parliamentarian.

7 See W Bagehot, *The English Constitution* (5th edn, Kegan Paul, Trench and Co 1888).

8 See Sir Leslie Scarman, *English Law – The New Dimension, The Hamlyn Lectures* (Stevens & Sons 1974) 14–15.

9 Lord Hailsham, 'Elective Dictatorship' (1976) 120 *Sol Jo* 693.

10 [2005] UKHL 56.

11 ibid [71].

12 JAG Griffith, 'The Political Constitution' (1979) 42(1) *MLR* 1.

behalf of the monarch. The monarch continues to exercise personal prerogative powers, but these powers must, by constitutional convention, be used upon the advice of the government. Walter Bagehot identified the monarch as having three rights: 'the right to be consulted, the right to encourage, the right to warn'.[13] A monarch who acts in a manner that is unconstitutional or contrary to the views of his Prime Minister will, as in the case of Edward VIII, risk having to abdicate.

Cabinet government

The business of exercising the executive function belongs to the cabinet, which is composed of the most senior ministers, who are usually responsible to managing a government department. As a collective, the cabinet members decide policy and take important decisions, and there exists a convention of collective ministerial responsibility. In practice it is the Prime Minister who, as leader of the party in government, will exercise real control over policy, and the quality of genuine cabinet government will be dependent on circumstances and personalities.

Parliamentary sovereignty

The United Kingdom's Parliament is regarded as being legally sovereign, that is, capable of enacting any law without legal restriction, on any subject matter, repealing any prior enactment no matter how important, and without being questioned by the courts.[14] Legal sovereignty, as in parliamentary sovereignty, should be distinguished from political sovereignty, and is a product of the constitutional struggles between Crown and Parliament in the seventeenth century. The orthodox account of parliamentary sovereignty has been challenged by the United Kingdom's former membership in the European Union[15] and judicial willingness, albeit in obiter, to suggest limitations.[16]

Respect for the rule of law

An important feature of the UK Constitution is the rule of law. The rule of law is capable of multiple different meanings but can be understood to mean that the government must govern in accordance with the law, that there is equality before the law, and that the courts are independent and accessible to ordinary citizens. Observance of the rule of law can be traced back through

13 Bagehot (n 7) 111.

14 The classic understanding of parliamentary sovereignty was outlined by AV Dicey in *Introduction to the Study of the Law of the Constitution* (8th edn, Macmillan 1915).

15 See *R v Secretary of State for Transport ex parte Factortame (No. 2)* [1991] 1 AC 603.

16 See *R (on the application of Jackson) v Attorney General* [2005] UKHL 56, per Lords Hope and Steyn. See counter-view as expressed by Lord Neuberger in 'Who Are the Masters Now?' (Second Lord Alexander of Weedon Lecture, 6 April 2011).

constitutional history, as evidenced by Magna Carta 1215, the Petition of Right 1628, Bill of Rights 1689, and the Act of Settlement 1701. To illustrate the importance of the rule of law, it was used by the Supreme Court in *R (on the application of Unison) v Lord Chancellor*,[17] as the basis to declare increased tribunal fees to be unlawful.

A parliamentary system of government as opposed to a presidential system of government

The United Kingdom has a parliamentary system of government, which is known as the Westminster system. As a matter of constitutional convention, the government is composed wholly of parliamentarians, and the Prime Minister must be a member of the House of Commons. As discussed earlier, this is contrary to the concept of the separation of powers, however, it is a product of political and constitutional history and reflects the changing relationship between the Crown and the House of Commons following the Glorious Revolution of 1688. The majority of ministers will be members of the House of Commons and usually all senior cabinet ministers will be from that House, although there have been exceptions, such as Peter Mandelson during Gordon Brown's premiership. The number of ministers who can be members of the House of Commons is restricted by the House of Commons (Disqualification) Act 1975. A political party (or parties in the case of the 2010–2015 Conservative and Liberal-Democrat coalition) will form the government if it commands the confidence of the House of Commons. Therefore, the public do not elect a government through a direct vote, rather each constituency will elect a Member of Parliament who will belong to a political party.

The relationship between the government and the House of Commons is premised on the representative nature of the Westminster system. This system developed prior to the emergence of modern political parties and the power of the political parties in dominating Parliament was discussed in the Introduction, when considering the parliamentary decline thesis. Central to the Westminster system is the principle of responsible government and the willingness of the executive to comply with constitutional constraints on how it conducts governmental business.

The parliamentary system that operates in the United Kingdom is different from the presidential system that operates in countries such as the United States. In the United States, the federal constitution requires that there be a separation between personnel, and a member of the executive branch cannot be a member of Congress.[18] The relationship between the President, who is directly elected by a national popular vote, and Congress will depend on which political party has a majority in the House of Representatives or the Senate.

17 [2017] UKSC 51.
18 Note the exception that is the Vice President.

Concluding comments

Part one has reviewed the UK Constitution. This review will provide the context for the rest of this chapter on the political accountability of the executive and the possible role that impeachment might play in achieving this. The constitution of the United Kingdom is very different from the two countries that will be considered in this book as comparators for the use of impeachment. It will be argued that the UK Constitution is dependent on respect for the customary institutions and processes of constitutional conduct, most importantly by the executive. This is especially the case given the lack of a written constitution and a reliance on political rules. This means that accountability of the executive is of utmost importance to ensure not just good government in terms of the efficient implementation of policies and the running of government departments but also compliance with accepted constitutional norms.

The accountability of the executive

Part two is concerned with the accountability of the executive, that is, the Prime Minister and other ministers at a central UK level. The earlier review of the literature surrounding accountability in Chapter 2 demonstrates the contested nature of the adequacy of the existing arrangements and the arguments for and against enhanced accountability. The political accountability mechanisms and their effectiveness will be considered ahead.

Accountable to Parliament

In the Westminster system of parliamentary government, the relationship between Parliament and the executive is the very axis of the constitution. As Norton has observed, 'Parliament exists because of government' and therefore it responds 'to the demands and actions of government'.[19] The government is formed of parliamentarians, and the political party (or parties in a coalition) that commands the confidence of the House of Commons will govern the country. Central to the relationship between the executive and Parliament is the need for the government to maintain the confidence of the House of Commons, and subject to the Fixed-term Parliaments Act 2011 a vote of no confidence can bring about an early general election.[20] Ministers are responsible to Parliament for departments, policies, and personal conduct. However, Parliament does not possess the means to dismiss a minister who has breached the duties outlined under the Ministerial Code (or existing in the convention of individual ministerial responsibility), as this power rests with the Prime Minister. Parliamentarians can hold the government to account, that is, to answer for its actions and policies, and ultimately to

19 Norton (n 3) 12.
20 It is likely that the Fixed-term Parliaments Act 2011 will be repealed during the lifetime of this Parliament, see the Fixed-term Parliaments Act 2011 (Repeal) Bill.

hold a minister responsible for a specific failure, through a number of mechanisms that include Prime Minister's Questions, ministerial questions, the role of departmental select committees in the House of Commons and select committees in the House of Lords, early day motions, and debates in either chamber. These mechanisms are concerned with political accountability, and the efficacy of accountability will depend on the circumstances and importantly whether the government enjoys the confidence of the House of Commons, the support of its own members, and the subject matter of the issue in question.

Accountable to the courts

Although the focus here is on political accountability, it will be necessary to consider how the executive is accountable to the courts. This is because recent litigation before the courts has concerned compliance with constitutional principles, which perhaps could be addressed through a modernised form of impeachment.

The government is accountable to the courts, or more accurately is accountable to individuals who bring legal action through the courts. Through judicial review the courts are able to review government decisions, including politically sensitive ones, as illustrated by the decisions *in Council of Civil Service Unions v Minister for the Civil Service (GCHQ)*,[21] *R (on the application of Miller and Santos) v Secretary of State for Exiting the European Union (No. 1)*,[22] *R (on the application of Miller) v Prime Minister (No. 2)*,[23] and *R (on the application of Unison) v Lord Chancellor*[24] which demonstrate the judicial willingness to review executive action whether using powers conferred by statute or by the prerogative. Judicial review plays an important role in ensuring legal accountability of the executive and that constitutional principles are upheld. It is of considerable importance that individual ministers can be held in contempt of court if they disobey a court order.[25] Ministers do not enjoy legal immunity from legal action and the Crown Proceedings Act 1947 extended the ability to bring civil litigation against the government. It is submitted here that the courts have gradually increased the accountability of the executive, by scrutinising the use of prerogative powers, even ones traditionally considered to be non-justiciable, and through the use of judicial review. This accountability by way of the judiciary has proved controversial, as there is a concern about judicial overreach and the use of judicial power, which has led the current government to review the use of judicial review and to consider reforms to the Supreme Court. However, it is submitted that such concerns could be seen as missing the issue, which is that without effective political accountability, legal accountability has a heightened significance.

21 [1985] AC 374.
22 [2017] UKSC 5.
23 [2019] UKSC 41.
24 [2017] UKSC 51.
25 *M v Home Office* [1994] 1 AC 377.

Accountable to the electorate, party members, and the media

The executive is accountable to the electorate through the exercise of the franchise at a constituency level. Individual constituency elections, such as by-elections, can be used as a way to express disapproval of government policy. The executive can also be held to account by party members, and bodies representing the views of backbench Members of Parliament, such as the Conservative party's 1922 Committee. Media scrutiny plays an important role in holding the executive to account, whether through tabloid headlines or more thorough investigative journalism.

Internal executive accountability

The Ministerial Code serves an important role in regulating the conduct of ministers. The Ministerial Code, whilst not legally binding, is published and outlines the duties and standards expected of ministers in the performance of their duties. Whilst the Code does not replace the existing conventions of individual and collective ministerial responsibility, it does provide an overt set of standards that ministers can be judged against. The Code also incorporates the Nolan Principles, which are the Seven Principles of Public Life. Where there have been alleged breaches of the Ministerial Code, the Cabinet Office will undertake an investigation. In recent years several high-profile minsters have had to resign for breaching the Code, including Michael Fallon, Damian Green, and Priti Patel who all resigned in 2017. Ministers do resign if there is a breach. However, the Ministerial Code is enforceable at the discretion of the Prime Minister, and it would be possible for the Prime Minister to conclude, contrary to independent expert advice, that a breach has not occurred. This in fact took place in 2020, when the Home Secretary, Priti Patel, was found by the Prime Minister to have not breached the Ministerial Code, even if this was contrary to the advice of his ethics advisor.[26] Tangible breaches of the Ministerial Code can be distinguished from the more vague duties implied by the convention of individual ministerial responsibility and the constitutional requirement for ministers to take responsibility for their departments, to answer and to account for departmental failings, and ultimately resign.

Another form for the scrutiny of ministerial conduct is the Committee on Standards in Public Life which advises the Prime Minister and produces reports. An important form of accountability within executive decision-making is collective cabinet decision-making, which underpins the convention of collection ministerial responsibility. The Prime Minister and other ministers will have to justify their policies and decisions to colleagues, and this provides an important form of internal scrutiny.

26 S Payne, 'Boris Johnson's Ethics Adviser Quits Over Patel Bullying Report' *Financial Times* (20 November 2020) <www.ft.com/content/e0802cfb-1be2-4076-a153-edd3292f8810>.

A critical review of Parliament's role in holding the government to account and the associated accountability mechanisms

The previous sections have considered to whom the executive is accountable. This next section will provide a critical review of the role of Parliament in holding the government to account and the associated accountability mechanisms.

The centrality of the House of Commons

The executive is a creature of the House of Commons in the sense that the most senior ministers will be from that chamber, and the government must command its confidence, but this also has led to concern that the House of Commons is the creature of the executive, as most governments will enjoy a majority and therefore will have considerable freedom to introduce legislation, and government business has precedence due to Standing Order 14. It is submitted that both assertions are, if viewed as absolute, incorrect and misleading and do not reflect the realities of the relationship between the executive and the House of Commons, the independence of backbench Members of Parliament, and their willingness to defy the party whips. The emphasis here is on the House of Commons as the elected chamber and this should not be taken as negating the considerable role played by the House of Lords in scrutinising proposed government legislation and policies.[27] It is argued that within the Westminster system the UK House of Commons is in a unique position to hold the executive to account for the use of their powers and to ensure that the executive acts in accordance with constitutional norms. In this capacity the House of Commons fulfils the function of the guardian of the constitution. The Westminster system places considerable responsibility on parliamentarians, and it will be argued ahead that any form of accountability which enables them to discharge their role is to be welcomed. Within the context of ministerial responsibility, Norton observed the important function that is served: '[t]he doctrine underpins the accountability at the heart of the British constitution. Without it, there is no one entity that electors can hold to account for public policy.'[28] Therefore, in light of Norton's assessment it is clear the accountability of the executive very much depends on ministers being responsible to Parliament and the House of Commons possessing the mechanisms to achieve this.

27 See 'The Changing Role of the House of Lords' (Constitution Unit, University College London) <www.ucl.ac.uk/constitution-unit/research/parliament/changing-role-house-lords>. See generally Meg Russell, *The Contemporary House of Lords: Westminster Bicameralism Revived* (OUP 2013).

28 P Norton, *Governing Britain: Parliament, Ministers and Our Ambiguous Constitution* (Manchester University Press 2020) 165.

Addressing the institutional balance

The literature review of the parliamentary decline thesis and the range of arguments in support of such a thesis, which were most clearly put by Sir Ivor Crewe and Anthony King in *The Blunders of Our Governments*, can be countered by the more nuanced assessment advanced by Cowley, Flinders, Norton, and Russell, amongst others. Even if one does not accept the claim that the executive dominates the House of Commons and as a consequence the House of Commons lacks a tangible role in debating and influencing policy, there is some truth to the imbalance in the relationship between the executive and the House of Commons. This imbalance is caused by the nature of the Westminster system, the advent of modern political parties that emerged in the mid-nineteenth century, and the two-party system that exists in the English constituencies. The question is whether the existing procedures for accountability within the political constitution, that is, the conventional checks and balances within the Westminster system, are effective, whether there could be scope for improved accountability, and, if so, whether impeachment could serve such a role.

Problems with existing procedures for accountability

In order to see whether impeachment could buttress existing political procedures for executive accountability, it will be necessary to briefly consider criticisms of these mechanisms. The mechanisms are confidence motions, the problems of answerability, select committees, parliamentary privilege and the penal powers of Parliament, and an executive-focused mechanism in the form of observance of constitutional conventions. These mechanisms are, with the exception of conventions, concerned with the executive and how it functions, and are exercised by Parliament.

CONFIDENCE MOTIONS

Confidence motions are blunt instruments and are framed in terms of whether the House of Commons has confidence in the government, as opposed to the Prime Minister. Confidence motions are not concerned with whether there has been unacceptable constitutional conduct and do not seek to draw a line under such conduct. Neither are confidence motions effective where the government enjoys a majority in the House of Commons. Impeachment as proposed within this book would draw such a line and would be explicitly concerned with unconstitutional conduct; the impeachment process could tackle such conduct, even where the government enjoys a majority in the House of Commons.

The operation of confidence motions has been affected by the Fixed-term Parliaments Act 2011. Whilst it is still possible to have a confidence motion outside of the statutory parameters of the Act, it is not possible to trigger an early general election (as this is possible only under the Act) and this would be reliant on the Prime Minister advising the Queen to invite the Leader of the Opposition to form an alternative government. Confidence motions are dependent on a minority government, as they stand little chance of success where the government has sufficient support in the House of Commons, as evidenced by Theresa May in 2019.[29] The last successful vote of no confidence took place in 1979, when Prime Minister James Callaghan led a minority government. A criticism is that the Prime Minister, short of a formal confidence motion being tabled, has the discretion to determine which policies to treat as matters of confidence. This means that the Prime Minister could determine that, in the event that he suffers a defeat on a major policy area, this is not in fact serious enough to be treated as a matter for his resignation. For example, Theresa May did not view defeat on her Brexit policy as a matter for her resignation.

PROBLEMS OF ANSWERABILITY

Within the Westminster system, ministers are expected to be responsible for their departments and to answer to Parliament for any failings. This is regulated by the convention of individual ministerial responsibility and, as will be discussed ahead, is likely to be ignored, as ministers do not tend to resign, unless the Prime Minister and their colleagues demand it. Ministers must answer for their department policy and with some exceptions should be responsible for the actions of their civil servants, and will do so through ministerial question time, engagement with select committees, and responding to questions from Members of Parliament. In terms of sanctioning a minister, either through forced resignation or dismissal, this rests not with Parliament, but with the Prime Minister. This is a shortcoming of answerability, as a minister could in the event of a policy failing give insufficient or limited answers to the House of Commons and there is little that parliamentarians could do.

SELECT COMMITTEES

Since their establishment in 1979, select committees have served an important role in reviewing the work of government departments. The reforms led by Tony Wright MP in the House of Commons Reform Committee made some attempt to improve the independence of select committees through reform of how the chairs were elected and established the Backbench Business Committee.[30] The impact of the Wright reforms has been tempered by concern over the level of Members of Parliament's engagement with select committees[31] and the limited

29 'May's Government Survives No-Confidence Vote' *BBC News* (16 January 2019) <www.bbc.co.uk/news/uk-politics-46899466>.

30 *House of Commons Reform Committee, Rebuilding the House*, First Report of Session 2008–09, HC 1117.

31 S Bates, M Goodwin and S McKay, 'Do UK MPs Engage More with Select Committees Since the Wright Reforms? An Interrupted Time Series Analysis, 1979–2016' (2018) 70(4) *Parliamentary Affairs* 780.

powers of select committees to compel the attendance of witnesses.[32] Gordon and Street observed the lack of coercive powers and the shortcomings of this:

> At present select committees possess no clear coercive powers at all. The present situation poses a threat to the legitimacy of select committees. However, it does not necessarily follow from this that coercive powers should be introduced. There is a need to consider whether and if so how giving increased powers to select committees would affect Parliament's relationship with the courts more generally.[33]

Furthermore, Gordon and Street remarked that the powers that select committees do in fact possess were confusing:

> The source of powers of select committees in the House of Commons and the House of Lords is potentially confusing. In the case of the House of Commons, there are many gaps in terms of a coherent exposition of powers which are capable of impeding the practical day-to-day work of select committees.[34]

The House of Commons Committee of Privileges has since 2016 considered whether 'the exercise and enforcement of the powers of the House in relation to select committees and contempt' required reform.[35] In 2016, David Natzler, the Clerk of the House of Commons, provided written evidence to the committee, where he considered the options and noted that any substantial reform would require legislation.[36] The context was the possible refusal of members of the public to appear before a select committee, and Natzler noted that there were doubts 'about whether it is appropriate for the House to pursue and to punish non-Members for contempt'.[37] Whilst there are clear shortcomings as to the powers of select committees, which go hand-in-hand with the following discussion on parliamentary privilege, any reform would need to be tempered by codification to increase clarity, modernisation, and a transparent process that can be regarded as fair and understood by all parties.

32 A Horne, 'Select Committee Powers of Enforcement' *U.K. Const. L. Blog* (23 March 2017) <>https://ukconstitutionallaw.org/>; R Gordon and A Street, 'Select Committees and Coercive Powers – Clarity or Confusion?' (The Constitution Society, 2012) <www.consoc.org.uk/wp-content/uploads/2012/06/Select-Committees-and-Coercive-Powers-Clarity-or-Confusion.pdf>.

33 Gordon and Street (n 32) 21–2.

34 ibid 31.

35 See the work of the Committee of Privileges here <>https://committees.parliament.uk/work/296/select-committees-and-contempts/publications/>.

36 See <>http://data.parliament.uk/writtenevidence/committeeevidence.svc/evidencedocument/committee-of-privileges/select-committee-powers/written/48435.html>, 5.4.

37 ibid 2.19.

PARLIAMENTARY PRIVILEGE AND THE PENAL POWERS OF PARLIAMENT

Parliamentary privilege and the ability of Parliament to punish those who infringe on these privileges, through contempt of Parliament, can be regarded as convoluted, lacking in clarity, and, due to their antiquated nature, risk being viewed as irrelevant. The Joint Committee on Parliamentary Privilege had concluded in 2013 that legislative codification of Parliament's privileges was not required at present.[38] The Joint Committee also rejected the need to criminalise specific contempts:

> We reject the approach of criminalising specific contempts. It would entail a radical shift of power between Parliament and the courts. It would introduce delay. It would increase uncertainty about how contempts which were not covered by criminal statute could or should be dealt with, and remove the flexibility which is the chief advantage of the current system.[39]

However, regarding the existing penal powers of the House, the Joint Committee were clear that sanction short of imprisonment or a fine, which would be in the form of admonishment, could be effective:

> Although Sir Malcolm Jack considered that 'the possibility of hauling people to the bar of the House and admonishing them would provide a theatre of the absurd', the present Clerk of the House noted that admonishment could be done by resolution and suggested that, if it was clear that it was based on fair processes, admonishment would have a considerable reputational (and in some cases, financial) impact. Admonishment could take the form of a resolution of the House, without any requirement for the contemnor to appear in person.[40]

The Joint Committee noted that the retention of a more serious penalty should be accompanied by 'greater rights of intervention by legal advisers, and to ensure that the person investigated, or his or her legal advisers, had the opportunity to put questions to any witnesses'.[41]

It is clear that whilst there is an appetite for reform, there is a real case for modernisation of Parliament's powers and procedural developments to ensure that these powers, if involving sanction or criticism of non-members, are perceived as fair and do not infringe upon human rights or the rule of law. The most interesting scope for reform is through the use of an admonishment, as this offers an important deterrent so long as the exercise of such a sanction is not lost through

38 *Joint Committee on Parliamentary Privilege, Parliamentary Privilege*, Report of Session 2013–15, HL 30, HC 100, 71.

39 ibid.

40 ibid 27.

41 ibid.

the convoluted process or not perceived as a real sanction to be taken seriously. There is some attractiveness in forcing an individual to appear in person, though this raises issues such as how to compel attendance, the sanctions for non-attendance, jurisdiction, and whether this would be restricted to UK nationals. However, it is noted that this could, in Jack's words, be 'a theatre of the absurd', and whilst there are some advantages in the theatrical nature of such a sanction, the absurdity should be minimised through fair process, an appeal process, recourse to legal advice, and statutory codification.

CONSTITUTIONAL CONVENTIONS

We are concerned here with constitutional conventions and how executive-focused conventions (in the form of ministerial responsibility) regulate the conduct of ministers, and what they tell us about the relationship between the executive and Parliament and the way that they facilitate accountability in the Westminster system. The executive-focused conventions are not part of the laws and workings of Parliament. A key feature of the UK Constitution is the reliance on constitutional conventions to regulate the workings of the constitution and guide the conduct of actors within the constitution. Sir Ivor Jennings' account of conventions as 'the flesh which clothes the dry bones of the law; they make the legal constitution work; they keep it in touch with the growth of ideas', is useful in providing an understanding as to their function.[42] Conventions govern the conduct of ministers with regard to their responsibility to Parliament, the monarch's use of her personal prerogative powers, and the executive's relationship with the House of Commons. Norton is clear that '[conventions] are not created, but develop. A convention exists once there is an invariable practice. That is not the same as standard or usual practice. If one deviates from it, it is not an invariable practice.'[43] There is a difficulty in determining precise range of conventions or 'how they should be interpreted'.[44] Bogdanor noted the lack of formal checks and balances on executive power due to the lack of a codified constitution and observed: '[t]his does not of course mean that governments in practice have been tyrannical or authoritarian. They have conceived themselves to be limited, not by formal checks and balances, but by informal checks, generally known as conventions.'[45] This demonstrates the importance of conventions in regulating executive power and ensuring that the accepted norms of the constitution are respected and enforced through mutual agreement.

42 I Jennings, *The Law and the Constitution* (4th edn, University of London Press 1952) 80–1.
43 Lord Norton of Lough, 'The Strathclyde Recommendations Are Based on a False Premise That There Is a Convention That the Lords Does Not Reject Statutory Instruments' (Constitution Unit, 14 January 2016).
44 V Bogdanor, *The New British Constitution* (Hart Publishing 2009) 17.
45 ibid 15.

From a legal constitutionalist's position, a perceived shortcoming of conventions is their lack of legal enforceability by the courts. Despite their importance, AV Dicey observed that '[c]onstitutional understandings are admittedly not laws, they are not (that is to say) rules which will be enforced by the Courts.'[46] According to Vernon Bogdanor, 'A convention is a non-legal rule which supplements legal rules, imposing non-legal rather than legal obligations.'[47] In *Miller (No. 1)* the Supreme Court observed this non-legal status of conventions, whilst recognising their existence:

> Judges therefore are neither the parents nor the guardians of political conventions; they are merely observers. As such, they can recognise the operation of a political convention in the context of deciding a legal question . . . but they cannot give legal rulings on its operation or scope, because those matters are determined within the political world.[48]

The question arises over whether it matters that some conventions, such as individual ministerial responsibility, may be ignored by ministers. Dicey observed that 'the invariableness of the obedience to constitutional understandings is itself more or less fictitious' and

> [t]he uncertain character of the deference paid to the conventions of the constitution is concealed under the current phraseology, which treats the successful violation of a constitutional rule as a proof that the maxim was not in reality part of the constitution.[49]

A number of points will be made. First, the convention of individual ministerial responsibility often depends on 'a dash of principle' to be followed.[50] Second, as Diana Woodhouse notes, this occasional willingness to take responsibility and resign is evidence of this particular convention's existence.[51] Third, the convention that underpins the operation of cabinet government, collective ministerial responsibility, was not always followed during Theresa May's premiership where circumstances rendered the Prime Minister unable to discipline her own

46 AV Dicey, *Introduction to the Study of the Law of the Constitution* (8th edn, Macmillan 1915) 292.
47 Bogdanor (n 44) 15.
48 ibid [146]. See *R (on the application of Miller) v Secretary of State for Exiting the European Union (No. 1)* [2017] UKSC 5.
49 Dicey (n 46) 293.
50 Geoffrey Marshall on Lord Carrington's resignation as Foreign Secretary, see G Marshall (ed), *Ministerial Responsibility: Oxford Readings in Politics and Government* (OUP 1989) 131.
51 See D Woodhouse, 'Individual Ministerial Responsibility and a "Dash of Principle"' in D Butler, V Bogdanor and R Summers (eds), *The Law, Politics and the Constitution: Essays in Honour of Geoffrey Marshall* (OUP 1999).

cabinet.[52] Fourth, the right for the House of Commons to vote to approve military action before it takes place was an important development in the parliamentary oversight of the prerogative. However, there is unease over the war powers convention and an argument that this should be placed on a statutory footing. The question remains whether Theresa May breached the convention by taking military action against Syria in 2018 without an initial vote in the House of Commons. Finally, the ultimate responsibility of enforcing ministerial responsibility is the Prime Minister. This will inevitably depend on the circumstances and character of the Prime Minister.

CONCLUSION

It is clear that the accountability of the executive is an important requirement for the effective operation of the United Kingdom's constitutional system. There are shortcomings within the present range of mechanisms to ensure accountability, and it is clear that reform is required to address these. However, Part Three will address the question as to whether impeachment serves a role in buttressing these mechanisms.

52 See S Heffer, 'The Tory Party Is Disintegrating, Collective Responsibility Has Broken Down, Yet Theresa May Goes on' *New Statesman* (8 May 2019) <www.newstatesman.com/politics/uk/2019/05/tory-party-disintegrating-collective-responsibility-has-broken-down-yet-theresa>. Simon Heffer observed: 'May will be gone before long. She apparently said so herself, promising she would leave once the Brexit process was over. The decomposition of her authority is advanced. Collective responsibility has broken down. Most ministers resemble unfunny comedy turns rather than statesmen. There is hardly any government, as such.' For a contrary view see R Brett Taylor, 'Brexit and Collective Cabinet Responsibility: Why the Convention Is Still Working' (London School of Economics, 20 May 2019) <>https://blogs.lse.ac.uk/brexit/2019/05/20/brexit-and-collective-responsibility-why-the-convention-is-still-working/>. See also ' "Worst Example" of Cabinet Ill-Discipline in British Political History' *BBC News* (1 April 2019) <www.bbc.co.uk/news/av/uk-politics-47769369>. The then Chief Whip, Julian Smith said: '[a]s you're aware, discipline is not as good as it should be. This is I think the worst example of ill-discipline in cabinet in British political history.' See also 'Julian Smith: Chief Whip Attacks Cabinet's Post-Election Brexit Strategy' *BBC News* (1 April 2019) <www.bbc.co.uk/news/uk-politics-47768884>. The article reported that '[Julian Smith] said he witnessed ministers "sitting around the cabinet table . . . trying to destabilise her [Mrs May]" and described their behaviour as the "worst example of ill-discipline in cabinet in British political history".'

Part Three

A case for impeachment

7 A justification for a possible role for impeachment within the UK system

This chapter outlines the justification for a possible role for impeachment within the United Kingdom's contemporary constitution. It will consider how impeachment could serve a role in buttressing the existing political accountability mechanisms, which operate to regulate the conduct of ministers and ensure compliance with the accepted constitutional norms. Chapter 7 is intended to build upon the discussion in Chapter 6.

The rationale: enhancing accountability, democratic oversight, and providing a role for the House of Commons as the guardian of the constitution

In this first section it is necessary to consider the rationale for modernising impeachment and for arguing that it should be part of the contemporary constitutional landscape of the United Kingdom. The rationale for the retention and modernisation of impeachment could be viewed as threefold. The first rationale for this is the role impeachment could play in enhancing accountability, specifically of the executive, and ensuring the effective regulation of executive power. The importance of ensuring the accountability and democratic regulation of executive power cannot be underestimated, neither should it be taken for granted that the status quo cannot be improved upon by means of the use of impeachment.

The second rationale is the inherent legitimacy of the House of Commons in having such an oversight of the use of executive power and the ability of the House of Commons to impose tangible sanctions in the event that there has been serious misconduct through the abuse of this power. The House of Commons has such legitimacy due to its democratic nature and the importance of representative democracy in the Westminster system. This makes the House of Commons the most legitimate institution, both within a constitutional and democratic sense, of checking and regulating executive power and ministerial compliance with the accepted constitutional norms.

The third rationale is that impeachment would provide a role for the House of Commons as the guardian of the constitution and reinstate the House of Commons as the institution that should be able to determine the scope of, and compliance with, the constitution. This is essentially about re-empowering the

DOI: 10.4324/9781003269052-10

House of Commons through the modernisation of impeachment and the explicit recognition that impeachment can be used where there has been a breach of accepted constitutional norms.

Enhancing accountability

The first rationale is enhancing executive accountability. As noted earlier, there are five questions that are useful to consider when addressing accountability: (i) who is accountable, (ii) to whom are they accountable, (iii) for what are they accountable, (iv) which standards will they be judged by, and (v) why do they believe that they are held to account?[1] The rationale for impeachment is that it serves a purpose in reinforcing the constitutional accountability of the executive. Taking the five questions regarding accountability, I will consider whether impeachment, as reimagined within this book, could provide for greater accountability.

The first question to consider is who would be accountable when impeachment is used. Impeachment in England, and then Britain, has traditionally seen a broad range of individuals fall within the scope of those who could be impeached. These individuals included judges, royal advisers, ministers, Lord Chancellors, merchants, bishops, a Governor-General of Bengal, ambassadors, Members of Parliament, a Queen Consort, and a minister of religion. I will be clear in Chapter 9 that any revised formulation of impeachment would be concerned with only the Head of Government and ministers of the Crown at Westminster. In the definition of impeachment outlined in the Introduction, the scope of impeachment was restricted to ministers of the Crown. It was determined that it was appropriate for ministers, as senior actors within the political constitution, who exercise considerable statutory and prerogative powers, implement policies, and direct the business of state, should be the focus of impeachment as a constitutional accountability mechanism. The exclusion of the monarch can be justified by the operation of the constitutional monarchy and the limited discretion that the monarch has in the use of her personal prerogative powers.[2] The exclusion of the judiciary from the scope of a revised form of impeachment is that there already exist statutory accountability mechanisms in the form of disciplinary measures, in the case of junior judges, by the Lord Chancellor and the Lord Chief Justice of England and Wales, and both Houses of Parliament possess the ability to request the removal of senior judges by way of a resolution.[3] Furthermore, if impeachment were to focus on constitutional accountability and the judiciary were to be included within its scope, then there would be the possibility that, in

1 M Bovens, R Goodin and T Schillemans, 'Public Accountability' in M Bovens, R Goodin and T Schillemans (eds), *The Oxford Handbook of Public Accountability* (OUP 2016) 10–13.

2 Impeachment has never been used against a monarch, although it has been used against a Queen Consort. In the case of a monarch who may be perceived to be acting unconstitutionally the appropriate sanction would be for the government to advise that the monarch abdicates, as in the case of Edward VIII.

3 Senior Courts Act 1981 and the Act of Settlement 1701.

the event of a controversial judicial decision, Members of Parliament threaten judges with impeachment.[4] If this were to happen then it would undermine judicial independence, although it is conceded that in the same circumstances Members of Parliament may seek a resolution to remove the judges concerned.[5]

The second question is to consider to whom they are accountable. Impeachment originated in 1376 and was concerned with the accountability of royal advisors and minor officials to the Commons, in their capacity as the representatives of the country. It was the novel idea that grievances could be presented before the Commons, and then brought before the Lords by the Commons, where the Commons would demand a trial and determination of wrongdoing. There was some uncertainty during the 1370s and 1380s over who controlled procedure; however, it is clear that it is the Commons. Central to justification of the accountability of officials and advisers remains the notion of representative democracy and the role of Members of Parliament in representing constituents and collectively the country.[6] This would explain the exclusion of the Lords from the process. It is important to note that whilst the initial impeachment would be brought by the Commons, the Commons would not determine guilt. Therefore, in any revised form of impeachment this would be determined by a Court of Impeachment. Impeachment can be viewed as a hybrid form of accountability, essentially political in its initial stages, but increasingly legal in terms of the determination of wrongdoing.

The third question is for what are they accountable? Traditionally, individuals were impeached for treason and high crimes and misdemeanours and the definition of an impeachable offence was very wide and could include non-crimes.[7] However, political charges were often rooted out by the Lords[8] and in the penultimate impeachment the Lord Chancellor, Lord Thurlow, played a significant role in holding that ordinary law and rules of evidence applied during the trial of Warren Hastings. It is important to note this debate continues in the United States and is explored in Chapter 2. I will argue that ministers should be accountable for their official conduct and ensuring that they and their departments, when following official policy, comply with accepted constitutional norms. The revised form of impeachment would not be concerned with the criminal conduct of ministers, as this is best left to the ordinary courts,

4 This happened, for example, after Richard II sought advice from his judges as to the use of impeachment and a number of Charles I's judges were impeached for having supported the king in their judicial decisions.

5 For example, see the motion by nearly 200 Labour Members of Parliament to remove Sir John Donaldson in the 1970s.

6 For further discussion see AH Birch, *Representative and Responsible Government: An Essay on the British Constitution* (University of Toronto Press 1964) 13–17.

7 See the aforementioned definition of impeachment and the debate between Raoul Berger and Clayton Roberts in Chapter 1, 'Understanding Impeachment Within a British Context'.

8 See C Roberts, 'The Law of Impeachment in Stuart England: A Reply to Raoul Berger' (1975) 84(7) *Yale Law Journal* 1419, 1433–4.

nor would it be expedient to retain the formulation of 'high crimes and misdemeanours'. The key aspect of accountability would protect the integrity of the constitution and safeguard important constitutional principles such as the rule of law.

The fourth question is which standards would be applied when the accused is judged. Applying the proposed form of impeachment as explored in this book, the standards against which an individual would be judged are subject to contrary interpretation. This is because the United Kingdom possesses an uncodified constitution and there is considerable debate about the extent and scope of the constitution. Therefore, it would be reliant on expert determination and this would be built into the impeachment process, first, through an initial investigation before the House of Commons votes to impeach, and second, in the form of the Court of Impeachment. This could be problematic but there would be safeguards built in to protect ministers from a draconian application of constitutional principles, which make no allowance for reasonableness.

The final question is why ministers of the Crown should be accountable and why do they believe that they are held to account? Ministers exercise considerable power and are able through the exercise of their duties to act contrary to accepted constitutional norms. Given the importance of executive accountability in the Westminster system it could be argued that there is merit in looking at additional ways to complement the existing accountability mechanisms, through using impeachment as a way to enhance executive accountability.

Impeachment would promote constitutional integrity, and central to the rationale of impeachment would be protecting the integrity of the uncodified constitution. Through the ability to sanction breaches of the constitution, impeachment would serve as a deterrent, and importantly would promote a dialogue between the House of Commons and the executive as to the nature and scope of the constitution, and the obligations that Members of Parliament would impose upon ministers. Impeachment would be concerned with where the minister is personally blameworthy, within the area of ministerial responsibility. It would not be appropriate to impeach a minister for all matters for which he is accountable, that is, failings within his department, although a refusal to take responsibility for a policy failure might in itself give rise to an impeachment. It is submitted that impeachment would reinforce the obligations and duties within the Ministerial Code and empower Parliament in the most extreme cases of constitutional misconduct to hold a minister to account and responsible for their conduct.

Impeachment is democratic

The second rationale would be that impeachment is democratic, as the impeachment proceedings are brought by the democratically elected lower house, which is the House of Commons in the United Kingdom. It could be argued that impeachment could be an intrinsically democratic accountability mechanism;

this is because the charges would be brought on behalf of the elected House of Commons and the decision to impeach would be theirs, and it is argued that House of Lords should no longer be involved with the actual determination of wrongdoing. Impeachment would offer an in-house mechanism to enforce constitutional accountability, which could be instigated by a small number of Members of Parliament and see the House of Commons as the driver behind the process.

A further understanding of this rationale for impeachment would be that it counters areas of democratic concern, relating to fears that Parliament is weak and the presidentialism of the executive. There is a genuine concern over the presidentialism of the office of the Prime Minister, which emerged during Tony Blair's premiership and has resurfaced due to Boris Johnson's initial unwillingness to engage with the House of Commons and the creation of a White House–style press briefing at Downing Street. There are also concerns about the threat of popularism, with the executive willing to erode the rule of law, breach international law, or breach constitutional norms to achieve policy.

Guardians of the constitution

The final rationale, discussed earlier, is that Members of Parliament would act as the guardians of the constitution. The role for enforcing accepted constitutional norms would be undertaken by the elected representatives, rather than as at present left to the courts, and this could be useful in negating concerns about judicial power and the increased legalisation of the constitution. To enable Members of Parliament to undertake this role, impeachment would strengthen the powers of the House of Commons, which would have a strong punitive and deterrent factor. This would buttress the existing powers of the House of Commons, and this will be explored next.

Impeachment would reassert the House of Commons' role as the guardian of the constitution. Just which institution within the United Kingdom has this role and should actively seek to define the accepted nature and scope of the constitution is a moot point. Historically, impeachment had provided a way for the House of Commons to check the actions of the executive, and one that served an important role. Professor Philip Norton has observed that 'impeachment provided the basis for the development of Parliament's scrutiny of administrative actions.'[9] Parliament has been viewed as the grand inquest of the nation, to review grievances and misconduct, which was discharged by its ability to impeach, and the development and meanings of this term were considered by Geoffrey Marshall and Graeme Moodie.[10]

9 P Norton, *Parliament in British Politics* (2nd edn, Palgrave 2013) 19.
10 G Marshall and GC Moodie, *Some Problems of the Constitution* (4th edn, Hutchinson University Library 1967) 139.

The Supreme Court's decision in *R (on the application of Miller) v Prime Minister (No. 2)*[11] serves as an illustrative example of the problems of constitutional accountability, the question of which institution should determine the scope of the constitution, and the limitations to the political constitution. The decision to advise the monarch to prorogue Parliament in 2019 was challenged through the courts by ordinary citizens and importantly by a very large number of parliamentarians who, because Parliament was prorogued, could not challenge this use of the prerogative through the political constitution. It was the political constitution that the Supreme Court turned to by way of justification, when it found that the decision to prorogue Parliament was unlawful as, in addition to restricting parliamentary sovereignty, it also prevented political accountability through the House of Commons being able to hold the government to account. This central role played by the House of Commons in scrutinising executive decision-making was recognised as a principle of the constitution and given legal protection.

A particular criticism of the Supreme Court's decision in *Miller (No. 2)* was that the court was seeking to exercise an improper role in defining the nature of the constitution and acting as a constitutional court.[12] Given the controversy, it is necessary to briefly consider some of this criticism. Professor Finnis has criticised the Supreme Court for an unnecessary constitutional development: '[t]his exercise of judicial constitutional creativity is not an authentic constitutional development because there was *no need for it*. There was *no need* – no constitutional need.'[13] Furthermore, the decision damaged democracy and undermined the rule of law. Stephen Laws QC regarded the decision in *Miller (No. 2)* as being without reason and 'damaging to the UK's constitutional arrangements'.[14] Richard Ekins has advocated for wholesale reform to the Supreme Court and has raised concerns regarding the court's role as guardian of the constitution:

> There are reasons to fear that the Supreme Court has begun to understand itself to be a constitutional court, with a responsibility to serve as *the* guardian of the constitution. The Court has been invited to play this role and to some extent has accepted the invitation, with damaging consequences for the rule of law and the integrity of the political constitution.[15]

11 [2019] UKSC 41.

12 For example, see D Wyatt and R Ekins, 'Reforming the Supreme Court' *Policy Exchange* (July 2020) <https://policyexchange.org.uk/wp-content/uploads/Reforming-the-Supreme-Court.pdf>.

13 J Finnis, 'The Law of the Constitution Before the Court' *Policy Exchange*, 2019, 24 <https://policyexchange.org.uk/wp-content/uploads/The-Law-of-the-Constitution-before-the-Court.pdf>.

14 S Laws, 'The Supreme Court's Unjustified Lawmaking' *Judicial Power Project* (4 October 2019) <>https://judicialpowerproject.org.uk/stephen-laws-the-supreme-courts-unjustified-lawmaking/>.

15 R Ekins, 'Protecting the Constitution: How and Why Parliament Should Limit Judicial Power' *Policy Exchange* (2019) 19 <https://policyexchange.org.uk/wp-content/uploads/2020/01/Protecting-the-Constitution.pdf>.

In his proposal for the abolition of the Supreme Court, David Wyatt QC acknowledged that the Supreme Court did have a role to play in upholding and developing the constitution:

> I agree with Professor Ekins that if there is a problem with the judicial approach of the UK Supreme Court, it may in part be attributed to the fact that it sees itself as a constitutional court, and as guardian of the Constitution, but I would add that it is part of the judicial responsibility of every court in the United Kingdom to uphold our Constitution, and the role of all superior courts to make an appropriate contribution to the evolution of that Constitution.[16]

The aforementioned criticism is founded in long-standing concerns over judicial power and the constitutional legitimacy of the judiciary's role in shaping the constitution, especially where this involves the judicial oversight of inherently political decisions. Whilst this can be presented as a threat to the separation of powers, the rule of law, and respective institutional competence, it should be noted that this criticism can be countered on the premise of the legitimacy of the Supreme Court in upholding the accepted norms of the constitution and giving effect to key constitutional principles through the protection of the law. I do not agree with the aforementioned criticism, but I do acknowledge that many do for considered and justified reasons. The point is that there is scope for redressing the institutional balance in protecting and evolving the constitution. Therefore, a form of impeachment that gives the House of Commons the power to determine whether the constitution has been breached, or where there has been non-compliance with an accepted constitutional norm, would explicitly give the House of Commons an overt role in protecting and defining and evolving the constitution. The advantage of this is that it would counter concerns about the role of the Supreme Court by making it clear that the task of protecting the constitution is not only that of the court, through the legal constitution, but also is that of the House of Commons through the political constitution.

By reasserting the role of the House of Commons as the guardian of the constitution, it would provide an additional mechanism to protect the constitution. I will explore how impeachment could buttress the existing accountability mechanisms, and the importance of the political constitution, which is dependent on non-legally enforceable constitutional conventions and the inherent discretion of ministers, being protected through the use of impeachment cannot be underestimated. This would be the case where the revised form of impeachment, as will be set out in Chapter 9, first, empowers a small number of Members of Parliament to instigate impeachment proceedings. Second, such instigation could lead to a time-sensitive review by experts of the perceived wrongdoing even if there

16 Wyatt and Ekins (n 12).

are not enough votes in the House of Commons to support impeachment. And third, it carries a range of serious sanctions that may act as a deterrent to ensure initial compliance with accepted constitutional norms.

Application: how impeachment could buttress existing executive political accountability mechanisms

We will now consider how impeachment could buttress the existing executive political accountability mechanisms by applying impeachment to recent events, that have been argued as amounting to actual, or possible, breaches of the accepted constitutional norms, or outlining how impeachment might be used to enhance accountability in relation to other mechanisms. At this stage, the consideration of how impeachment might play a role is only intended as introductory, with the detailed analysis being advanced in Chapter 9. Therefore, the application in this section will highlight where impeachment might play a role in assisting the existing accountability mechanisms, in being used independently, or whether the existence of impeachment would serve as a deterrent. The consideration of the arguments for and against impeachment and precise shape that the revised form of impeachment would take will be outlined in Chapter 9.

Failure to comply with a constitutional convention

The first example where impeachment could serve a role is the failure of the executive to comply with a constitutional convention. It must be noted that ministerial performance of their duties and impeachment were once connected, before the emergence of the convention of individual ministerial responsibility. Birch observed:

> In the early part of the eighteenth century . . . ministers were liable to be impeached by Parliament for the mismanagement of public affairs. . . . Impeachment fell into disuse because politicians had come to regard 'the loss of office and public disapprobation as punishments sufficient for errors in the administration not imputable to public corruption'. This clear assumption that a minister would have to resign if an administrative error in his department were exposed and criticized in Parliament was shared by most constitutional lawyers and commentators in the second half of the nineteenth century. It forms the basis of the doctrine of the individual ministerial responsibility of ministers for the work of their departments.[17]

17 AH Birch, *Representative and Responsible Government: An Essay on the British Constitution* (University of Toronto Press 1964) 139.

Dicey was clear that impeachment would not be used to enforce conventions as they are not laws,[18] and Marshall and Moodie gave an interesting account of the political and legal aspects of ministerial responsibility, which concerned the use of impeachment.[19]

In terms of a specific example of where impeachment could be used, the following arguably provides this. In 2018, Theresa May deployed the UK military to take part in airstrikes against Syria. This military action had not been approved by the House of Commons before military action took place, as required by the constitutional convention that regulates military action. Theresa May was accused of breaching the convention and Jeremy Corbyn, the Leader of the Opposition, stated:

> It seems the convention established in 2003 and that is in the Cabinet manual is being tossed aside as simply inconvenient. It is necessary and urgent that the House has the opportunity to discuss its rights and responsibilities in respect of decisions on UK military intervention.'[20]

A vote was subsequently held. However, it was clear that the Prime Minister did not consider herself in the present circumstances to be bound by the convention and did not believe that it covered the situation. Whilst demonstrating the uncertainty and plurality of views as to what is required by a convention, it is clear that there did appear to be breach of the convention and that impeachment might have been used as a way to register disapproval of the Prime Minister's decision.

Failure to enforce the Ministerial Code

This next example focuses not on a breach of the Ministerial Code by a minister, or the minister's failure to comply with the requirements of the convention of individual ministerial responsibility, but with the Prime Minister's failure to enforce the Ministerial Code. The Ministerial Code outlines the duties and requirements that ministers must comply with. It is an important constitutional document, despite not being legal in nature, and supports the political constitution. The only person who can enforce the Code, short of a minister resigning without being told to do so, is the Prime Minister. Priti Patel, the Home Secretary, was accused of bullying civil servants in her role as a minister and the most senior civil servant in her department resigned and commenced legal proceedings. In 2020, Sir Alex Allan, the Prime Minister's ethics advisor, carried out an inquiry that concluded that the Home Secretary's conduct amounted to bullying,

18 AV Dicey, *Introduction to the Study of the Law of the Constitution* (8th edn, Macmillan 1915) 276.
19 Marshall and Moodie (n 10) 59.
20 HC Deb 17 April 2018, vol 639, col 195.

and that she had breached the Ministerial Code. The Prime Minister decided that the conduct did not in fact breach the Code. In response Sir Alex Allan resigned.[21] The Prime Minister's decision not to enforce the Ministerial Code has been criticised as undermining accountability, the operation of the Code, and a system that is based on principle.[22]

The issue here in terms of where impeachment could possibly play a role is not Priti Patel's conduct, but the Prime Minister's refusal to enforce the Code and accept that it had been breached. It could be argued that the Prime Minister's conduct was contrary to accepted constitutional norms and that this might be an appropriate matter for impeachment to have been initiated, especially given the importance of the Code in ensuring ministerial accountability and the discretion accorded to the Prime Minister under the current system. Patel's conduct, whilst being found to have breached the Ministerial Code, would arguably not be suitable for impeachment, although a failure to resign if required by convention might possibly amount to impeachable conduct.

The Prime Minister's decision to advise the monarch to prorogue Parliament

Another example where impeachment could have been used is the prorogation controversy, where the Prime Minister advised the monarch to prorogue Parliament. This was found to be unconstitutional by the Supreme Court in *Miller (No. 2)* and the Prime Minister's advice to be unlawful. However, in order to challenge the decision to prorogue, ordinary citizens and parliamentarians had to rely on the courts, here the legal mechanism of judicial review, and this led to criticisms of the Supreme Court adjudicating on a political issue, acting as the guardian of the constitution, and reinforced long-standing concerns about judicial power. Impeachment could have been used in three ways: first, following on from the Supreme Court's decision in *Miller (No. 2)*, Members of Parliament could have responded by initiating an impeachment proceeding, which would have kept the issue of unconstitutional action alive and, even if it had not been successful, would have demonstrated the seriousness of the Prime Minister's conduct. Second, the existence of impeachment might have been used by parliamentarians as an alternative to litigation. This would have removed the need for the Supreme Court to adjudicate on political matters and would have seen Parliament, once it was no longer prorogued,

21 S Murphy, 'Alex Allan: The Veteran Windsurfing Mandarin Who Quit Over Patel Row' *The Guardian* (20 November 2020) <www.theguardian.com/politics/2020/nov/20/alex-allan-the-veteran-windsurfing-mandarin-who-quit-over-bullying>.

22 C Haddon, 'The Handling of the Priti Patel Bullying Inquiry Has Fatally Undermined the Ministerial Code' (Institute for Government, 20 November 2020) <www.instituteforgovernment.org.uk/blog/priti-patel-bullying-inquiry-undermined-ministerial-code>.

able perhaps to enquire into the probity of the Prime Minister's advice. Third, had the reforms that will be proposed in Chapter 9 been introduced, it might have been possible for impeachment to act as a deterrent and moderate the Prime Minister's decision-making. In reality, there were calls to impeach Johnson over prorogation.[23]

Failure to uphold the rule of law and judicial independence

The next example of where impeachment could have been used is in relation to the perceived failure of Liz Truss, the then Secretary of State for Justice and Lord Chancellor, to take sufficient steps to support the judiciary following the 'Enemies of the People' headline published by the *Daily Mail* in November 2016.[24] The headline was in response to the High Court's decision to find against the government in *Miller (No. 1)*. It is first necessary to consider the Lord Chancellor's constitutional obligations as outlined in statute. Section 17(2) of the Constitutional Reform Act 2005 requires that the Lord Chancellor take the following oath:

> I [name] do swear that in the office of Lord High Chancellor of Great Britain I will respect the rule of law, defend the independence of the judiciary and discharge my duty to ensure the provision of resources for the efficient and effective support of the courts for which I am responsible. So help me God.

This oath is intended to protect two important constitutional principles, the rule of law and judicial independence. The Lord Chancellor, due to the nature of the office, is in a unique position as a minister, and the role requires office holders to take their constitutional obligations seriously.

Returning to the aftermath of the 'Enemies of the People' headline, Liz Truss delayed responding to the headline and eventually gave what was perceived to be an unsatisfactory response. Senior judges were critical of the Lord Chancellor's conduct. A former judge, Sir Stephen Sedley, criticised Truss, observing: '[t]he failure of . . . Liz Truss . . . to do anything to defend the three senior judges . . . is evidence enough of the fragility of judicial independence.'[25] In March 2017, Lord

23 L Saville Roberts, 'Boris Johnson Led the Charge to Impeach Tony Blair for Betraying Our Trust. What's So Different Now?' *The Times* (29 September 2019) <www.thetimes.co.uk/article/boris-johnson-led-the-charge-to-impeach-tony-blair-over-iraq-qrl9zhz2k>.

24 J Slack, 'Enemies of the People: Fury Over "Out of Touch" Judges Who Have "Declared War on Democracy" by Defying 17.4m Brexit Voters and Who Could Trigger Constitutional Crisis' *Daily Mail* (4 November 2016) <www.dailymail.co.uk/news/article-3903436/Enemies-people-Fury-touch-judges-defied-17-4m-Brexit-voters-trigger-constitutional-crisis.html>.

25 S Sedley, 'Judicial Independence Is a Fragile Thing' *The Financial Times* (27 January 2017) <www.ft.com/content/abd56378-e3e0-11e6-9645-c9357a75844a>.

Thomas, the Lord Chief Justice of England and Wales, criticised Truss' failure to defend judicial independence as required by her statutory oath:

> 'I regret to have to criticise her as severely as I have, but to my mind she was completely and absolutely wrong. And I am very disappointed,' he said. 'I can understand how the pressures were on in November, but she has taken a position that is constitutionally, absolutely wrong. It was Truss's duty, as lord chancellor, to defend the judges, he said.[26]

Despite the criticism of Truss and conduct that was against accepted constitutional norms, she remained in office as she had the support of the Prime Minister. Impeachment could have been used here as an initial deterrent, or to be used by Members of Parliament to commence an investigation into Truss' perceived failure, which, even if it had not proceeded and reached only a report stage, would have been a public condemnation of the Lord Chancellor.

An inquiry into the legality of the Iraq War

The next example is controversy surrounding the legality of the Iraq War and the decision to hold a public inquiry. The Chilcot Inquiry was criticised as too costly, too slow, and the findings obscured by delay and depth of coverage. Whilst there was an attempt to impeach Tony Blair in 2004 in relation to the invasion of Iraq in 2003, had a revised form of impeachment been available then this could have served as an alternative to a public inquiry and considered the constitutional conduct of the Prime Minister. The advantage would be to take the impetus for reviewing misconduct and controversies away from the executive. Public inquiries are at the discretion of the government and are criticised as too long-winded and costly, buying time for government and not addressing problems at the relevant time. The form of impeachment which will be outlined in Chapter 9 would give power to initiate to the House of Commons and would contain a process for an independent review of the alleged misconduct within a specific period of time, even if the Members of Parliament initiating the impeachment ultimately lack the votes to impeach.

26 O Bowcott, 'Lord Chief Justice Attacks Liz Truss for Failing to Back Article 50 Judges' *The Guardian* (22 March 2017) <www.theguardian.com/politics/2017/mar/22/lord-chief-justice-castigates-liz-truss-for-failing-to-defend-judges>.

8 Reinvigorating impeachment

This chapter considers the case for a revised form of impeachment by taking into account the counter-arguments against impeachment, before seeking to address these criticisms within the literature and arising from interviews undertaken as part of the research. This chapter aims to address the possibility whether impeachment can be reinvigorated within the United Kingdom. The purpose of this chapter is to provide a balanced and independent examination of the argument that a new impeachment procedure would buttress the existing political accountability mechanisms at Westminster. Chapter 7 considered the rationale and justification for impeachment, which was made within the context of the political constitution and ensuring executive accountability. This chapter will consider the perceived obstacles to impeachment, in the former of counter-arguments, before addressing these and proposing ways in which these counter-arguments can, if possible, be overcome.

Does Parliament still have the ability to bring an impeachment because the power is obsolete?

The first counter-argument and obstacle to impeachment is whether Parliament has the ability to bring an impeachment because the power is regarded by many commentators as obsolete. The argument in support of impeachment being obsolete is premised on the fact impeachment was last used in 1806 and has been superseded by alternative political accountability mechanisms. This argument will be considered ahead. However, it is important to distinguish between the fact impeachment is regarded as obsolete and the ability for the House of Commons, should it choose to do so, to bring an impeachment. The passage of time does not negate the existence of a parliamentary procedure, especially where it had previously fallen into abeyance in the 1450s and was then revived in the 1620s.

The counter-argument against impeachment is that it has been superseded by ministerial responsibility to Parliament. According to Homersham Cox, the last attempt at a party impeachment was that of Walpole, and this led to the need for the government to enjoy the confidence of the Commons, or risk dismissal:

> The career of Walpole illustrates two remarkable principles of modern government. In the first place, he inaugurated the modern system of political

DOI: 10.4324/9781003269052-11

> union among the ministers of the Crown; in the second place, the abandonment of his impeachment, which, after the majority of Parliament turned, against him, had been projected by the House of Commons, marks the discontinuance of the old system of party impeachments, and the substitution of the modern system of Parliamentary control over ministers, exercised by compelling their resignation.[1]

Cox observed:

> This instance established a precedent of no little importance, with reference to the future relations between the Cabinet and Parliament. Another material change in those relations occurred about the same time. What may be termed political impeachments were discontinued. Several of the ministers of William III and Anne, were after their loss of power impeached on account of their counsels to the Crown. The last such impeachment was that of Harley, Earl of Oxford, in 1717. From that time impeachments were confined to a different class of offences, as corruption or malversation; and the House of Commons found that they possessed a sufficient control over the Cabinet by votes expressing or implying a want of confidence in it.[2]

Cox's assessment of impeachment in the eighteenth century is certainly a sound one and reflects the decline in purely politically motivated impeachments against rivals, as had been the case at the start of the eighteenth century. It is clear that Walpole's decision to resign, after realising that he no longer commanded the confidence of the House of Commons, was a pivotal moment in parliamentary and constitutional history, as was the House of Commons' ultimate decision not to impeach him, as had been the case of previous senior ministers who had left government. It would be observed, though, that whilst the confidence motion was a significant development, it did not negate the need for impeachment, as Warren Hastings was impeached in 1787 and Viscount Melville in 1806, nor should it support the conclusion that impeachment no longer exists within the Westminster system. The key point was that the House of Commons no longer had to resort to bringing an impeachment against government ministers, nor was it deemed appropriate to punish former ministers with impeachment. This is not to say that impeachment might not be reserved for instances where a minister committed a breach of the accepted norms of the constitution and a confidence vote would not be suitable because the government enjoyed a majority in the House of Commons. In this instance, the motion to impeach could be made by a small number of Members of Parliament and machinery of the House of Commons deployed to initiate the first steps to bringing an impeachment, even if the House of Commons would never vote to support the impeachment. I would argue that any revised proposed form of impeachment should contain actions short of an impeachment

1 H Cox, *The Institutions of the English Government* (Sweet 1863) lv.
2 ibid 249.

vote, such as a preliminary report by independent experts to determine whether there is substance in the charges, that would stand as criticism of the minister's conduct, even if the vote to impeach was unsuccessful.

Returning to the development of the confidence vote, this meant that the government was dependent on the support of the House of Commons. This also meant that the House of Commons could protect a minister from being dismissed by the king, as in the case of Viscount Melbourne in 1834 when he was dismissed by William IV.[3] The ability to hold a vote to determine lack of confidence in the government, which was supported by the emergence of a constitutional convention that required the government to resign should it lose the House of Commons' confidence, was an important constitutional development.

The nineteenth-century constitution was rooted in ministerial responsibility to Parliament. This was dependent on the House of Commons being able to hold ministers responsible, and this ability was eroded by the development of modern political parties. As to how impeachment fitted into the nineteenth-century constitution, leading constitutional writers such as Walter Bagehot and AV Dicey explored the status of impeachment as part of their respective accounts of the workings of the constitution. In his book *The English Constitution* Walter Bagehot explored the present status of impeachment in the constitution as it stood in the 1860s.[4] Bagehot regarded impeachment as an ancient check on ministers and 'coarse' – a critical view of the role impeachment could play in holding ministers to account.[5] According to Bagehot, the other remedy for holding ministers to account was the House of Commons voting to remove the government, which he described as 'modern and delicate'.[6] Dicey regarded impeachment as obsolete and considered that criminal conduct should be dealt with through the courts:

> In some instances, it is true, the only legal mode in which his offence could be reached may be an impeachment. But an impeachment itself is a regular though unusual mode of legal procedure before a recognised tribunal, namely, the High Court of Parliament. Impeachments indeed may, though one took place as late as 1805, be thought now obsolete, but the cause why this mode of enforcing Ministerial responsibility is almost out of date is partly that Ministers are now rarely in a position where there is even a temptation to commit the sort of crimes for which impeachment is an appropriate remedy, and partly that the result aimed at by impeachment could now in many cases be better obtained by proceedings before an ordinary Court.[7]

3 Viscount Melbourne was dismissed by William IV. The king was forced to reappoint Melbourne in 1835. See IDC Newbould, 'William IV and the Dismissal of the Whigs, 1834' (1979) 11(3) *Canadian Journal of History* 311.

4 W Bagehot, *The English Constitution* (5th edn, Kegan Paul, Trench and Co 1888).

5 ibid xxxix.

6 ibid xl.

7 AV Dicey, *Introduction to the Study of the Law of the Constitution* (8th edn, originally published in 1915, Liberty Classics 1982) 211.

Sir Thomas Erskine May, in the first edition of *A Practical Treatise on the Law, Privileges, Proceedings and Usage of Parliament*, did not doubt that impeachment still existed in the 1840s.[8] Impeachment had its own nine-page chapter devoted to the law and procedure of impeachment. It is to this account that Members of Parliament wishing to introduce an impeachment motion would turn, although in recent editions the coverage has been substantially reduced.[9] Erskine May noted the scope of impeachment: '[f]rom these causes, impeachments are reserved for extra-ordinary crimes and extraordinary offenders; but by the law of Parliament, all persons, whether peers or commoners, may be impeached for any crimes whatever.'[10] Erskine May was praising of impeachment as a tool:

> Impeachment by the commons, for high crimes and misdemeanors beyond the reach of the law, or which no other authority in the state will prosecute, is a safeguard of public liberty well worthy of a free country, and of so noble an institution as a free Parliament. But, happily, in modern times, this extraordinary judicature is rarely called into activity.[11]

This demonstrates that it was not universally accepted that impeachment no longer had a role to play, even a potential one, within the United Kingdom's parliamentary system.

Academics continued into the twentieth century to regard impeachment as obsolete. In his *Constitutional History of England*, the legal historian Sir Frederick Maitland viewed the current status of impeachment as obsolete:

> It seems highly improbable that recourse will again be had to this ancient weapon unless we have a time of revolution before us. If a statesman has really committed a crime then he can be tried like any other criminal: if he has been guilty of some misdoing that is not a crime, it seems far better that it should go unpunished than that new law should be invented for the occasion, and that by a tribunal of politicians and partizans; for such misdoings disgrace and loss of office are now-a-days sufficient punishments. Lastly a modern House of Commons will hardly be brought to admit that in order to control the king's advisers it needs the aid of the House of Peers.[12]

Frederick Maitland's assessment is interesting, as he was warning against the House of Commons seeking out new ways of punishing conduct that was deemed

8 T Erskine May, *A Practical Treatise on the Law, Privileges, Proceedings and Usage of Parliament* (1st edn, Charles Knight and Co 1844).

9 M Hatton et al., *Erskine May: Parliamentary Practice* (25th edn, Lexis Nexis Butterworths 2019).

10 Erskine May (n 8) 375.

11 ibid 374.

12 FW Maitland, *The Constitutional History of England* (4th reprint, Cambridge University Press 1919) 477.

unacceptable, but which did not amount to a criminal offence. Maitland did note that 'a procedure by way of impeachment had been evolved whereby parliament could bring home their responsibility to [the king's] ministers.'[13] He sought to argue that impeachments had been relatively few in number: '[d]o not think of impeachments as common events.'[14] This underlines the exceptional nature of impeachment and the fact that it was used at times when other accountability mechanisms were considered inappropriate, or impeachment preferable as a way of proceeding against political or constitutional opponents. Another constitutional lawyer, Sir Ivor Jennings, also regarded impeachment as 'obsolete' as '[t]he ballot boxes are now available for political opponents and the criminal courts for criminals.'[15]

A common theme emerging from the views discussed earlier regarding impeachment is that impeachment had been superseded by other forms of political accountability. It was also no longer appropriate for impeachment to be used to prosecute those accused of committing criminal offences, as these offences were capable of being prosecuted before the ordinary courts. Indeed, the last impeachment brought, that of Viscount Melville in 1806, could possibly have been brought instead as a criminal prosecution before the ordinary courts. This raises questions as to what exactly the scope of impeachment would be if it were to be used today. It is being proposed in this book that impeachment should be revised in order to buttress the existing political accountability mechanisms and specifically provide a remedy for ministerial conduct that is contrary to accepted constitutional norms. This is different perhaps from what had been perceived as the purpose of impeachment in the eighteenth century, where it had been used to punish political rivals and proceed against those accused of criminal offences, which reflects the way that academics have subsequently perceived impeachment. The different ways impeachment had been used and the concerns that it was being misused by political opponents, or trespassing into the domain of the ordinary courts, stems from its development as a way for the House of Commons to hold royal advisers to account. It was the lynchpin of accountable government, and this notion of empowering the House of Commons to check unconstitutional conduct is of considerable importance. It is this core purpose of empowering the House of Commons and limiting the scope of impeachment to where a minister acts contrary to the accepted norms of the constitution, that the revised form of impeachment would seek to achieve. To reflect upon Jennings' aforementioned observations, the revised form of impeachment would not be concerned with criminal offences as these would be expressly excluded from its scope, and there would be sufficient safeguards to prevent inappropriate politically motivated impeachments.

13 ibid 196.
14 ibid 317.
15 I Jennings, *Parliament* (2nd edn, Cambridge University Press 1969) 397.

Towards the end of the twentieth century, academics still occasionally commented upon impeachment.

Writing in 1993, Philip Norton observed: '[t]hough impeachment has since fallen into disuse, it provided the basis for the development of Parliament's scrutiny of administrative actions.'[16] In his brief study of impeachment in the 1980s, the academic AW Bradley was of the opinion that impeachment was obsolete.[17] Based on the way impeachment had been viewed by academic commentators, it was apparent that impeachment was viewed as a historical relic and not something that would be seriously undertaken by the House of Commons.

The existence of impeachment was occasionally discussed in the House of Commons. One such example took place in 1960; during a debate on Cyprus there was an exchange between Mr William Yates MP, Mr Silverman MP, and the Speaker of the House of Commons on the status of impeachment.[18] Mr William Yates observed: 'I very much regret to say that the House has no longer the right of impeachment. I myself consider this matter to be grossly mishandled, and I very much regret that the House has lost that power.'[19]To which Mr Silverman later responded:

> [A]t the end of his observations to you [Mr Yates] expressed the view that this House had lost the power of impeachment. May I ask, for the guidance of the House, whether that is so? It is an idea that has occurred to some of us from time to time as a useful power which the House of Commons ought to exercise rarely and with restraint, but which it ought never to abandon.[20]

The Speaker's response was 'I think, in fear of encouraging the hon. Member, that I had better look at that.'[21] This was a rare discussion on the status of impeachment in Parliament and shows its peripheral status. However, this does not mean that impeachment was not considered by parliamentary committees. Parliamentary committees have recommended that impeachment should be 'formally abandoned' by way of legislation.[22] Almost 20 years ago impeachment was described as obsolete because '[t]he circumstances in which impeachment has taken place are now so remote from the present.'[23] The fact that it was

16 P Norton, *Does Parliament Matter?* (Harvester Wheatsheaf 1993) 14–15.

17 See AW Bradley, 'Personal Responsibility and Government: A Case for Impeachment?' in G Carnall and C Nicholson (eds), *The Impeachment of Warren Hastings: Papers from a Bicentenary Commemoration* (Edinburgh University Press 1989).

18 HC Deb 4 May 1960, vol 622, cols 1084–6.

19 ibid.

20 ibid.

21 ibid.

22 Select Committee on Parliamentary Privilege, Report (1966–67, HC 34) paras 114–15; Committee of Privileges, *Third Report* (1976–77, HC 417) para 16.

23 Joint Committee on Parliamentary Privilege, *First Report* (1999, HL 43-I, HC 214-I) para 16.

recommended that legislation be introduced to abolish impeachment arguably demonstrates that impeachment is still available to Members of Parliament, and that whilst it is described as obsolete, this does not negate the possibility that it could be used.

The legacy of Iraq and the failure to impeach Tony Blair in 2004

Another counter-argument against the use of impeachment is the failure of the motion to impeach the then Prime Minister, Tony Blair, in 2004 in connection with the military invasion of Iraq in 2003. The failure to impeach Blair was selected as a counter-argument as it demonstrates the particular difficulties in attempting to use what was regarded by most commentators as an obsolete procedure, against a Prime Minister who enjoyed the confidence of the House of Commons. This section will consider the move to impeach Tony Blair and the academic and legal arguments put forward in support of the impeachment, both in terms of the availability of impeachment to the House of Commons and how it could be used in response to Blair's perceived misconduct. It will then consider the debates in the House of Commons on impeachment and the reasons why the motion failed.

The legality of the Iraq War in 2003 is highly debatable and many eminent lawyers have held that it was illegal under international law.[24] To date there have been three public inquiries into various aspects of the build-up and conduct of the war.[25] In 2004, Adam Price MP made public a report 'A Case to Answer', that had been written on Price's behalf by two academics, Glen Rangwala and Dan Plesch.[26] In chapter 1 of their report, Rangwala and Plesch set out the case against Tony Blair in relation to the lead-up to the Iraq War in 2003. In chapter 2 of the report, Plesch explored the history of impeachment and its present status.[27] He noted that the fact that it has not been used since Viscount Melville's impeachment should not be taken to mean that it was obsolete.[28] This was because impeachment had previously been revived in the 1620s.[29] Plesch noted that today matters of policy were 'less impeachable' than they had been in the

24 Lord Steyn, 'The Legality of the Invasion of Iraq' (2010) *European Human Rights Law Review* 1; V Lowe, 'The Iraq Crisis: What Now?' (2003) 52 *ICLQ* 859; Lord Alexander of Weedon QC, 'Iraq: The Pax Americana and the Law' (2004) 36 *BLJ* 6; Lord Bingham, *The Rule of Law* (Penguin 2011).

25 The Hutton Inquiry, the Butler Inquiry, and the Chilcot Inquiry.

26 G Rangwala and D Plesch, 'A Case to Answer: A First Report on the Potential Impeachment of the Prime Minister for High Crimes and Misdemeanours in Relation to the Invasion of Iraq' (August 2004).

27 ibid. See 222.

28 ibid 235.

29 ibid.

past, whereas matters of competence and honesty were 'more impeachable'.[30] The impeachable charges against Tony Blair were:

> [T]hat the Prime Minister's refusal to resign for his misleading statements meant that he breached parliamentary conventions. Therefore, not only should he face impeachment for misleading Parliament, but judgments should also be cast for his failure to respect constitutional conventions by resigning. In addition to these charges, there is evidence that prior to March 2003, he made an agreement with President Bush to overthrow Saddam Hussein. As in the case against Palmerston in 1848. . . this charge is equally impeachable.[31]

Plesch concluded that there was a case for impeaching Tony Blair, which was supported by historic precedent.[32] He argued that 'the ability of Parliament to control the activities of government is in continuous decline, consequently public concern is growing'[33] and '[t]he apparently decreasing power of parliament and the increasing power of government provide the background to considering whether it is appropriate to revive impeachment in relation to the invasion of Iraq.'[34] This, Plesch argued, was justification for Members of Parliament using impeachment 'as a last resort'.[35] His justification was *inter alia* that '[i]mpeachment is the process by which Parliament can restore its authority and by which public confidence in Parliament may be restored.'[36] Plesch's observations about the role impeachment could play in restoring the authority of Parliament highlights the possible opportunities for a revised form of impeachment to buttress the existing political accountability mechanisms. He was writing within the context of the established impeachment procedure, and even then, he believed that it could serve a similar purpose. What is of particular interest is that there was an academic case being made for impeachment in 2004, which was being justified by the declining ability of the House of Commons to hold the government to account. Therefore, impeachment was being presented as a way to remedy this perceived decline.

Whilst, as we will see ahead, the attempt to impeach Tony Blair failed, there was legal opinion in support of the use of impeachment. This legal opinion demonstrated that impeachment was regarded by some as not being obsolete in 2004, and that it was capable of being used to impeach the Prime Minister. Rabinder Singh QC and Conor Gearty were instructed by a solicitor acting for Adam Price

30 ibid 227.
31 ibid 228 (emphasis in the original).
32 ibid 261–74.
33 ibid 250.
34 ibid 251.
35 ibid 259.
36 ibid 260.

MP to prepare a legal opinion on the possibility of impeaching Blair.[37] Their legal opinion was published in September 2004. This legal opinion, drafted by two leading lawyers, firmly held that, based on the authorities, impeachment was not obsolete and is 'still available to Parliament as a matter of law'.[38] Impeachment would operate 'where there is a prima facie case (i.e. a case to answer) of either crimes or serious breaches of constitutional principles'.[39] The authors noted the potential scope of conduct that could be impeached and observed that 'while the charge of impeachment is theoretically very broad, it should be confined to wrongs of a legal, or at least of a serious constitutional, nature.'[40] However, they argued that there was authority to extend impeachment to unconstitutional conduct.[41] Singh and Gearty were of the opinion that 'the continuing disuse of impeachment is not an inevitable state of affairs but is, rather, contingent on the continuation of those other, alternative forms of public accountability which have come over time to take its place.'[42] Impeachment served a purpose 'where there is no other means of calling a person to account, either legally or politically'.[43] In order to bring impeachment a Member of Parliament would need to pass 'the evidential threshold' and 'the impunity threshold'.[44] It is very much a last-case mechanism, this sparing use 'being much preferable to the process of impeachment which is a residual blunderbuss, to be held in reserve until all else has failed, and been seen to fail.'[45] Singh and Gearty set out the procedure for impeachment (according to the authorities) and how it would apply in the case of Tony Blair being impeached.

Finally, we can see that Singh and Gearty demonstrated that impeachment could be used where the Prime Minister had acted unconstitutionally, and that impeachment was an option available to Members of Parliament. They rejected the view that impeachment was obsolete, although they were clear that it was very much a last resort. It was clear that Singh and Gearty believed that impeachment could operate in a constitutional landscape where there were alternative accountability mechanisms, and that impeachment could be called upon where these could not achieve accountability in any given particular situation.

Returning to the attempt by Adam Price MP and others within the House of Commons to impeach Tony Blair, it is necessary to consider why the motion to impeach did not succeed. On 9 September 2004, there was debate over the status

37 R Singh QC and C Gearty, 'In the Matter of an Impeachment of the Prime Minister: Arising from the War Against Iraq' (22 September 2004).

38 ibid 2.

39 ibid.

40 ibid 7.

41 ibid 8–9.

42 ibid 16.

43 ibid 17.

44 ibid.

45 ibid.

of impeachment. Adam Price MP asked Peter Hain MP, the Leader of the House of Commons:

> When the Leader of the House chaired the Young Liberals he supported a campaign to impeach the then Lord Advocate of Scotland. Does he still believe that impeachment is a sanction available to the House when seeking to hold Ministers to account, or will he oppose any moves to introduce a motion for debate under that procedure?[46]

Peter Hain responded:

> The hon. Gentleman is an admirable researcher who digs up all sorts of facts, some of which are uncomfortable for the Government. I cannot for the life of me recall that campaign, which was over 30 years ago. However, he has dug it up from a file somewhere, so I acknowledge his research expertise.
>
> The House of Commons has already voted overwhelmingly to back the Government's position on Iraq. That was the House's clear decision. For the first time, the Government brought to the House a motion on a decision to go to war, and gave it an opportunity to authorise it or not. That decision was made, but the hon. Gentleman is seeking to circumvent it.
>
> *I am advised by the Clerk of the House*[47] *that impeachment effectively died with the advent of full responsible parliamentary government, perhaps to be dated from the second Reform Act of 1867, and a motion of no confidence would be the appropriate modern equivalent.* The Joint Committee on Parliamentary Privilege in 1999 concluded that
>
> 'The circumstances in which impeachment has taken place are now so remote from the present that the procedure may be considered obsolete.'
>
> Perhaps the hon. Gentleman should research the matter more carefully.[48]

The opinion of the Clerk of the House of Commons was relied upon to effectively demonstrate that there was no scope for using impeachment as it had been superseded by responsible government and the vote of no confidence. This reflects one of the main obstacles facing those who wished to impeach Tony Blair: the fact that impeachment would be viewed as a constitutional and parliamentary irrelevance.

On 25 November 2004, an early day motion was introduced to impeach Tony Blair. This motion was unsuccessful, but it did have the support of 23 Members of Parliament. The motion stated:

46 HC Deb 9 September 2004, vol 424, col 871.
47 At the time the Clerk of the House of Commons was Sir William McKay.
48 HC Deb 9 September 2004, vol 424, cols 871–2 (emphasis added).

4 CONDUCT OF THE PRIME MINISTER IN RELATION TO THE WAR AGAINST IRAQ

Mr Edward Garnier
Mr Douglas Hogg
Mr Elfyn Llwyd
Mr Alex Salmond
Mr Richard Taylor
Dr Jenny Tonge
Mr David Amess
Mr Richard Bacon
Mrs Angela Browning
Mr Nigel Evans
Annabelle Ewing
Mr Roger Gale
Angus Robertson
Mr Simon Thomas
Mr Michael Weir
Hywel Williams
Pete Wishart
Mr George Galloway
Mr John Gummer
Mr Boris Johnson
Mr Paul Marsden
Richard Ottaway
Adam Price

That a select committee of not more than 13 Members be appointed to investigate and to report to the House on the conduct of the Prime Minister in relation to the war against Iraq and in particular to consider

(a) the conclusion of the Iraq Survey Group that in March 2003 Iraq did not possess weapons of mass destruction and had been essentially free of them since the mid 1990s,
(b) the Prime Minister's acknowledgement that he was wrong when in and before March 2003 he asserted that Iraq was then in possession of chemical or biological weapons or was then engaged in active efforts to develop nuclear weapons or was thereby a current or serious threat to the UK national interest or that possession of WMD then enabled Iraq to inflict real damage upon the region and the stability of the world,
(c) the opinions of the Secretary General of the United Nations that the invasion of Iraq in 2003 was unlawful, and
(d) whether there exist sufficient grounds to impeach the Prime Minister on charges of gross misconduct in his advocacy of the case for war against Iraq and his conduct of policy in connection with that war; and

That the Committee shall within 48 days of its appointment report to this House such resolutions, articles of impeachment or other recommendations as it shall think fit.[49]

49 Quoted in J Simson Caird, 'Impeachment' (House of Commons Library, Briefing Paper CBP7612, 6 June 2016) <>https://commonslibrary.parliament.uk/research-briefings/cbp-7612/>.

There was considerable parliamentary debate as to the status of impeachment and why the motion of impeachment had been introduced. Edward Garnier MP explained why the motion had been tabled to impeach Tony Blair:

> On 23 November, the first day of the Session, I and a number of other right hon. and hon. Members tabled a motion calling for a Select Committee to examine the work and conduct of the Prime Minister that led to the decision to invade Iraq in March 2003, with a view to considering his impeachment. We intend to keep the motion on the Order Paper – motion 37 on today's Order Paper – until the matter is resolved by debate on the Floor of the House. It is a process that survives the general election and one that focuses more accurately on particular conduct of the Prime Minister for which he personally must answer.[50]

Garnier was clear that impeachment should not be dismissed as a waste of time, or something from history:

> For a cross-party group of Members to contemplate the impeachment of the Prime Minister is to invite derision from Government loyalists, pitying but concerned smiles from self-proclaimed political realists and yawns from those who *believe that there are many more interesting things for grown-up Members to be getting on with.* The first reaction is understandable. The paramount rule in the political jungle is survival, and any available weapon is a good one. Ridicule is the most effective tool, even when borrowed by those way down the political feeding chain. It brings with it a sense of moral and intellectual superiority. *In 21st century Britain, the very word 'impeachment' suggests the troubles of the favourite of Charles I, the Duke of Buckingham, or men in 18th-century wigs spending almost a decade arguing over Warren Hastings's life of luxury in far-off India. It is a process lost in the mists of history with no purpose in our advanced parliamentary democracy, which is sustained by universal suffrage and the discipline of general elections.*[51]

Neither did Garnier think that the recent experience of impeachment in the United States was relevant: '[t]he Prime Minister's sexual morality is unimpeachable, so the Clinton example has no relevance to us.'[52] Garnier considered the views of realists who write off the prospect of impeachment due to Labour's majority in the House of Commons:

> For the realist, one has only to ask, 'Can we impeach the Prime Minister?', to know the answer. Of course not. Labour has a vast majority, this is a political

50 HC Deb 21 Dec 2004, vol 428, col 2127.
51 ibid (emphasis added).
52 ibid.

> question and the tribal loyalty of party in the Commons will outweigh the merits of the case, whatever its qualities. It simply will not work. We will sort out the Prime Minister at the general election. That is when he will be held to account.[53]

Garnier was clear about his own reasons for supporting the motion:

> For me, the argument in support of our motion to inquire into the grounds for impeachment is not based on the wrongness of going to war. If it were, I would not support it. *It is based upon the need for Parliament to check the Executive*, and to remind even the most powerful in our country that they are not supreme and ourselves that a functioning parliamentary democracy depends on trust and truth.[54]

The crucial question for Garnier was '[d]id the Prime Minister know, do and say things in the lead-up to the war that were inconsistent with what he told us?'[55] This was important as Garnier had voted to support the invasion

> because I believed that the Prime Minister was advancing a case for war based on the unvarnished truth and because I could not believe that any Prime Minister, particularly one who had put so much store on his personal trustworthiness, could do otherwise. If the Prime Minister had already committed our country to war in a private deal with the President of the United States in 2002, he should have told at least his Cabinet at the time, and Parliament when he made the case for war in March 2003.[56]

To Garnier the attempt to impeach the Prime Minister was on a point of constitutional principle:

> It is the constitutional duty of all Members of Parliament – Government and Opposition Members – to hold the Government to account. I accept that that task is made difficult in Westminster, where the Executive largely sit in and on the Commons. The Government have an enormous majority over all other parties and, save for a few notable exceptions, it has been a supine majority that has forgotten, if it ever knew, that it should do more than lamely follow its leader. I believe, and I sincerely hope, that the realists are beginning to get real. We lack accountability in the House . . . in respect of the Executive.[57]

53 ibid.
54 HC Deb 21 December 2004, vol 428, col 2128 (emphasis added).
55 ibid.
56 HC Deb 21 December 2004, vol 428, col 2129.
57 ibid.

Garnier's observations for why the use of impeachment could be justified are sound and show an informed engagement with the arguments against impeachment, and the underlining concern about the nature and quality of accountability within the constitution.

The debate surrounding whether Tony Blair should have been impeached continued to be occasionally mentioned in the House of Commons. The Labour government was clear that the Iraq Inquiry set up by the then Prime Minister Gordon Brown was not going to act as a court or be an impeachment. In 2009, David Miliband MP, the then Foreign Secretary, observed:

> The House is united on the point that the significant nature of Britain's involvement in Iraq demands an inquiry. It needs to be comprehensive, independent and 'not a trial or an impeachment, but an effort to learn for the future.'[58]

This was the distinction the Foreign Secretary was drawing between an inquiry and impeachment. In 2013, the then Father of the House of Commons, Sir Peter Tapsell MP, asked David Cameron,

> Is the Prime Minister aware of the growing sentiment that, as the publication of the Chilcot report has been so long delayed, the ancient but still existing power of Back Benchers to commence the procedure of impeachment should now be activated to bring Mr Tony Blair to account for allegedly misleading the House on the necessity of the invasion of Iraq in 2003?[59]

In 2016, Lord Owen, speaking in the House of Lords, distinguished between whether Blair had committed an impeachable offence and if so, whether it would be appropriate to have impeached him:

> It is arguable that the statement which the Prime Minister made on 28 July 2002 that he would support President Bush 'whatever' is almost an impeachable offence. Certainly, Lord Sanderson made it perfectly clear, in describing what impeachment meant in February 1906 – when he was dealing with the question of the military conversations in that year in which the French and British staff forces got together to plan a British expeditionary force, but did not tell the Cabinet for five years – that the terms of an impeachable offence would be, 'to go to war in certain circumstances, and were not to mention this pledge to Parliament, and if at the expiration of some months the country suddenly found itself pledged to war in consequence of this assurance, the case would be one which would justify

58 HC Deb 24 June 2009 col 812.
59 HC Deb 18 June 2014 col 1105.

impeachment'. I do not believe that impeachment is the right solution to our present problems. I make it quite clear that I do not think you can do that in the 21st century.[60]

The legacy of the attempt to impeach Tony Blair over the military invasion of Iraq demonstrates considerable resistance to the use of impeachment, which is based on its perceived obsolete status, the fact that Labour enjoyed a majority in the House of Commons, and the existence of alternative political accountability mechanisms. Whilst the early day motion to impeach Tony Blair did not succeed, it did demonstrate that a number of Members of Parliament were willing to resort to impeach in circumstances where the other accountability mechanisms were either unavailable or unlikely to succeed. The legal opinion from Singh and Gearty went some way to highlight that impeachment was not obsolete and that it could be used to proceed against the Prime Minister, subject to procedural safeguards. What the attempt to impeach Tony Blair shows us is that it is not universally accepted that impeachment is no longer an option in exceptional constitutional circumstances, that the case for impeachment is undermined by the perception that impeachment is obsolete and a relic of parliamentary history, and that the legacy of British and American impeachments is a factor in how actors within the constitution perceive impeachment. The revised form of impeachment that is being set out within this book will aim to remove the uncertainty about the nature and scope of impeachment. It will do this by setting out impeachment on a statutory basis and clarifying how and when it might serve a purpose. This would remove the fog of history from how this form of impeachment would be understood.

Negative perceptions of impeachment from US and English and British history

The next counter-argument to the use of impeachment that will be considered is the negative perceptions of impeachment from how it operates in the United States and its legacy in English and British history. Within the United Kingdom, impeachment is perhaps most closely associated with the controversial trial of Warren Hastings in the eighteenth century.[61] In the popular consciousness, impeachment is most commonly associated with the impeachments of President Clinton and President Trump. In the case of Clinton, the impeachment might have been viewed as less about accountability for Clinton's misconduct than as an attempt by a Republican-controlled House of Representatives to use impeachment as a means to remove Clinton from office. The decision to impeach Clinton in the House of Representatives saw the majority of the

60 HL Deb 12 July 2016, vol 774, col 167.
61 See Chapter 2.

Members of Congress vote along party lines,[62] a trend that was followed in the Senate vote on 12 February 1999.[63] It is clear that the Republican majority in the House of Representatives ensured that Clinton was impeached, whilst the Republicans' lack of the two-thirds majority in the Senate ensured that Clinton was acquitted. Almost 20 years after Clinton's acquittal by the US Senate, Clinton's impeachment could arguably be presented as sexual misconduct and the President's narrow interpretation of sexual relations. This legacy was brought to the fore during the 2016 US presidential election, when Donald Trump invited those who had made allegation against President Clinton as guests to the debate between himself as Hillary Clinton.[64] The two impeachments of President Donald Trump polarised public opinion in the United States, but from a UK perspective, observers could arguably see the constitutional rationale for impeachment, even if the likelihood of success in the Senate depended on political considerations.

In terms of the use of impeachment beyond the United States, in recent years there have been impeachment trials in Brazil and South Korea which have seen the presidents of both countries removed from office, and these impeachments have been reported by the mainstream media.[65]

It is intended that the proposed revised impeachment process would counter the concerns about impeachment which stem from the above. The procedure would be reimagined for a modern UK context and whilst it would owe its origins to what had been developed through its historical use, the purpose and scope of impeachment would reflect contemporary concerns over the problems of enforcing compliance with accepted constitutional norms.

The need for a rebranding exercise?

Connected to the aforementioned counter-argument are the negative connotations of the term impeachment. In light of the previously mentioned issues, it might appear to be necessary to divorce the word impeachment from the process. It could be expedient to refer to the mechanism as to outcome, such as a 'removal and/or disqualification mechanism'. This could remove automatic connotations with its historic and comparative use. However, it would be tenable to keep the word impeachment, so long as the revised process and procedure specified how it would now operate, as opposed to its historical scope and usage. However,

62 A Mitchell, 'Clinton Is Acquitted Decisively by Senate on Both Charges' *The New York Times* (13 February 1999) <www.nytimes.com/learning/general/featured_articles/990216tuesday.html>.

63 ibid.

64 See Chapter 3.

65 See C Sang-Hun, 'South Korea Removes President Park Geun-hye' *The New York Times* (9 March 2017); S Romero, 'Dilma Rousseff Is Ousted as Brazil's President in Impeachment Vote' *The New York Times* (31 August 2016).

given that the term impeachment is clearly well known, it will be argued that it should be kept, to reflect the importance of the exercise undertaken by the House of Commons, and to avoid confusion and reinforce public clarity about the mechanism.

Reforms to the House of Lords and the office of the Lord Chancellor

Another counter-argument against the use of impeachment is the constitutional developments that have occurred since Viscount Melville was impeached in 1806. In terms of these developments, the House of Lords has been reformed by the Life Peerages Act 1958, which enabled individuals to be appointed to the House of Lords without a hereditary peerage being created, and by the removal of the majority of the hereditary peers by the House of Lords Act 1999. The Constitutional Reform Act 2005 has created the Supreme Court and removed Parliament's judicial function in the form of the abolition of the Appellate Committee of the House of Lords; it has reformed the office of the Lord Chancellor and removed the requirement that the Lord Chancellor must be legally qualified. If the House of Lords were to undertake its historic role, then the House would be fundamentally different in terms of composition from what it was in 1806 when the trial of Viscount Melville took place. Equally, if the Lord Chancellor were to preside over the trial, then this would raise many issues, including the ability of the post holder to do this and the fact that the House of Lords has its own Lord Speaker.

Concerns about the procedural arrangements for impeachment were raised by those I interviewed as part of my research. Lord Owen was highly critical of the House of Lords having a role in the impeachment proceedings, observing that the involvement of the House of Lords was 'one of the reasons [why] I drew back from impeachment, I looked at all these procedures [and] you cannot use the House of Lords. The House of Lords is a completely disreputable organisation.'[66] Lord Owen also had concerns about the involvement of the Lord Chancellor in presiding over the trial, observing that

> [t]he Lord Chancellor itself now is a completely political appointment. In those days when the Lord Chancellor was really above politics that was an appropriate mechanism but now, I mean look at . . . the trivial people [who are appointed now].[67]

Lord Owen clearly regarded the Lord Chancellor as no longer suitable to be involved. Another individual who I interviewed, who had been a very senior judge, was also critical of the historic procedure of impeachment being used today

66 Interview with Lord David Owen (London, England, 1 March 2018).
67 ibid.

in the contemporary United Kingdom. Asked whether impeachment might work today, they responded:

> If it could, about the only way it could get to the starting gate is if you adopted the kind of trimming to it which you have obviously been contemplating . . . the historical version of impeachment I regard as utterly indefensible.[68]

They were concerned over the role of all the members of the House of Lords as a jury and wider issues connected to prosecuting criminal offences in Parliament, when they should be prosecuted in the ordinary courts.[69]

A few observations can be made regarding the comments. The suitability of the House of Lords in performing its historical function will depend on who is being interviewed, as there is a range of opinions as to the legitimacy of the House of Lords and its effectiveness as a legislative chamber. To counter these concerns about the use of impeachment, I would be proposing to reform impeachment and as part of these reforms the House of Lords would no longer be involved with determining wrongdoing at the trial stage, as the outcome would be determined by a separate Court of Impeachment. The Lord Chancellor would not be involved with the trial and would not preside over the Court of Impeachment.

Human Rights

Another counter-argument against the use of impeachment is the concern that the impeachment procedure does not comply with human rights. The United Kingdom is a member of the Council of Europe and since October 2000 the majority of the European Convention on Human Rights (ECHR) has been given effect in domestic law through the Human Rights Act 1998. The key Convention rights would be Article 6 (which protects the right to a fair trial), Article 5 (which protects liberty), and Article 7 (which guards against retrospective punishment). There is considerable literature on criminal trials and the ECHR, and the Venice Commission has been established to explore this area. Furthermore, there have been hearings before the European Court of Human Rights concerning impeachments including Denmark and Iceland.[70] In none of these cases was there found to be a breach of the ECHR. Given that both Denmark and Iceland have parliamentary systems of government and that their impeachment procedures have been found to comply with their respective obligations under the ECHR, they offer guidance on how impeachment might be revised for the modern United Kingdom.

68 ibid.
69 ibid.
70 See Chapter 3 and Chapter 4.

When I interviewed Chris Bryant MP, he warned that having an impeachment trial in the House of Lords could violate the European Convention on Human Rights:

> It seems to me, you are in danger of falling foul of whether it is European Convention [on] Human Rights or for that matter the British Human Rights Act. [Because] you have to be able to show due process and I do not think if you have just had politicians voting, whether they are members of the House of Lords or the House of Commons, voting, I do not think that that is a due process.

These are valid concerns about the importance of due process and the risks involved with having politicians deciding the outcome as to whether an impeachable offence has been committed. However, to counter these concerns, it is submitted that any revised form of impeachment would need to conform to a procedure that as a minimum safeguard the ECHR rights. The proposed procedure would *inter alia* ensure that the process does not include a sanction that results in loss of liberty by excluding a custodial sentence (even if a custodial sentence could be possible according to the European Court of Human Rights), that the trial is fair, managed in a professional manner, in full accordance with the rules of fairness and natural justice, and in adherence to the rules of evidence. In light of the importance of impeachment, despite the absence of a custodial sentence, it is proposed that the rules of evidence in criminal proceedings be used subject to any necessary modifications. The proposed use of a Court of Impeachment to determine whether the accused is guilty, or not, would draw upon the operation in Denmark and Iceland. In Chapter 4, I reviewed the use of impeachment in Denmark, and the discussion and analysis within this chapter have fed into my consideration of the proposed blueprint for a revised form of impeachment.

Natural justice, the rule against bias, partisanship, and public confidence

Another counter-argument against the use of impeachment is the concern that the process will offend the requirements of natural justice, be biased in favour of, or against, the accused, be subject to overt partisanship by those bringing the impeachment, and therefore not enjoy any degree of public confidence. Central to natural justice is the concept of fairness. The question of fairness is important as impeachment has been regarded as a political trial, which is conducted along party lines and is inherently partisan. The old committees of inquiry that existed until the Marconi scandal are cited as an example of this political trial and the dangers of the politicians voting along party lines.[71] The Marconi scandal had

71 F Donaldson, *The Marconi Scandal* (Bloomsbury 2013).

concerned the award of a government contract to the American Marconi company, when several cabinet ministers owned shares in the English Marconi company.[72] There was a subsequent committee of inquiry and a vote in the House of Commons. Vernon Bogdanor has observed that the use of a select committee was 'discredited' as a result of 'the Marconi affair [as it] divided on party lines in 1913'.[73] The resulting vote in the House of Commons also divided upon party lines, which is hardly surprising given the United Kingdom's parliamentary system of government. As a consequence, the Tribunals of Inquiry (Evidence) Act 1921 was enacted.[74] The Salmon Report was critical of the use of parliamentarians to investigate scandals:

> We of course recognise that there are many purposes for which Select Parliamentary Committees are most useful and indeed indispensable – but the investigation of allegations of public misconduct is not one of them. Such matters should be entirely removed from political influences. A Select Parliamentary Committee is constituted of members representing the relative strength of the parties in the House. Accordingly it may tend in its report to reflect the views of the party having the majority of members, or indeed, as in the Marconi case, it may produce two reports and when these are debated in the House, the House may divide along party lines.[75]

Professor Bogdanor has warned about the problem of fairness in public inquiries and these are sound concerns and reflect the inherent difficulty with seeking to have a completely fair review of a controversial subject matter.[76] The Scott Inquiry into Arms to Iraq had been criticised on the grounds of fairness in terms of the procedure adopted by Sir Richard Scott and how the inquiry was conducted.[77] Other inquiries can be criticised on grounds of fairness, an example being Crichel Down.[78] It is clear that, given the importance of the rule against violating the requirements of natural justice in the common law, impeachment could not be regarded as permitting the procedure to be explicitly or implicitly abused

72 ibid.

73 V Bogdanor, 'Forms of Inquiry: Can Inquiries be Probing, Expeditious and Fair? Scott Compared with Earlier Inquiries' (LSE Public Policy Group Seminar Series, October 1997) 1. I am grateful to Professor Bogdanor for drawing my attention to this paper. The paper is available upon request at the London School of Economics and Political Science.

74 M Flinders, 'Mechanisms of Judicial Accountability in British Central Government' (2001) *Parliamentary Affairs* 54, 66.

75 Royal Commission on Tribunals of Inquiry 1966, Report of the Commission under the Chairmanship of The Rt. Hon. Lord Justice Salmon (Cmnd, 3121) [11], quoted in BK Winetrobe, 'Forms of Investigatory Inquiry & the Scott Inquiry' (House of Commons Library, Research Paper 96/22, 9 February 1999) 22.

76 Bogdanor (n 73).

77 See Lord Howe of Aberavon, 'Procedure at the Scott Inquiry' (1996) *PL* 445.

78 See J Delafons, 'A View from Whitehall: Crichel Down Revisited' (1987) 65 *Public Administration* 339.

by those bringing it.[79] The rule against bias is an important part of the common law, and decisions where there has been actual, presumed, or apparent bias can result in a judicial decision being quashed.[80] It is crucial that if impeachment were to be used, the proceedings would not be regarded as biased and open to legal, political, or media challenge.

Equally important is the question of public confidence and the confidence of all participants in the impeachment process. If the process is not regarded as legitimate in terms of fairness, procedure, and outcome, then there is a risk that any attempt to bring an impeachment could be viewed as partisan. In terms of context, public and participant confidence in public inquires is a moot point. Examples of this include Lord Howe's criticism of the Scott Inquiry, the perception by some that the Hutton Report was a 'whitewash', the controversy over the chair of the Child Abuse Inquiry, and the choice of a retired judge to chair the Grenfell Inquiry.[81] On the other hand, public inquiries have benefited from having a respected individual as chair, and these include the Denning Inquiry (albeit questionable given the procedure adopted by Lord Denning), the Chilcot Inquiry, and the choice of Sir Brian Leveson.[82] Returning to the Scott Inquiry, the operation of the inquiry's procedures and debate over fairness may appear quite abstract to the public, however it is important that, where possible, care is taken to maintain confidence of all involved. This could be achieved by relying on the Inquiries Act 2005, rather than on ad hoc public inquiries, as in the case of the Scott Inquiry. Any impeachment must be capable of carrying public confidence and therefore the procedure and nature of impeachment would need to be reviewed to test whether it would be realistically possible to achieve this.

When I interviewed Chris Bryant he was concerned about the appropriateness of impeachment and the risk of it being misused for partisan politics:

> But the idea that just because you have got 250 MPs or 326 MPs who say that they hate Bloggins and therefore they are going to impeach them and then they have to be tried before a court of the House of Lords or whatever, I think that is a nonsense.[83]

79 *R v Sussex Justices, ex parte McCarthy* [1924] 1 KB 256.

80 See *R v Bow Street Metropolitan Stipendiary Magistrates and others ex parte Pinochet Ugarte (No. 2)* [1999] All ER 577; K Malleson, 'Judicial Bias and Disqualification After Pinochet (No. 2)' (2000) *MLR* 119.

81 See C Cozens, 'Widespread Scepticism to Hutton "Whitewash"' *The Guardian* (29 January 2004) <www.theguardian.com/media/2004/jan/29/huttoninquiry.davidkelly2>; N Watt, 'Lady Butler-Sloss Stands Down from Child-Abuse Inquiry' *The Guardian* (14 July 2014) <www.theguardian.com/society/2014/jul/14/lady-butler-sloss-stands-down-child-abuse-inquiry>; 'Grenfell Tower Inquiry Chairman Heckled as He Is Met with Angry Response from Residents' *The Telegraph* (7 July 2017) <>www.telegraph.co.uk/news/2017/07/07/grenfell-tower-inquiry-chairman-heckled-meets-residents-first/>.

82 See C Bingham, 'Leveson – a "Fair-Minded" Liverpudlian' *Financial Times* (29 November 2012) <www.ft.com/content/95d00b02-3988-11e2-85d3-00144feabdc0>.

83 Interview with Chris Bryant MP (London, England, 28 June 2017).

Chris Bryant had concerns over the fairness of the process and the danger of party political impeachments. When I interviewed Lord Phillips he was also clear that an impeachment would not be fair: 'I very much doubt it, conducting a trial is quite tricky and requirements of fairness are not necessarily all that obvious.'[84] Sir Ross Cranston highlighted the dangers of impeachment being misused: 'it can be very political and unless it were somehow institutionalised it could just be . . . simply used as a weapon without much justification.'[85] To counter these concerns there would be a distinction between the impeachment in the House of Commons brought by Members of Parliament and the determination of wrongdoing in the Court of Impeachment, which would not be undertaken by politicians but by senior judges and political appointees. Lord Owen thought that the Danish system of impeachment, with a hybrid Court of Impeachment, sounded sensible.[86] Even in the House of Commons stage there would be safeguards built in to prevent inappropriate and overtly partisan impeachments, which would be intended to remove, as far as possible, bias and partisanship in the proceedings.

In our correspondence, Viscount Hailsham was of the view that

> there is also the argument based on perceived bias. The majority of peers have a party affiliation, and it will be said that they could not be fair judges in a quasi-political trial. All of the above will be contrasted with the US where the Senate has the authority of an elected body. I also think that grounds for impeachment (i.e. the charges), are not sufficiently specific or identified in advance. This could result in perceived and probably actual injustice.[87]

Viscount Hailsham's concerns about the unspecific nature of charges and the dangers of retrospectivity in the charges presented are certainly sound ones. The proposed revised form of impeachment would counter these concerns by restricting the scope of the impeachable offences to breaches of the constitution, offering guidance on how this might occur and requiring numbers of procedural hurdles to be cleared in order for an impeachment to take place.

The danger of impeachment being used to punish political rivals once they have left office was a concern raised by Chris Bryant MP. This would be because they no longer had a majority in the House of Commons and impeachment could be used against them:

> Let us say for sake of argument that there was a parliamentary process for investigating whether Tony Blair had taken us into an illegal war or had, you know, sent troops to their death or lied to Parliament, [or] any of those

84 Interview with Lord Nicholas Phillips (London, England, 18 October 2017).
85 Interview with Sir Ross Cranston (London, England, 27 July 2017).
86 Interview with Lord David Owen (London, England, 1 March 2018).
87 Correspondence with Viscount Hailsham (13 June 2017 and 2 August 2017).

> things. The moment he loses a general election he no longer commands a majority in the House of Commons, then if you subscribe to that way of doing business then every government would always be prosecuting its predecessors and sending them to prison. And I think that would prevent the proper exchange of democratic process in our country.[88]

To counter this concern, whilst there could be impeachments brought against ministers once they were no longer in office, the fear that every outgoing government would be impeached by its successor could be safeguarded against by the procedural requirements built into the blueprint for impeachment. These would include the need for the permission of the Speaker of the House of Commons and the need for the allegations to be examined by an independent committee of experts before they are voted on by the House of Commons. There is nothing wrong about former ministers being impeached; however, I agree that this should not become the norm.

As discussed earlier, the proposed blueprint for a revised form of impeachment would give the role of determining wrongdoing to a specially constituted Court of Impeachment. This would be composed of senior judges and political appointees and would draw upon the Danish model of impeachment. I discussed the role of the Supreme Court in a possible impeachment process with Lord Phillips, who was of the view that as the Supreme Court does not have first instance jurisdiction it would require an Act of Parliament to provide the court with a role. I asked Lord Phillips whether, in light of the decision in *Miller (No. 1)*[89] and the reaction of the press, the Supreme Court could be asked to determine whether a breach of the constitution had occurred. Lord Phillips responded: '[w]ell if Parliament . . . quite clearly conferred that jurisdiction on them, giving them that function I think they would exercise it, they might rather enjoy it.' In our interview, Sir Ross Cranston warned against the dangers of having the judiciary involved with the impeachment process:

> I think Judges would be extremely reluctant to become engaged with that. I mean the sensitivities are considerable even now under our system and there's a reluctance of the judges to become involved in anything that might be in any way political simply because [of the effect that this would have on their legitimacy]. And to become involved in [a] . . . highly controversial political issue of impeaching someone. . . [the judges would] be reluctant . . . to become involved in really controversial issues.

88 Interview with Chris Bryant MP (London, England, 28 June 2017).

89 *R (on the application of Miller and Santos) v Secretary of State for Exiting the European Union* [2017] Uksc 5 And *R (On The Application Of Miller And Santos) V Secretary Of State for Exiting the European Union* [2016] EWHC 2768. See J Slack, 'Enemies of the People: Fury Over "Out of Touch" Judges Who Have "Declared War on Democracy" by Defying 17.4m Brexit Voters and Who Could Trigger Constitutional Crisis' *The Daily Mail* (3 November 2016).

I asked the retired senior judge whether judges, in light of the press coverage of *Miller (No. 1)*, might be willing to serve on the tribunal. They replied:

> [Judges] will not be put off by that, quite a lot of what one does . . . sometimes has fairly far reaching political consequences and you just have to do what you are expected to do . . . but if the task in each case involves defining what the offence is . . . then this is risky.[90]

Their concern was that the judges would be involved in what could be regarded as politics and judges could be 'seen by the public as just another . . . bunch of actors on the political stage'.[91] They drew comparisons with the unjustified reporting of *Miller (No. 2)* and highlighted the risk of such reporting if judges were used in the impeachment process. They pointed out the dangers of judges no longer being viewed as neutral, especially if they were represented as performing an essentially political task. If on the model proposed judges could be represented in this way, then it arguably would undermine the viability of the Court of Impeachment.

The rule of law

The rule of law is an important feature of the UK Constitution. Indeed, according to Lord Hope, '[t]he rule of law enforced by the courts is the ultimate controlling factor on which our constitution is based.'[92] The rule of law can mean many different things and it has both procedural and substantive requirements.[93] There is a risk that impeachment could fall foul of the procedural requirements where there are flaws with the process and a risk of an unfair procedure. Dicey's account of the rule of law places an emphasis on the supremacy of the ordinary courts and the distrust of legal systems where officials are tried by special courts.[94] The argument for impeachment being obsolete lies in part with the role of the ordinary courts and the ability of the Crown Prosecution Service to prosecute senior officials without fear of consequences. An example would be the prosecution and conviction of Chris Huhne for perverting the course of justice.[95]

Advocates for impeachment could argue that it would allow Parliament to take an active role in ensuring accountability, or filling a lacuna whereby conduct would not be addressed by traditional mechanisms. However, there is a risk that this could be seen as politicians and other members of the 'elite' receiving

90 Interview with former senior judge (Online, 29 June 2020).

91 ibid.

92 *R (on the application of Jackson) v Attorney General* [2005] UKHL 56, [107].

93 For example, see J Raz, *The Authority of Law: Essays on Law and Morality* (Clarendon Press 1979); Lord Bingham, 'The Rule of Law' (2007) 66(1) *CLJ* 67.

94 Dicey (n 7).

95 'Chris Huhne Admits Perverting the Course of Justice' *BBC News* (4 February 2013) <www.bbc.co.uk/news/uk-21320992>.

special treatment. An analogy would be trial by peers, whereby a peer enjoyed the privilege of being tried not in an ordinary court, but instead by their peers in the House of Lords.[96] There are criminal offences that cover misconduct in office and abuse of position that could be used to prosecute individuals in certain circumstances,[97] and despite the unsuccessful argument in *Chaytor*,[98] parliamentarians were convicted under the Theft Act 1968. The last impeachment that took place in 1806, that of Viscount Melville, could have been tried instead by an ordinary court and therefore if impeachment were to be viewed as a way to proceed against those accused of breaching the law, then there is a risk, whether consciously or not, of usurping the role of the ordinary courts.

The senior retired judge who I interviewed believed that the mixture of judicial function with politics was a threat to the rule of law, 'even with the kind of carefully constructed form of impeachment that you are talking about'.[99] Interestingly, they observed that impeachment could have the effect of a deterrent for governments in office. However, they observed, 'the problem is you have to contemplate it being used and you have to work out how it would operate when it was. But that is where I am having a little difficulty.'[100] Whilst 'the process is well thought out' and the review was a 'super exercise and you may be right. . . [and is] certainly well worth investigating', they concluded that they would struggle to see impeachment work.[101] Interestingly, they emphasised the point of avoiding a show trial and, in the case where it might work, that of previous governments who had left office, it would risk being about retribution. Therefore, the retired senior judge was very cautious about judicial involvement in the impeachment process.

It is conceded that it may be difficult to overcome concerns about the role of judges in the Court of Impeachment. However, the inclusion of judges in what would be an exceptionally rare event could be justified by the need to draw a distinction between the political side of the impeachment in the House of Commons and the non-political determination of wrongdoing by the Court of Impeachment.

The existence of alternative accountability mechanisms

Another counter-argument against the use of impeachment is the existence of alternative accountability mechanisms within the political constitution. Ministers are responsible to Parliament, and there are two constitutional conventions that have regulated ministerial conduct: individual ministerial responsibility and

96 Baron de Clifford. See R Paley, 'The Dying Embers of an Outdated Privilege: The 1935 Trial of Lord de Clifford in the House of Lords' (2013) *Parliamentary History* 169.
97 See J Horder, *Criminal Misconduct in Office: Law and Politics* (OUP 2018).
98 *R v Chaytor* [2010] UKSC 52.
99 Interview with former senior judge (Online, 29 June 2020).
100 ibid.
101 ibid.

collective cabinet responsibility. Whether both conventions are effective is often a moot point; however, they are both central to ministerial responsibility in the Westminster system. The obligations on ministers are found in the Ministerial Code and breach of the Code could ultimately lead to the minister concerned being dismissed by the Prime Minister.[102] Parliament could also censure or withdraw its confidence from a particular minister, but given that most governments enjoy an actual, or collaborative, majority in the House of Commons, it is unlikely that this will happen. Impeachment, as discussed at the beginning of this chapter, is viewed by many commentators as having been superseded by ministerial responsibility to Parliament. There are other mechanisms to proceed against a politician who has been accused of 'wrongdoing' that is not of a criminal nature. In these circumstances the government may be forced to hold a public inquiry, a select committee might investigate, a minister could be dismissed (as in the case of Gavin Williamson), or the politician's own colleagues might withdraw their support and force their departure (as in the case of Theresa May). Consequently, it is necessary to ask what role impeachment serves and why there is a case for bringing impeachment back into the constitutional landscape. In Chapter 7, I addressed the rationale and justification for impeachment, and it can be argued that the declining authority of the House of Commons requires a genuine review of the existing accountability mechanisms, and to see whether impeachment might be used to buttress these mechanisms.

Academic commentators have explored the reasons why impeachment is no longer a feature of the UK Constitution. Professor Keeton considered the 'passing of impeachment' and why it was no longer used:

> Had Walpole been successfully impeached it is possible that, notwithstanding the evolution of theories of ministerial responsibility to Parliament, every Prime Minister, on defeat in the House, would have run the risk of impeachment, especially if issues of any moment had been decided during his tenure in office.'[103]

Keeton argued that the reason for there being no more impeachments was not the use of ministerial responsibility, but rather the settlement of 1688: 'the Revolution of 1688 had established a parliamentary settlement which lasted in all essentials until the middle of the nineteenth century.'[104] This removed the need for impeachment.[105] Keeton observed, albeit in the 1950s, that the House of Commons enjoyed less independence than Congress, and '[i]t should also be added that the legal accountability of Ministers for their public conduct has ended with the passing of impeachment.'[106] In terms political accountability, it

102 Ministerial Code, Cabinet Office, January 2018.
103 GW Keeton, *The Passing of Parliament* (2nd edn, John de Graff 1954) 49.
104 ibid 51–2.
105 ibid.
106 ibid 206.

was to the House of Commons, which Keeton regarded as 'subservient' to the government.[107]

AW Bradley considered the status of impeachment in the late 1980s as part of an edited collection to mark the 200th anniversary of the commencement of the trial of Warren Hastings. In terms of impeachment's status today, Bradley's conclusions were negative:

> Is there any point . . . in looking for a revival of some form of political or legal sanctions administered through an impeachment type-process? The temptation to give a positive answer to that question is undeniable. . . [However] the overwhelming weight of constitutional comment . . . is against bringing back British-style impeachment.[108]

Bradley questioned whether impeachment could be used against a serving minister and whether the House of Commons would really want the House of Lords involved.[109] Bradley highlighted the differences between the United Kingdom and United States, where impeachment was used to remove the President from office.[110] He observed:

> If impeachment were to be revived . . . an acute problem would be whether the jurisdiction of the House of Lords should be performed by the whole House, with its imperfect and unjustifiable composition, albeit with the judges in attendance as in the eighteenth century, or solely by the Law Lords (which would reinforce the judicial nature of the proceedings at the expense of the political aspects).[111]

Bradley argued that there were both legal and political mechanisms which could be used instead of impeachment:

> So there is no shortage of procedures, each with particular strengths and weaknesses. However, the effectiveness of many of the procedures depends on whether the House of Commons can exercise an independent will to take action affecting a resolute government. The same would, of course, be true of impeachment, *so that if the problem is the lack of political will in the House of Commons, an attempt to revive impeachment would not help.*[112]

107 ibid.
108 AW Bradley, 'Personal Responsibility and Government: A Case for Impeachment?' in G Carnall and C Nicholson (eds), *The Impeachment of Warren Hastings: Papers from a Bicentenary Commemoration* (Edinburgh University Press 1989) 180.
109 ibid.
110 ibid.
111 ibid 180–1.
112 ibid 182 (emphasis added).

Professor Bradley made a strong argument, and his conclusions are apt. This highlights the problems of whether impeachment could ever be used and the issues of process and procedure. However, a revival of impeachment that aimed at strengthening the hand of the House of Commons might go further than the traditional form of impeachment. It would do so through its focus on protecting the accepted constitutional norms and present itself as an appropriate mechanism for rare, but significant, occasions when ministers acted contrary to these norms.

Those who I interviewed were clear that accountability within the British constitution was a moot point. Lord Phillips was clear that the question of whether Parliament effectively held the government to account depended upon the circumstances.[113] The view of Sir Ross Cranston was that 'there are lots of mechanisms there but not necessarily always used effectively.'[114] Whereas Chris Bryant did not believe that the existing accountability mechanisms were adequate, observing that 'the government has phenomenal power in our system, it's very much winner takes all.'[115]

Public confidence and financial implications

A final counter-argument is the financial implications, that is, the cost, of the impeachment and the impact that this would have on public confidence. It is necessary to contrast with costs of a hypothetical impeachment with real-life public inquiries. The final costs for the Iraq Inquiry amounted to £10,000,000,[116] whilst the first part of the Leveson Inquiry cost £5,400,000.[117] By comparison, an impeachment into whether a Prime Minister would have acted unconstitutionally in circumstances similar to Iraq could well cost several million pounds. This would take into account paying the salaries and expenses of all those involved with the impeachment and the Court of Impeachment, the legal fees incurred, and the logistics of convening the Court. Whether the public would have less confidence in an impeachment than say a long-drawn out public inquiry, such as Arms to Iraq, is a moot point.

113 Interview with Lord Nicholas Phillips (London, England, 18 October 2017).

114 Interview with Sir Ross Cranston (London, England, 27 July 2017).

115 Interview with Chris Bryant MP (London, England, 28 June 2017).

116 'Iraq War: Everything You Need to Know About the Chilcot Inquiry' *ITV News* (5 July 2016) <www.itv.com/news/2016-07-05/iraq-war-what-is-the-chilcot-inquiry>; A Beckett, 'Revelation or Whitewash – What Can We Expect from the Chilcot Inquiry?' *The Guardian* (4 July 2016) <www.theguardian.com/uk-news/2016/jul/04/chilcot-inquiry-iraq-war-whitewash>.

117 'Government Response to the Consultation on the Leveson Inquiry and Its Implementation' (Home Office, 1 March 2018) <https://assets.publishing.service.gov.uk/government/uploads/system/uploads/attachment_data/file/684678/GOVERNMENT_RESPONSE_TO_THE_CONSULTATION_ON_THE_LEVESON_INQUIRY_AND_ITS_IMPLEMENTATION_.pdf>.

Conclusion

This chapter has considered the case for impeachment, in the form of a revised model, by taking into account the counter-arguments against impeachment, before seeking to address these criticisms. The purpose of this chapter was to provide a balanced and independent examination of the argument that a new impeachment procedure would buttress the existing political accountability mechanisms at Westminster.

9 Re-engineering the British Constitution

Can impeachment be sufficiently revised as to re-engineer the British constitution and to shift a greater focus towards political accountability and the protection of the constitution? This question will be addressed in this chapter, which draws upon the previous chapters in the book in order to present a blueprint for a revised procedure for impeachment. This procedure is set out in the form of a proposed Impeachment Act and this chapter will undertake detailed consideration of how the proposed Impeachment Act and impeachment might operate in practice within the contemporary United Kingdom. The chapter will consist of three parts. The first will be to consider the other chapters within this book. The second will be to outline the proposed blueprint for a revised form of impeachment. The third will be to set out the proposed Impeachment Act. Together the three parts will envisage how impeachment could operate alongside the existing political accountability mechanisms and buttress the existing powers of the House of Commons. The purpose of Chapter 9 is to show how, despite the arguments against, impeachment could feasibly operate again in the United Kingdom. It is conceded that the proposal for reform may not convince everyone; however, the aim is to think about in what circumstances impeachment might prove tenable and how this might be achieved.

How this chapter approaches the blueprint for impeachment

This section will draw upon the previous chapters in this book to explain how the drafting of the blueprint for a revised form of impeachment was approached, and how the lessons that arose helped to inform the eventual recommendation.

The purpose of the book has been to explore whether impeachment, in a revised form, might buttress the existing powers of the House of Commons. The focus was on the political constitution and political rather than legal accountability mechanisms. In Chapter 6 there was an exploration of political accountability and the limitations within the current constitutional framework. This demonstrated that there was scope for improving and augmenting the ways that the House of Commons, as the democratically elected chamber, holds the government to account and ensures that ministers are individually

DOI: 10.4324/9781003269052-12

and collectively responsible to Parliament. A number of examples were referred to in Chapter 6 where ministerial conduct failed to comply with the accepted norms of the constitution and where it was important for there to be a method of accountability that could empower the House of Commons to counter such conduct, which crucially would not initially be dependent on a majority of members.

The buttressing of the existing powers of the House of Commons by a modernised form of impeachment, limited to the Prime Minister and government ministers for breaches of the constitution, would demonstrate and reinforce the principle that the House of Commons has a vital, indeed a primary role in enforcing the accepted constitutional norms and ministerial respect for the constitution. The justification for giving the House of Commons such a role is to redress the concerns over who is responsible for being the guardian of the constitution. This book is concerned with the political constitution and envisages that the House of Commons should have the dominant role in safeguarding the constitution. Furthermore, the House of Commons needs to be capable of entering into a dialogue with the courts to address concerns over judicial overreach in determining the legal aspects of the constitution, and impeachment could offer a way for the House of Commons to do this.

However, what is not being argued here is that the existing political mechanisms by which the House of Commons holds the government to account are inherently defective. The existing mechanisms, such as select committees, are valuable and serve an essential role in terms of executive accountability. Rather, what is being argued here is that impeachment might offer a way to allow the House of Commons to take on an enhanced role in how the executive is held to account, to provide greater democratic oversight of ministerial decisions and ministerial conduct, and to give emphasis to the House of Commons' role as the ultimate guardian of the constitution. To this end, impeachment could provide enforcement powers that would enable Members of Parliament to take on a more activist approach to protecting the constitution from abuse and to shaping how the constitution further develops. These enforcement powers would need to be effective, safe from partisan misuse, fair to the accused, and sufficiently independent of the government to have a chance to be taken seriously.

In Chapter 8 the problems associated with impeachment were explored in the form of counter-arguments, and these demonstrated the obstacles that would need to be overcome by a revised form of impeachment. Any revised form of impeachment would need to address the concerns raised by those who are sceptical of reviving impeachment and demonstrate that it could serve a useful purpose. It is submitted that the blueprint within this chapter will seek to do this, as it will show how a revised procedure could, by allowing a small number of Members of Parliament to initiate impeachment proceedings, give precedence to the impeachment proceedings and ensure that there was sufficient parliamentary time to allow the procedure to be effective. Whilst empowering a small number of Members of Parliament there must however be restrictions on impeachment being used as part of ordinary party politics, and to reserve impeachment to deal with conduct that is deemed to be of a sufficiently serious nature as to fall within the scope of an impeachable offence. Therefore, to achieve this the blueprint contains safeguards to prevent inappropriate impeachments. It is conceded that whilst impeachment, even in a revised form, might not be capable of divorcing political considerations from the decision to initiate an impeachment, it could by the inclusion of suitable safeguards counter the risk of overt political partisanship.

Whilst this book is not a history of impeachment, history is still important to understanding how impeachment has been used and the purposes that it has served. The review of how impeachment had been used at various stages in English and British history in Chapter 2 has helped to illustrate the way impeachment could serve as a political accountability mechanism, although one which is of a legal nature due to the trial process. Although there were risks of political partisanship, as evidenced in the party impeachments at the beginning of the eighteenth century, impeachment had in part been prevented from misuse by the requirement that the accused be tried before the House of Lords. By the end of the eighteenth century the trial process was informed by the legal and evidential standards of the common law and the ordinary courts, which proved to be instrumental in the acquittal of Warren Hastings, the penultimate person to be impeached. The history of impeachment demonstrates the value that impeachment could serve in empowering the House of Commons.

However, Chapter 8 also demonstrated that impeachment as it operated at the start of the nineteenth century was ill-suited for use in the contemporary United Kingdom. It can be seen from Chapter 8 that there was uncertainty about whether impeachment still existed in 2004, when there was an attempt to impeach Tony Blair, and presenting impeachment as a relic of history did little to help the argument that Tony Blair's conduct was worthy of impeachment. Therefore, there is a strong argument that impeachment presents a way to buttress the existing mechanisms by which the House of Commons holds the executive to account and empowers the House of Commons to act as the guardian of the constitution, and which relies on reimagining how impeachment might operate today.

In terms of reimagining impeachment and how a modernised form of impeachment might operate, the two comparative case studies in Chapter 3 and Chapter 4 provide an opportunity to see how impeachment is used as a political accountability mechanism in both a presidential and a parliamentary system of government.

The inspiration for the inclusion of impeachment within the US Constitution in 1787 was English and British practice, and examples of how impeachment operated in Britain are still being relied upon as precedents, such as the reference by the prosecutors in President Trump's second impeachment trial to the impeachment of Warren Hastings to support the argument that a former official can be impeached. What is apparent from the second Trump impeachment trial is that, even though he was acquitted, the fact that he could be impeached for conduct perceived to be of a sufficiently grave nature was significant.[1] The focus on removal and then possible disqualification from holding future public office that exists in the US Constitution would be narrower than what would be proposed for the United Kingdom, as removal from office would be the ultimate sanction, rather than the norm. Nonetheless, the US practice of divorcing criminal sanctions from the impeachment process is beneficial as it prevents the prospect of political accusations leading to a custodial sentence or the imposition of a fine.

Whilst the US Constitution offers an example of how impeachment could operate, it does exist in a political system that is fundamentally different from the United Kingdom's parliamentary system of government, which allows the House of Commons to remove a government from office without the need to hold a trial and prove that specific offences have taken place. Nonetheless, the use of impeachment at a federal level highlights how it might serve as a way to proceed where conduct is considered sufficiently grave as to require impeachment and a trial in the Senate.

The other case study, Denmark, with its parliamentary system of government and the ability of the Folketing to remove the government through a vote of no confidence, has served as a particularly useful comparator to how impeachment might operate in the United Kingdom. It is apparent that the last two Danish impeachments were regarded as something of a surprise, due to impeachment being considered redundant and archaic. However, these two episodes show how impeachment empowers the Folketing. It enables the Folketing to proceed against individual ministers, even where they have left office and would be immune from the effects of a confidence vote. An example of this was the impeachment of Inger Støjberg, the former immigration minister, in 2021.[2] Denmark therefore demonstrates how impeachment could coexist alongside other political accountability mechanisms. What is important is that in Denmark there is a clear distinction between the Folketing voting to impeach, which is ultimately a political decision, and the specially constituted Court of Impeachment, that is composed of senior judges and political appointees, determining the merits of the charges. The Danish case study also provides a way of showing how concerns regarding due process and a fair trial can be mitigated against, as the Court of Impeachment was found not to violate the European Convention on Human Rights (ECHR).[3]

1 A similar point was made in *The Guardian's* editorial, 'The Guardian View on Trump's Impeachment: Uneasy, but Essential' *The Guardian* (10 February 2021) <>www.theguardian.com/commentisfree/2021/feb/10/the-guardian-view-on-trump-second-impeachment-uneasy-but-essential>.

2 See 'Denmark's Former Immigration Minister to Face Impeachment Trial for Anti-Migrant Policies' *The Guardian* (2 February 2021) <>www.theguardian.com/world/2021/feb/02/denmarks-former-immigration-minister-to-face-impeachment-trial>.

3 See *Ninn-Hansen v Denmark* (1999) (Admissibility decision, no. 28972/95).

Proposed format for impeachment

This section will set out the proposed format for a revised form of impeachment. Clearly it is inappropriate to suggest that impeachment should operate in exactly the same manner as it did during the impeachment of Viscount Melville in 1806 and his subsequent trial in that same year. This is for a number of reasons: first, that the procedure has always evolved over time, and second, there have been considerable constitutional changes since then, including *inter alia* the House of Lords Act 1999, the Constitutional Reform Act 2005, and the ECHR.

There are five possible approaches to the future of impeachment in the United Kingdom. The first is to accept that impeachment is obsolete because of the passage of time and whilst it still exists as a mechanism, it is unlikely to be used again. The second is to introduce legislation to abolish impeachment, as has been recommended in a number of parliamentary reports.[4] The third is to consider whether there is a justification for impeachment in its current form. The fourth is to consider that, if there is justification for impeachment, whether a revised procedure which would provide a mechanism suitable for use today. The fifth is to recognise that in the Westminster system the executive dominates the House of Commons and therefore impeachment might not be effective, even if revised, because of the inherent dependence of the House of Commons on the government, and that a more radical reform is needed. It is the fourth of these options that this book is advocating. The proposed blueprint for impeachment would be set out on a statutory basis in an Impeachment Act. The retention of the word impeachment would reflect the purpose of the procedure, that is, empowering the House of Commons, although, as discussed in Chapter 8, the name does carry with its use certain negative connotations. What follows sets out the legislative scheme for the modernised process of impeachment.

Drawing upon the Danish model of impeachment

The Danish Constitution and its use of impeachment alongside the vote of no confidence have demonstrated a way that impeachment could operate within a framework that respects human rights. Impeachment within the Danish context has shown how impeachment can add to the accountability toolkit. The proposed use of impeachment within the United Kingdom would draw upon the Danish experience and undertake a partial constitutional transplant, as Denmark provides a clear example of how impeachment could work to hold ministers to account. The concept of a constitutional transplant is important, as it is submitted that there is benefit in incorporating the Danish version of impeachment into the United Kingdom. It must be emphasised, first, that there will be differences between the scope and process of how impeachment works in Denmark, and how impeachment would work in the United Kingdom, and second, that

4 See ahead.

impeachment does have its limitations in Denmark and was considered to be obsolete prior to its use in 1993 and again in 2021.

The Danish model has been found by the European Court of Human Rights not to violate Articles 6 and 7 of the ECHR. Given the United Kingdom's membership of the Council of Europe, and the concern by those I interviewed or contacted (see Chapter 8) over the human rights element, it is expedient to draw heavily upon the Danish experience of impeachment. Furthermore, as will be argued ahead, the exclusion of criminal conduct from the scope of impeachment, and the removal of a custodial sentence, will further remove the risk that the process could breach the United Kingdom's obligations under the ECHR.

The allocation of roles in the revised impeachment procedure

It is no longer appropriate for the House of Lords or the Lord Chancellor to perform their historic roles in the impeachment process. Under the Impeachment Act the Lord Chancellor would have minimal involvement with the impeachment, which would be limited to the choice of venue. However, the Ministry of Justice, for which the Lord Chancellor is responsible as Secretary of State for Justice, would have responsibility for funding the Court of Impeachment and providing civil servants, but this would be the extent of the department's role.

Continuing with an impeachment role for the House of Lords as arbiter today would be an anachronism, especially since its loss of judicial function. It is proposed that the role of the House of Lords should be reduced to providing a method of appointing the lay members of a Court of Impeachment through a Special Appointment Committee. This would draw upon the professionalism and expertise of the Lords, without requiring its members to serve as members of the court. This would allow appropriately qualified individuals with the requisite political and constitutional experience to be appointed. Drawing upon the Danish model of impeachment, it is proposed that there should be a Court of Impeachment composed of both judicial and lay members. This, as is the case in Denmark, would provide a sufficiently professional body, with suitable political, legal, and constitutional expertise, with the integrity and public confidence in its judicial members, and through their independent appointment, also the lay members.

The inclusion of judicial members of the Court of Impeachment could be controversial given the reaction to the two judgments in the *Miller (No. 1)*[5] litigation. However, it is necessary to have judicial involvement, given the seriousness of the subject matter and the need to have proper due process, independence, and public confidence in the impeachment trial. It is for this reason that judges are asked to chair public inquiries. The Danish judiciary perform this function, and it

5 *R (on the application of Miller and Santos) v Secretary of State for Exiting the European Union (No. 1)* [2017] UKSC 5 and *R (on the application of Miller and Santos) v Secretary of State for Exiting the European Union (No. 1)* [2016] EWHC 2768.

is expected that the United Kingdom's judiciary would be capable of undertaking a similar role. In any event, senior members of the judiciary would be able to take on the role of a quasi-constitutional court.

The House of Commons would retain its role as the body that initiates the impeachment. It is important that the impeachment process is not seen as being largely politically motivated or partisan game playing. Politics does involve political calculations being made by individuals, groups of parliamentarians, or political parties. This is a feature of politics and it can never be truly altruistic, even if the intention of the actors within the system is to produce an outcome that is the best for the country. The impeachment procedure would need to safeguard against impeachments being undertaken to punish or embarrass political opponents. The safeguards will be discussed ahead.

The House of Commons is the body that initiates the impeachment and, given the outcome (a trial before the Court of Impeachment, with the prospect of destroying the accused's career and reputation), there must be sufficient safeguards to ensure that impeachment occurs only where it is appropriate and is supported by evidence. Put simply, it should not be a question of a new government using its majority in the House of Commons to impeach the former Prime Minister, unless the Prime Minister's conduct is objectively, or as much as this can be realistically measured, impeachable conduct within the understanding of the constitution. To prevent impeachment from being used in a purely partisan manner, there would need to be a number of stages that the impeachment process would go through before the House of Commons voted to impeach. In any event, the decision as to whether the conduct was unconstitutional would be determined by the Court of Impeachment.

It is proposed that the initial motion to impeach must be supported by a minimum number of Members of Parliament, which would be 12. This would ensure that there is a sufficient number of Members of Parliament who believe that there are grounds to impeach. The next stage would rely upon the neutrality and independence of the Speaker of the House of Commons, who would determine whether, on the balance of probabilities, an impeachable offence had been committed. This initial ruling would be an important safeguard as it would act as a filter to block clearly partisan and inappropriate impeachments. The actual decision of whether there are grounds to impeach would be taken by the Impeachment Committee of the House of Commons, which, assisted by an Independent Panel of Experts, would be responsible for drafting the articles of impeachment. This would provide external guidance on whether an impeachable offence had been committed. It would be important to show that there had been sufficient consideration of the evidence to justify bringing an impeachment. The Independent Panel of Experts would be appointed by the Impeachment Committee of the House of Commons and any individual could be appointed so long as it is reasonable to conclude that they are an expert. This would permit a large number of individuals to be approached to undertake this role, including former judges, former politicians, legal practitioners, and academics. It is important to note that the decision of the Impeachment Committee of the House of Commons would be separate from the earlier decision of the Speaker of the House of Commons, which means that there would be two hurdles to overcome for anyone wishing to bring an impeachment. These two stages would reinforce the point that impeachment should not involve purely political considerations and would be reserved for cases where it is highly likely that an impeachable offence had been committed.

Protecting the accused

The accused would be involved throughout the proceedings in the House of Commons and would be provided with financial assistance. It is clear that anyone who stands to be criticised in the course of an impeachment would seek legal representation and that these costs might not be payable by their employer or the Cabinet Office in the case of ministers. Therefore, the impeachment process would need to cover legal costs, to avoid imposing a prohibitive financial burden on individuals. It is intended that the process should allow the accused and their lawyers to have a dialogue with the House of Commons and to be able to counter any errors of fact in order to limit the possibility of an erroneous allegation in the articles. It would be important that full financial assistance be provided, and that the accused could have recourse to legal representation. It is submitted that unlike a public inquiry (where it is the events that are being investigated, albeit these may inevitably mean that the focus is on one individual) impeachment would be used to proceed directly against one or more individuals This means that there is far more reputational risk involved and the process must safeguard against this.

What conduct would amount to an impeachable offence?

This section will consider the scope of an impeachable offence. The new Impeachment Act would considerably narrow the scope of what would be an impeachable offence. First, impeachment would not be used to pursue breaches of the ordinary law and therefore the process would not involve a trial of crimes and the possible imposition of a custodial sentence. This is because the ordinary courts are best placed to try individuals accused of committing a criminal offence, while the rule of law, at least according to AV Dicey, requires that officials be treated no differently from other citizens.[6] Historically, impeachment has covered a broad range of conduct. For instance, as Keeton observed, '[f]or what may a person be impeached? The trials show that either a peer or a commoner may be impeached for high treason, for felonies, and for high political misdemeanours.'[7] The decision to remove criminal conduct from the scope of an impeachable offence is controversial, as during the course of history there have been arguments against impeaching individuals purely for political reasons.

6 AV Dicey, *Introduction to the Study of the Law of the Constitution* (Liberty Classics 1982).
7 GW Keeton, *The Passing of Parliament* (2nd edn, John de Graff 1954) 46.

It is submitted that, whilst in the past it was important that impeachment was not just a mechanism for proceeding against political opponents on the basis of policy disagreements (such as the Treaty of Utrecht) and used to punish a party's political rivals once they were out of power, it is arguable that accountability is needed more within the realm of constitutional propriety and ministerial conduct than of criminal wrongdoing.

The ordinary law is already equipped for trying breaches of the law by ministers. There is an independent Crown Prosecution Service and an independent judiciary. There are a range of offences that capture wrongdoing, including misconduct in public office, theft, bribery, and fraud. To leave the criminal law to the courts and to focus instead on impeachment as a way to proceed against conduct that is unconstitutional would be to support the existing accountability and responsibility mechanisms.

So, what conduct would fall within the scope of impeachable conduct for the purposes of the Impeachment Act? The Impeachment Act would abolish high crimes and misdemeanours and this would permit a clear foundation upon which to construct the new grounds for impeachment. Importantly, this would ensure that impeachment was restricted to the statutory framework, as opposed to the laws of Parliament. It is submitted that impeachment is to be used where there is an allegation, that can be supported with evidence, that an individual has or individuals have committed: (a) a serious breach of the constitution of the United Kingdom, (b) a breach of the Ministerial Code, (c) a breach of the rule of law, or (d) non-criminal misconduct in office. The first grounds is designed to be general to capture conduct that falls outside of the accepted norms of the constitution, whilst the second and third grounds are specific and reinforce the importance of compliance with particular duties or constitutional requirements. The final grounds would be designed for the rare instances where misconduct falls outside of the scope of the Ministerial Code.

In their 2004 legal opinion on the Tony Blair impeachment, Singh and Gearty advised that a serious breach of the constitution could be treated as an impeachable offence.[8] The decision to treat impeachment as a way to proceed against non-criminal, but rather unconstitutional conduct cannot be objected against as impeachment could always be used to do this, and it would be open to Parliament to 'revive' impeachment in whatever manner it wished to. It is noted that 'a serious breach of the constitution of the United Kingdom' is subjective due to the uncodified status of the constitution. However, the task of determining whether this is the case would fall to the Court of Impeachment and it would be instructed to carry out an appropriate review of the present status of the constitution. It is submitted that this is a task that can be undertaken by a suitability qualified 'constitutional' court, and the need to provide written evidence for any determination ensures a thorough and authoritative account. The same

8 R Singh QC and C Gearty, 'In the Matter of an Impeachment of the Prime Minister: Arising from the War Against Iraq' (22 September 2004).

would apply to a determination as to whether the rule of law had been breached. Whether the Court of Impeachment would eventually become a constitutional court is a moot point and its rulings would prove authoritative as to the functioning of the constitution.

As to whether there would be judicial willingness to define the scope of the constitution, it is possible to point to the Supreme Court's willingness to protect a constitutional principle, ministerial responsibility to Parliament, in *R (on the application of Miller) v Prime Minister (No. 2)*,[9] where the Supreme Court has shown that it is capable of this task. Therefore, it is feasible to presume that a specially constituted Court of Impeachment, with a clear mandate, would be capable of undertaking such a task.

Who could be impeached?

It has been argued throughout this book that impeachment should be restricted to ministers of the Crown. This would narrow the scope of who could be impeached. In light of the procedure under the Act of Settlement 1701 it is (a) unnecessary and (b) inexpedient to impeach members of the judiciary, as senior members of the judiciary can be removed by Parliament through an existing procedure. The United States does not have a dismissal mechanism for the federal judiciary that is separate from impeachment, hence the use of federal impeachment to proceed against members of the executive and the judiciary. It is submitted that it would also be inappropriate to proceed against civil servants, heads of government agencies, ministers of the devolved governments, and private citizens. The reason for this is that the focus in this book is on how impeachment could be used to protect the constitution and to strengthen the powers of the House of Commons to ensure the accountability of the executive. The emphasis is on Westminster, and this would exclude ministers in the devolved governments. The use of impeachment against private citizens and civil servants would be inappropriate and would not be justified by the intended purpose of impeachment. The exclusion of heads of government agencies would be justified on the distinction in terms of function, exercise of power, and role within the constitution between ministers and heads of agencies. Finally, Her Majesty the Queen could not be impeached. There will be a discussion ahead as to legal immunity and a head of state.

Could a former minister be impeached?

It is submitted that, following on from historical practice, it should be possible to impeach former ministers who can be impeached for acts committed whilst in ministerial office. The fact that a minister has left office should not be a bar to their subsequent impeachment, as otherwise this would reduce the deterrent

9 [2019] UKSC 41.

factor of impeachment and would impede action in relation to a newly discovered wrongdoing.

What are the available sanctions?

It is proposed that the consequences of impeachment should not result in either a custodial sentence or a financial sanction. The proposed sanctions would include (a) a determination of wrongdoing, (b) removal from office for a period of time not exceeding 15 years, and/or (c) an appearance at the Bar of the House of Commons to apologise. The sanctions need not deprive a minister of office and could result in the making of an official apology, or at the most significant, the sanction could result in loss of office and the exclusion from public office for a period of 15 years. The exclusion element is drawn from the Company Directors Disqualification Act 1986, and it seems reasonable that such a sanction should be available where appropriate to the Court of Impeachment. The removal from office element is influenced by the role of impeachment in the United States, where it is noted there can also be the sanction of a ban from the holding of public office in the future. In the United States, it is possible to be impeached and removed from office, and then hold public office again, as in the case of Alcee Hastings (see Chapter3). The removal of a custodial sentence would be different from the way in which impeachment operates in Denmark, where a minister can be impeached and sentenced to serve time in prison as a result of their conduct in office (see Chapter 4).

What is meant by action short of an impeachment?

The decision whether to impeach a minister or former minister will be taken by the House of Commons by way of a majority vote. This means that ministers currently in government would not be impeached unless members of their own party were to support the impeachment. Nonetheless, the proposed impeachment procedure is intended to give effect to action short of impeachment, whereby, even without the need for a successful vote to support articles of impeachment, there is a mechanism to condemn behaviour considered impeachable. This would occur where the Impeachment Committee of the House of Commons and the Independent Panel of Experts agree that there is a case for impeachment, and this would be set out in an advisory opinion and draft articles of impeachment. This finding and the draft articles would stand regardless of whether the House of Commons supported the impeachment. The consequences of this could be significant for the reputation and career of the accused. Therefore, it would be possible that this could serve as a deterrent, perhaps more so than the possibility that a minister might be impeached by a majority vote of the House of Commons. This would also highlight how the constitution has been breached where a minister does not comply with the accepted norms of the constitution.

Another action short of impeachment would be where the Impeachment Committee of the House of Commons decides to recommend an alternative forum, such as the Parliamentary and Health Service Ombudsman, the Police, or another select committee of the House of Commons, rather than bringing forward an impeachment. It should be noted that these alternative forums could be engaged without requiring Members of Parliament to use the statutory framework in the Impeachment Act; however, their inclusion within the Act is intended to serve as a way for the impeachment mechanism to exist alongside these alternative accountability mechanisms.

The role of the Impeachment Review Commission

The Impeachment Review Commission would be established to support the work of the bodies set up under the Impeachment Act. The purpose of the Impeachment Review Commission would be to provide guidance on the procedural rules of the Court of Impeachment, to give illustrative examples of how the Impeachment Act would apply, and for the purposes of consistency provide definitions of the terms stated within the Impeachment Act. The membership of the Impeachment Review Commission would be composed of judges, Members of Parliament, and members of the House of Lords.

The relationship of impeachment and immunity from legal suit in relation to a head of state

Finally, the relationship between impeachment and legal immunity needs to be considered. In a presidential system such as the United States, impeachment exists as a mechanism to remove the head of state. In the case of the United States, the President enjoys immunity from criminal prosecution whilst he is in office; therefore, a serving President who commits a criminal offence can only be proceeded against by way of impeachment and not (whilst he is in office) through the ordinary criminal courts. In the United Kingdom, the head of state, Her Majesty the Queen, enjoys absolute legal immunity for both criminal and civil action. This is not a position enjoyed by the head of government, the Prime Minister, who can be proceeded against through the ordinary courts and removed from office by way of impeachment.

Throughout the use of impeachment in England and the United Kingdom it was accepted through practice that impeachment would not be used directly against the monarch but could be used indirectly to proceed against the monarch's advisors and favourites. The monarch's immunity from prosecution and from being impeached goes to the very nature of the Crown within the constitution. Ultimately, given the observance of the constitution by successive monarchs, there is no need for impeachment, even in a revised form, to be extended to the United Kingdom's head of state. This is because the monarch serves no role politically, and in the United Kingdom, real power lies with the Prime Minister and he or she can be impeached. Importantly, if a monarch were to act in way that fell below constitutional expectations, the historical remedy would be abdication, as in the case of Edward VIII in 1936 and the enactment of His Majesty's Declaration of Abdication Act 1936, which occurred because the government refused to support the monarch's intention to marry a divorcée. In conclusion, therefore, the royal head of state should not fall within the scope of the new impeachment process.

The proposed Impeachment Act

The following section contains the proposed Impeachment Act. It is submitted that the procedure should be set out in an Act of Parliament, as opposed to a new Standing Order of the House of Commons or relying on a description of the impeachment procedure contained in historic sources. The proposed Act is intended to achieve the following objectives. The first objective is to ensure that there are adequate and appropriate checks on impeachment being used as a partisan weapon. This has been achieved by the number of stages that any impeachment needs to go through and the degree of independence of each stage. The second objective is to remove the House of Lords as a venue for the Court of Impeachment. This is supported by the comments of those whom I have interviewed. The third objective is to provide a mechanism that is fair on those accused of an impeachable offence and respects the rule of law. The fourth objective is to ensure that the impeachment mechanism complies with Articles 6 and 7 of the ECHR. The final objective is to remove criminal conduct from the ambit of impeachment.

The proposed Impeachment Act would be structured as follows:

Part 1. An impeachable offence

Section 1. The power to impeach

(1) The sole power to impeach is vested with the House of Commons of the United Kingdom.
(2) The power of impeachment enables the House of Commons to address perceived wrongdoing and to act as a voice for the citizens of the United Kingdom and, where appropriate, citizens of other countries.
(3) The power of impeachment shall be used in good faith and in the public interest.
(4) All members of Parliament are under a duty to respect the requirements in subsection (3) and the integrity of the process.

Commentary

The power of impeachment remains exclusively with the House of Commons. Subsection (2) briefly sets out the rationale for impeachment. Importantly, subsection (3) seeks to prevent impeachment from being abused and to include a requirement of good faith.

Section 2. What is an impeachable offence?

(1) An impeachable offence for the purposes of this Act is defined exclusively within subsection (2).
(2) An impeachable offence by a Minister of the Crown is:

(a) A serious breach of the constitution of the United Kingdom.
(b) A breach of the Ministerial Code.
(c) A breach of the rule of law.
(e) Non-criminal misconduct in office.

(3) The historic ground of high crimes and misdemeanours is hereby abolished.

Commentary

Section 2 is designed to limit the scope of impeachment to exclude circumstances in which impeachment would be inappropriate. Subsection (2) sets out what is an impeachable offence. Paragraph (a) is intended to catch conduct that is unconstitutional by reference to a serious breach of the UK Constitution (a definition is provided in section 3). The inclusion of the Ministerial Code in paragraph (b) would develop upon the current situation where the only sanction for breach is dismissal by the Prime Minister. The abolition of 'high crimes and misdemeanours' is intended to limit the scope of impeachment and to remove criminal offences from the ambit of impeachment. Subsection (2) limits impeachment to Ministers of the Crown and significantly narrows the scope of impeachment to exclude individuals such as judges.

Section 3. A serious breach of the constitution of the United Kingdom

(1) For the purposes of this Act a breach of the constitution means a breach of the accepted constitution as it stands in written or unwritten sources, whether legally binding or political.
(2) The question of whether there has been a breach will be determined by the Court of Impeachment.
(3) The Court of Impeachment must take into account:

(a) The leading authorities on the present state of the UK Constitution.
(b) Any reasonable ambiguities. In the event of any ambiguity the Court must accept the accused's conduct as falling within their understanding of the constitution.

(4) The Court of Impeachment must provide detailed reasoning in the event that it finds that there has been a serious breach of the constitution.

Section 4. The standard of proof

(1) The prosecution must establish beyond reasonable doubt that an impeachable offence has occurred.

Section 5. Defences

(1) The defences outlined in subsection (2) will apply to the grounds listed in section 2 (2).
(2) The defences are not exhaustive and include:

(a) Accepted practice'
(b) Good faith.
(c) The breach was not deliberate.
(d) Technical breach.

(3) In order for subsection (2)(c) to be satisfied the breach must not be deliberate. This is a question to be determined by the Court of Impeachment with reference to the relevant legal principles, but it shall be free to determine its own test.

Section 6. Majority verdict

(1) The Court of Impeachment shall not find that an impeachable offence has been committed unless a majority reaches this decision.

Section 7. Sanctions

(1) The Court of Impeachment may impose the following sanctions as outlined in subsection (3). When determining a sanction, the Court of Impeachment must have regard to any relevant guidelines.
(2) Relevant guidelines are those that have been produced by the Impeachment Review Commission.
(3) One or more of the following sanctions can be imposed by the court:

(a) Determination of wrongdoing.
(b) Removal from public office for a period of time not exceeding 15 years.
(c) Appearance at the Bar of the House of Commons to apologise.

(4) Removal from office means:

(a) A Secretary of State will be automatically dismissed from cabinet.
(b) The Queen shall dismiss the Prime Minister.
(c) A minister will be automatically dismissed from their department.
(d) A minister will be disqualified from membership of the House of Commons and the House of Lords.
(e) Failure to comply with subsection 3(a) and (c) will amount to a contempt of court.

Part 2. The Impeachment Review Commission

Section 8. Establishment of the Impeachment Review Commission

(1) The Impeachment Review Commission is hereby established.
(2) A senior civil servant from the Ministry of Justice shall be assigned to the Impeachment Review Commission on a permanent basis.

Section 9. Responsibility for providing guidance

(1) Guidance shall be provided from time to time by the Impeachment Review Commission, that shall meet every five years to review the guidance provided.
(2) Guidance shall include:

  (a) The procedural rules of the Court of Impeachment.
  (b) Illustrative examples of how this Act shall apply.
  (c) Definitions of terms stated within this Act.

(3) The Impeachment Review Commission shall meet in the Palace of Westminster.
(4) The Impeachment Review Commission shall appoint the relevant external advisers to provide support to its members.
(5) The guidance shall be published on the website of the Impeachment Review Commission.

Section 10. Composition of the Impeachment Review Commission

(1) The Impeachment Review Commission shall be composed of:

  (a) Eight members of the House of Commons.
  (b) Eight members of the House of Lords.
  (c) The Lord Chief Justice of England and Wales.
  (d) The Lord Chief Justice of Northern Ireland.
  (e) The Lord President of the Court of Sessions of Scotland.
  (f) The Deputy President of the United Kingdom Supreme Court.
  (g) The Master of the Rolls.

(2) The lay members (a) and (b) shall serve only one 10-year term.

Part 3. The Court of Impeachment

Commentary

It is proposed that there is scope to undertake a constitutional transplant from the Danish system of impeachment. The House of Lords would no longer have a role in impeachment, beyond the Impeachment Review Commission. Instead the venue for determining whether an impeachable offence has been committed shall be the Court of Impeachment. The terminology deliberately emphasises the judicial character of the proceedings, and that whilst the trial would no longer take place in the House of Lords, the legal and evidential safeguards that were developed will be retained.

Section 11. Composition

(1) The Court of Impeachment shall be composed of seven judicial members and seven lay members.

(2) The Court of Impeachment shall be composed of a quorum of four judicial members and four lay members.
(3) The Court of Impeachment shall be presided over by the President of the Supreme Court.

Commentary

The hybrid membership of the Court of Impeachment is based upon the Danish model. The inclusion of senior judges will instill a foundation of fairness and due process. The choice of a quorum of four for both judicial and lay members reflects the possibility that members may need to step down or become ill or otherwise unable to continue in their role.

Section 12. Judicial members

(1) The judicial members shall include:

    (a) At least one judge from England.
    (b) At least one judge from Wales.
    (c) At least one judge from Northern Ireland.
    (d) At least one judge from Scotland.

(2) The judicial membership shall be determined by the Lord Chief Justice of England and Wales, the Lord Chief Justice of Northern Ireland, the Lord President of the Court of Sessions of Scotland, and the President of the Supreme Court.
(3) The determination of judicial membership for subsection (2) shall be decided every five years and the names sealed until the Court of Impeachment sits.
(4) To be eligible to serve on the Court of Impeachment a judicial member must:

    (a) Not have any direct or indirect interest in the proceedings which could give rise to actual, presumed, or apparent bias.
    (b) Be from one of the following courts:

        (i) Court of Session.
        (ii) Court of Appeal of England and Wales.
        (iii) Court of Appeal of Northern Ireland.
        (iv) Supreme Court.

Section 13. Lay members

(1) The lay members shall be appointed from outside of Parliament and shall serve for a period of ten years.
(2) In the event of an impeachment occurring during the lifetime of a member's appointment, their appointment shall not terminate under (1) until the impeachment process has finished.

(3) The lay members shall be appointed by a Special Appointment Committee of the House of Lords that shall consist of all the chairs of the House of Lords' existing committees.
(4) The lay members shall include at least one member who is a resident of:

(a) England.
(b) Wales.
(c) Scotland.
(d) Northern Ireland.

(5) The Special Appointment Committee shall seek to ensure that the lay membership reflects the general population and, so far as is possible, takes into account the protected characteristics under the Equality Act 2010.

Commentary

The House of Lords will have a limited involvement with the trial element of the impeachment, which shall be confined to the appointment of the lay members of the Court of Impeachment.

Section 14. The chairperson

(1) The Court of Impeachment shall be chaired by the President of the Supreme Court.
(2) The chairperson shall be responsible for ensuring the effective operation of the Court of Impeachment in terms of resources, procedure, and process.
(3) In the event of a tied decision the chairperson shall have the casting vote.

Section 15. Security of tenure and complaint procedures

(1) All members of the Court of Impeachment shall enjoy security of tenure for the lifetime of their appointment to the Court of Impeachment.
(2) Any members shall have the right to resign their appointment by giving notice to the Special Appointment Committee.
(3) Any complaints against lay members of the Court of Impeachment shall be submitted in the first instance to the Special Appointment Committee. If in the opinion of a majority of the Special Appointment Committee there is some basis for the complaint, then the Special Appointment Committee shall instruct independent counsel to conduct a report into the complaint.
(4) Any complaints against judicial members of the Court of Impeachment shall be submitted to the relevant head of the judiciary.

Section 16. Expenses

(1) During the time that the Court of Impeachment is in session lay members shall be entitled to expenses at the current rate paid to those members of the House of Lords who attend a session from the Ministry of Justice.

(2) During the time that the Court of Impeachment is in session judicial members shall not be entitled to claim expenses from the Ministry of Justice.
(3) If a lay member is employed their employer can recover reasonable costs from the Ministry of Justice.

Section 17. Support for the Court of Impeachment

(1) When the Court of Impeachment is in session the Ministry of Justice shall provide sufficient funding to employ appropriate staff to assist the court for the purposes of impeachment.
(2) When the Court of Impeachment is in session the Ministry of Justice shall provide sufficient funding to instruct a legal counsel to assist the court for the purposes of impeachment.

Section 18. Powers of the court

(1) The Court of Impeachment will have the same powers as the High Court.
(2) All evidence shall be given under oath and providing deliberately false or misleading information will be regarded as perjury.

Section 19. Contempt of court

(1) The Court of Impeachment does not have the power to impose a custodial sentence save for where a contempt of court has been committed during the course of the proceedings.
(2) In the event of a contempt of court being committed the judicial members of the Court of Impeachment shall deal with this matter on their own.
(3) The guidance for contempt of court can be found in the relevant sentencing guidelines that are used within the ordinary courts.

Part 4. The process

Section 20. The impeachment motion

(1) In order to commence proceedings a Member of Parliament is required to submit a motion to the Clerk of the House of Commons.
(2) This motion must be supported by 12 Members of Parliament.
(3) The Clerk of the House of Commons cannot refuse the motion outright but is under a statutory duty to advise on the form and language used.
(4) Once the motion is submitted it will be referred to the Speaker who has discretion to issue a certificate to permit the referral to the Impeachment Committee of the House of Commons where she or he believes that on the balance of probabilities an impeachable offence has been committed.

Section 21. The Impeachment Committee of the House of Commons

(1) The Impeachment Committee of the House of Commons shall be composed of all the chairs of the current House of Commons select committees.
(2) The Impeachment Committee will be tasked with investigating the initial allegations and producing a report.
(3) The report shall either:

  (a) Find no grounds in the allegation.
  (b) Recommend an alternative forum such as the Parliamentary and Health Service Ombudsman, the Police, or another Select Committee.
  (c) Where there appears to be a case for impeachment refer the matter to an independent Panel of Experts.

Section 22. The composition of the Independent Panel of Experts

(1) The Independent Panel of Experts shall be appointed by the Impeachment Committee of the House of Commons in order to undertake a review of the case for impeachment.
(2) There shall be a minimum of seven members and the panel shall appoint its own chairperson.
(3) Members of the Independent Panel of Experts shall be entitled to recover reasonable expenses from the House of Commons.
(4) Members of the Independent Panel of Experts shall be protected by parliamentary privilege for the purposes of this Act.
(5) Any individual who the Impeachment Committee of the House of Commons considers to be an expert shall be able to serve in this capacity, so long as it is reasonable to conclude that they have sufficient expertise in the relevant area.

Section 23. Duties of the members of the Independent Panel of Experts

(1) Members of the Independent Panel of Experts are under a statutory duty to act in a quasi-judicial capacity.
(2) In the event of an actual or potential conflict of interest members are obliged to recuse themselves.

Section 24. The advisory opinion

(1) The Independent Panel of Experts shall produce an advisory opinion within four months of the referral being made. This shall be submitted to the Impeachment Committee of the House of Commons.
(2) The advisory opinion need not be unanimous, although there must be a majority of at least five members.

(3) Where there are dissenting opinions, these shall be included as an appendix to the advisory opinion.
(4) Upon receipt of the advisory opinion the Committee shall produce a second report that shall either:

   (a) Find no grounds in the allegation.
   (b) Recommend an alternative forum such as the Parliamentary and Health Service Ombudsman, the Police, or another Select Committee of the House of Commons.
   (c) Where there is a case for impeachment draft provisional articles of impeachment that will be presented to the Speaker.

(5) The second report need not be unanimous, although there must be a majority of all members.
(6) Where there are dissenting opinions, these shall be included as an appendix to the second report.
(7) The report shall not be made public until it is published by the Speaker. It shall be a contempt of Parliament to publish or otherwise reveal the report's contents.

Section 25. Submission of the draft articles of impeachment

(1) If for the purposes of section 24(4)(c) draft articles are presented to the Speaker, then a copy of the draft articles must be sent to all persons mentioned within the articles at the same time that these are submitted to the Speaker.
(2) Any person mentioned shall be entitled to claim reasonable legal expenses for instructing legal counsel to advise on the draft articles.
(3) Once in receipt of the draft articles the Speaker shall wait for a minimum seven working days before publishing the draft articles.
(4) Any person mentioned in the draft Articles shall be entitled to petition the Speaker in the event of any material errors in the report.
(5) If a petition is made under subsection (4) the Speaker shall determine whether it is appropriate to ask the Impeachment Committee of the House of Commons to reconsider its second report.

Section 26. Publication of the draft articles of impeachment

(1) Where articles of impeachment have been presented to the Speaker and are then published, a new Standing Order will be invoked to make time for an initial vote in the House of Commons.

Section 27. The vote on the draft articles of impeachment

(1) The wording of the vote shall be 'Does this House believe that the provisional Articles of Impeachment should proceed to a full vote in the House of Commons?'

(2) If the House votes yes, then an Ad-hoc Committee will be formed to consider the Articles and consider amendments.

Section 28. The Ad-hoc Committee

(1) The Ad-hoc Committee shall be appointed by the House of Commons. It shall consist of 21 members and shall appoint its own chairperson.
(2) The Ad-hoc Committee shall be assisted by a legal counsel.
(3) The Ad-hoc Committee shall have a maximum of two months to consider the articles and consider amendments.
(4) It shall submit the report and the final articles of impeachment to the Speaker and anyone named within the articles.
(5) Any person mentioned shall be entitled to claim reasonable legal expenses for instructing legal counsel to advise on the draft articles.

Section 29. The final vote

(1) Within two months of the initial vote the House of Commons will vote on each article in turn. Those articles that are voted for by the House will proceed to trial.
(2) The House of Commons shall instruct counsel to act as prosecutors. The instruction shall be undertaken by the Speaker on behalf of the House of Commons.

Part 5 The trial

Section 30. The venue

(1) The venue for the trial shall be Westminster Hall.
(2) If Westminster Hall is unavailable a suitable alternative venue shall be chosen by the Lord Chancellor.

Section 31. The proceedings of the Court of Impeachment are not affected by the dissolution of Parliament

(1) The proceedings of the Court of Impeachment are not affected by the dissolution of Parliament.

Section 32. Legal costs

(1) The person(s) who are being impeached shall have access to a fund to cover the reasonable cost of instructing counsel and their reasonable legal costs shall be paid in full.
(2) In the event of a dispute concerning the question of reasonableness, reasonableness shall be determined by the Court of Impeachment.

Section 33. The duty of fairness

(1) The Court of Impeachment is under a legal duty to ensure that the proceedings are fair. This includes, but is not exhausted by, the following:

  (a) The person who is being impeached shall have the right to know all evidence against him or her and to cross-examine all witnesses.
  (b) Any person who has a reasonable belief that he or she shall be adversely affected by the impeachment will have a right to make representations to the Court of Impeachment.

(2) In determining what is required by the duty of fairness in subsection (1) the Court of Impeachment shall make reference to:

  (a) The common law duty of fairness.
  (b) The requirements of fairness in public inquires.
  (c) The relevant rules under Article 6 of the European Convention on Human Rights.

Section 34. The procedure of the Court of Impeachment

(1) The procedure shall be determined by the Court of Impeachment.
(2) In determining the procedure the Court of Impeachment shall have reference to:

  (a) The rules of evidence in both criminal and civil proceedings.
  (b) The European Convention on Human Rights and the jurisprudence of the European Court of Human Rights.

Section 35. Right of appeal

(1) There is no right of appeal to the Supreme Court.
(2) The defendant may make an application to the European Court of Human Rights.

Section 36. Right of pardon

(1) No Pardon under the Great Seal of the United Kingdom is pleadable to an impeachment by the House of Commons in Parliament.

Bibliography

Ackerman B, 'What Ken Starr Neglected to Tell Us' *The New York Times* (14 September 1998)
Adams GB, *A Constitutional History of England* (Jonathan Cape 1921)
Amar A, 'If You Convict, You Must Evict' *Legal Times* (8 February 1999)
Anderson CB, 'Ministerial Responsibility in the 1620's' (1962) 34(4) *The Journal of Modern History* 381
Anderson S, 'Judicial Accountability: Scandinavia, California and the U.S.A.' (1980) 28(3) *The American Journal of Comparative Law* 393
Anon, *Arguments Pro and Con in Several Speeches for and Against an Impeachment* (J. Roberts, Near the Oxford Arms in Warwick Lane 1715)
Anon, *The Justice of Parliaments: On Corrupt Minister, in Impeachments and Bills of Attainder, Confider'd* (J. Roberts in Warwick-Lane 1725)
Anon, *An Enquiry into the Origin of Parliamentary Impeachments: With a History of the Most Remarkable Proceedings of That Kind from the Beginning to Our Time* (J Peele at Locke's Head, in Pater-Nofter-Row 1745)
Anon, *The Parliamentary or Constitutional History of England; Being a Faithfull Account of All the Most Remarkable Transactions in Parliament, from the Earliest Times to the Restoration of King Charles II*, Volume XII (William Sandby 1753)
Anon, *The Trial, By Impeachment, of Henry Lord Viscount Melville, for High Crimes and Misdemeanors Before the House of Peers in Westminster Hall, Between the 29th of April and the 17th of May 1806* (Longman, Hurst, Rees and Orme 1806)
Babington Macaulay T, *Warren Hastings* (John Long 1905)
Bagehot W, *The English Constitution* (5th edn, Kegan Paul, Trench and Co 1888)
Barkham P, 'Clinton Impeachment Timeline' *The Guardian* (18 November 1998)
Bates S, M Goodwin and S McKay, 'Do UK MPs Engage More with Select Committees Since the Wright Reforms? An Interrupted Time Series Analysis, 1979–2016' (2018) 70(4) *Parliamentary Affairs* 780
BBC News, 'Iceland ex-PM Haarde "Partly" Guilty Over 2008 Crisis' (23 April 2012)
BBC News, 'Paraguay President Fernando Lugo Impeached by Congress' (23 June 2012)
BBC News, 'Chris Huhne Admits Perverting the Course of Justice' (4 February 2013)
BBC News, 'Ding Dong! The Witch Is Dead Enters Chart at Two' (14 April 2013)
BBC News, 'Brazil President Dilma Rousseff Removed from Office by Senate' (1 September 2016)
BBC News, 'Donald Trump: Could the US President Pardon Himself?' (22 July 2017)
BBC News, 'May's Government Survives No-Confidence Vote' (16 January 2019)

BBC News, 'Julian Smith: Chief Whip Attacks Cabinet's Post-Election Brexit Strategy' (1 April 2019)

BBC News, '"Worst Example" of Cabinet Ill-Discipline in British Political History' (1 April 2019)

Beckett A, 'Revelation or Whitewash – What Can We Expect from the Chilcot Inquiry?' *The Guardian* (4 July 2016)

Bekiempis V, 'Trump's Acquittal Shows Paltry Punch of Impeachment Process' *The Guardian* (14 February 2021)

Bennett MJ, 'Stanley, Thomas, First Earl of Derby' in *Oxford Dictionary of National Biography* (OUP 2004, Online 3 January 2008)

Berger R, *Impeachment the Constitutional Problems* (Harvard University Press 1973)

Bernstein J, *Dawning of the Raj: The Life and Times of Warren Hastings* (Ivan R Dee 2000)

Bingham C, 'Leveson – a "Fair-Minded" Liverpudlian' *Financial Times* (29 November 2012)

Birch AH, 'Responsibility in British Politics' in G Marshall (ed), *Ministerial Responsibility* (OUP 1989)

Biskupic J, 'Rehnquist to Transform Senate into Jury' *The Washington Post* (7 January 1999)

Blackburn R and A Kennon, *Griffith & Ryle on Parliament: Functions, Practice and Procedures* (2nd edn, Sweet & Maxwell 2003)

Bogdanor V, 'Scott Report' (1996) 74 *Public Administration* 593

Bogdanor V, 'Forms of Inquiry: Can Inquiries by Probing, Expeditious and Fair? Scott Compared with Earlier Inquiries' (LSE Public Policy Group Seminar Series, October 1997)

Bogdanor V, 'Ministerial Accountability' (1997) 50(1) *Parliamentary Affairs* 71

Bogdanor V, *The New British Constitution* (Hart Publishing 2009)

Bovens M, 'Analysing and Assessing Accountability: A Conceptual Framework' (2007) 13(4) *European Law Journal* 447

Bovens M, R Goodin and T Schillemans, 'Public Accountability' in M Bovens, R Goodin and T Schillemans (eds), *The Oxford Handbook of Public Accountability* (OUP 2016)

Bowcott O, 'Lord Chief Justice Attacks Liz Truss for Failing to Back Article 50 Judges' *The Guardian* (22 March 2017)

Bowman FO, 'Falling Out of Love with America: The Clinton Impeachment and the Madisonian Constitution' (2001) 60(5) *Maryland Law Review* 5

Bowman FO, *High Crimes and Misdemeanors: A History of Impeachment for the Age of Trump* (Cambridge University Press 2019)

Bowyer TH, 'Philip Francis and the Government of Bengal: Parliament and Personality in the Frustration of an Ambition' (1999) 18(2) *Parliamentary History* 1

Braddick MJ, 'Cranfield, Lionel, First Earl of Middlesex' in *Oxford Dictionary of National Biography* (OUP 2004, Online 4 October 2012)

Bradley AW, 'Personal Responsibility and Government: A Case for Impeachment?' in G Carnall and C Nicholson (eds), *The Impeachment of Warren Hastings: Papers from a Bicentenary Commemoration* (Edinburgh University Press 1989)

Brett Taylor R, 'Brexit and Collective Cabinet Responsibility: Why the Convention Is Still Working' *London School of Economics* (20 May 2019)

Broyde MJ and RA Schapiro, 'Impeachment and Accountability: The Case of the First Lady' (1998) 15 *Const. Comment* 479

Bryant C, *Parliament: The Bibliography, Volume 1: Ancestral Voices* (Doubleday 2014)
Bryant C, *Parliament: The Bibliography, Volume 2: Reform* (Doubleday 2014)
Bryce J, *The American Commonwealth*, Volume I (Liberty Fund 1995)
Buchan L, 'Brexit: David Davis Won't Be Investigated for Contempt After He Admits There Are No Impact Studies' *The Independent* (6 December 2017)
Cabinet Manual, October 2011
Cannon J, *The Fox-North Coalition: Crisis of the Constitution, 1782–84* (Cambridge University Press 1970)
Cheney K, 'Trump Vote Fails Overwhelmingly' *Politico* (6 December 2017)
Chowdhury T, '*Miller (No 2)*, the Principle-isation of Ministerial Accountability and Military Deployments' *U.K. Const. L. Blog* (24 October 2019)
Clarke MV, *Fourteenth Century Studies* (LS Sutherland and M McKisack eds, Clarendon Press 1968)
Clemmensen N, *Denmark's Constitution 150 Years: England and the Danish Constitution of 5 June 1849* (Royal Danish Ministry of Foreign Affairs 1999)
Clemmensen N, 'The Image of Britain in the Danish Constitutional Debate' in J Sevaldsen and C Bjorn (eds), *Britain and Denmark: Political, Economic and Cultural Relations in the 19th and 20th Centuries* (Museum Tusculanum Press 2003)
CNN, 'White House Weighs Impeachment Trial Strategy' (21 December 1998)
Cobbett W, *The Parliamentary History of England, from the Earliest Period to the Year 1803*, Volume XXVIII (TC Hansard 1816)
Committee of Privileges, *Third Report* (1976–77, HC 417)
Constitution Unit, *The Changing Role of the House of Lords* (University College London 1995)
Cowan B, 'The Spin Doctor: Sacheverell's Trial Speech and Political Performance in the Divided Society' in *Faction Displayed: Reconsidering the Impeachment of Dr Henry Sacheverell* (Parliamentary History 2012)
Cox H, *The Institutions of the English Government* (Sweet 1863)
Cozens C, 'Widespread Scepticism to Hutton "Whitewash"' *The Guardian* (29 January 2004)
Cripps Y, 'The Consequence of Disclosure in the Public Interest' in C Forsyth and I Hare (eds), *The Golden Metwand and the Crooked Cord: Essays in Honour of Sir William Wade QC* (OUP 1998)
Cruise O'Brien C, *Edmund Burke* (Vintage 2002)
Cust LH, revised by Smith EA, 'Sayers [Sayer], James' in *Oxford Dictionary of National Biography* (OUP Online 23 September 2004)
Damgaard E and P Svensson, 'Who Governs? Parties and Policies in Denmark' (1989) 17 *European Journal of Political Research* 731
Davies CC, 'Warren Hastings and the Younger Pitt' (1955) 70 *The English Historical Review* 609
Day P and R Klein, *Accountabilities: Five Public Services* (Tavistock Publications 1978)
Democratic Constitutional Design, *The Court of Impeachment and the Power of Indictment* <https://stjornarskra.hi.is/en/deliberative-poll/the-court-of-impeachment-and-the-power-of-indictment/>
Dicey AV, *Introduction to the Study of the Law of the Constitution* (reprinted by Liberty Classics in 1982, originally published as 8th edn, Macmillan 1915)
Dickinson HT, 'St John, Henry, Styled Viscount Bolingbroke' in *Oxford Dictionary of National Biography* (OUP 2004, Online 3 October 2013)

Dirks NB, *The Scandal of Empire: India and the Creation of Imperial Britain* (Permanent Black 2008)

Ditchfield GM, 'The House of Lords and the Impeachment of Warren Hastings' (1994) 13(3) *Parliamentary History* 277

Donaldson F, *The Marconi Scandal* (Bloomsbury 2013)

Dougherty JH, 'Inherent Limitations Upon Impeachment' (1913–1914) 23 *Yale Law Journal* 60

Ducharme J, 'Hillary Clinton: "Very Credible" Sexual Assault Allegations Against Donald Trump Should Be Investigated' *Time* (18 November 2017)

Dunleavy P, GW Jones, J Burnham, R Elgie and P Fysh, 'Leaders, Politics and Institutional Change: The Decline of Prime Ministerial Accountability to the House of Commons, 1868–1990' (1993) 23(3) *British Journal of Political Science* 267

Dwight TW, 'Trial by Impeachment' (1867) 15 *The American Law Register* 257

The Economist, 'Impeachment, Paraguayan-Style' (30 June 2012)

Ekins R, 'Protecting the Constitution: How and Why Parliament Should Limit Judicial Power' *Policy Exchange* (2019)

Ekins R, P Hennessey, K Mahmood and T Tugendhat, 'Aiding the Enemy: How and Why to Restore the Law of Treason' *Policy Exchange* (2018)

Ellis DL, 'Collective Ministerial Responsibility and Collective Solidarity' in G Marshall (ed), *Ministerial Responsibility* (OUP 1989)

Ellison J, 'Why the Chilcot Inquiry Has Taken So Long – and Why We Should Wait to Judge It' *The Conversation* (28 August 2015)

Elo Rytter J and M Wind, 'In Need of Juristocracy? The Silence of Denmark in the Development of European Legal Norms' (2011) 9(2) *International Journal of Constitutional Law* 470

Epstein J, *Scandal of Colonial Rule: Power and Subversion on the British Atlantic During the Age of Revolution* (Cambridge University Press 2012)

Erskine DH, 'The Trial of Queen Caroline and the Impeachment of President Clinton: Law as a Weapon for Political Reform' (2008) 7 *Washington University Global Studies Law Review* 1

Erskine May T, *A Practical Treatise on the Law, Privileges, Proceedings and Usage of Parliament* (1st edn, Charles Knight and Co 1844)

European Commission, 'European Commission Acts to Preserve the Rule of Law in Poland' (25 July 2017)

European Commission for Democracy Through Law, 'Report on the Relationship Between Political and Criminal Ministerial Responsibility' (11 March 2013)

Fandos N, 'Trump Acquitted of Two Impeachment Charges in Near Party-Line Vote' *The New York Times* (5 February 2020)

Fandos, N, 'Senator Patrick Leahy, the Longest-Serving Democrat, Will Preside Over Trump's Impeachment Trial' *The New York Times* (24 January 2021)

Fandos N and MD Shear, 'Trump Impeached for Abuse of Power and Obstruction of Congress' *The New York Times* (18 December 2019)

Farrand M, *The Framing of the Constitution of the United States* (Yale University Press 1913)

Feldman N and J Weisberg, 'What Are Impeachable Offenses?' 64(14) *The New York Review of Books* 16

Fenton B, 'Gore Blamed Clinton for His Defeat in Election' *The Telegraph* (8 February 2001)

Finer SE, 'The Individual Responsibility of Ministers' in G Marshall (ed), *Ministerial Responsibility* (OUP 1989)

Finnis J, 'The Law of the Constitution Before the Court' *Policy Exchange* (2019)

Fletcher FTH, *Montesquieu and English Politics (1750–1800)* (reprint, Porcupine Press 1980)

Flinders M, 'The Enduring Centrality of Individual Ministerial Responsibility Within the British Constitution' (2000) 6(3) *Journal of Legislative Studies* 73

Flinders M, 'Mechanisms of Judicial Accountability in British Central Government' (2001) *Parliamentary Affairs* 54

Flinders M, *The Politics of Accountability in the Modern State* (Ashgate 2001)

Flinders M, 'Shifting the Balance? Parliament, the Executive and the British Constitution' (2002) 50 *Political Studies* 23

Flinders M, 'Daring to be a Daniel' (2011) 43(5) *Administration and Society* 595

Flinders M and A Kelso, 'Mind the Gap: Political Analysis, Public Expectations and the Parliamentary Decline Thesis' (2011) 13 *BJPIR* 249

Forsyth C, 'Leading Administrative Law Cases: M v Home Office [1994] 1 AC 377' (*Cambridge University Legal Studies Research Paper Series*, Paper No. 50/2016, September 2016)

Freeman GP, 'Migration Policy and Politics in the Receiving States' (1992) 26(4) *The International Migration Review* 1144

Fritz CG, *American Sovereigns: The People and America's Constitutional Tradition Before the Civil War* (Cambridge University Press 2008)

Fry M, 'Dundas, Henry, First Viscount Melville (1742–1811)' in *Oxford Dictionary of National Biography* (OUP 2004, Online 8 April 2021)

Fry M, *The Dundas Despotism* (John Donald 2004)

Furgol EM, 'Fraser, Simon, Eleventh Lord Lovat' in *Oxford Dictionary of National Biography* (OUP 2004, Online 7 January 2010)

Gay O, 'Parliamentary Resolutions on Ministerial Accountability' (House of Commons Library, SN00608, December 2000)

Gay O, 'Individual Ministerial Accountability' (House of Commons Library, SN/PC/06467, November 2012)

Gay O and N Davies, 'Impeachment' (House of Commons Library, Standard Note, 16 November 2011)

Gearty C and R Singh, 'Legal Opinion: In the Matter of an Impeachment of the Prime Minister: Arising from the War Against Iraq' (22 September 2004)

Gerhardt MJ, 'The Lessons of Impeachment History' (1999) *Faculty Publications Paper* 978

Gerhardt MJ, *The Federal Impeachment Process: A Constitutional and Historical Analysis* (2nd edn, University of Chicago Press 2000)

Glass A, 'President Gerald Ford Pardons Richard Nixon, Sept. 8, 1974' *Politico* (9 August 2009, updated 9 June 2015)

Gold H, 'Clinton: Threats to Impeach Me Are "Ridiculous"' *Politico* (23 October 2014)

Goldstein JK, 'Constitutional Change, Originalism, and the Vice Presidency' (2013) 16(2) *Journal of Constitutional Law* 369

Gordon G and A Street, *Select Committees and Coercive Powers – Clarity or Confusion?* (The Constitution Society 2012)

Grant Robertson C, *England Under the Hanoverians* (Methuen & Co Ltd 1953)

Green-Pedersen C and J Krogstrup, 'Immigration as a Political Issue in Denmark and Sweden' (2008) 47 *European Journal of Political Research* 610

Green-Pedersen C and P Odmalm, 'Going Different Ways? Right-Wing Parties and the Immigrant Issue in Denmark and Sweden' (2008) 15(3) *Journal of European Public Policy* 367

Greene JP, *Peripheries and Centre: Constitutional Development in the Extended Polities of the British Empire and the United States 1607–1788* (University of Georgia Press 1986)

Greene JP, *Evaluating Empire and Confronting Colonialism in Eighteenth-Century Britain* (Cambridge University Press 2013)

Griffin SM, *American Constitutionalism: From Theory to Politics* (Princeton University Press 1996)

Griffith JAG, 'The Political Constitution' (1979) 42(1) *MLR* 1

Gronnegaard Christensen J, 'Delegation and Administrative Organization: An Overview of Danish Regulatory Administration 1950–2000' (Department of Political Science, University of Aarhus 1950–2000)

The Guardian, 'Denmark's Former Immigration Minister to Face Impeachment Trial for Anti-Migrant Policies' (2 February 2021)

The Guardian, 'The Guardian View on Trump's Impeachment: Uneasy, but Essential' (10 February 2021)

Guerin B, J McCrae and M Shepheard, 'Accountability in Modern Government: What Are the Issues?' (A Discussion Paper, Institute for Government, April 2018)

Haddon C, 'The Handling of the Priti Patel Bullying Inquiry Has Fatally Undermined the Ministerial Code' *Institute for Government* (20 November 2020)

Hailsham (Lord), 'Elective Dictatorship' (1976) 120 *Sol Jo* 693

Handley S, 'Butler, James, Second Duke of Ormond' in *Oxford Dictionary of National Biography* (OUP 2004, Online 25 May 2006)

Hanham AA, 'Parker, Thomas, First Earl of Macclesfield' in *Oxford Dictionary of National Biography* (OUP 2004, Online 8 January 2009)

Hastings W, *The Defence of Warren Hastings, Esq (Late Governor General of Bengal,) at the Bar of the House of Commons* (J Stockdale 1786)

Hatsell J, *Precedents of Proceedings in the House of Commons Under Separate Titles with Observations, Volume IV Relating to Conferences and Impeachment* (2nd edn, Luke Hansard and Sons 1818)

Hatton M, D Natzler, M Hamlyn, C Lee, C Mawson, C Poyser, E Samson and K Lawrence, *Erskine May: Parliamentary Practice* (25th edn, Lexis Nexis Butterworths 2019)

Heffer S, 'The Tory Party Is Disintegrating, Collective Responsibility Has Broken Down, Yet Theresa May Goes on' *New Statesman* (8 May 2019)

Hill BW, 'Fox and Burke: The Whig Party and the Question of Principles, 1784–1789' (1974) 39 *The English Historical Review* 1

Hjalmarsson R and I Kovras, 'Should We Prosecute Political Leaders After a Crisis? Lessons from Iceland' *LSE Blog* (6 December 2017)

Hoffer PC and NEH Hull, *Impeachment in America, 1635–1805* (Yale University Press 1984)

Holdsworth W, *A History of English Law*, Volume X (Methuen & Co Ltd 1938)

Holdsworth W, *A History of English Law*, Volume XII (Methuen & Co Ltd 1938)

Holms C and B Warming-Rasmussen, 'Audit Regulation and the Audit Profession in Denmark' in R Quick, S Turley and M Willekens (eds), *Auditing, Trust and Governance: Developing Regulation in Europe* (Routledge 2007)

Home Office, 'Government Response to the Consultation on the Leveson Inquiry and Its Implementation' (1 March 2018)

Horder J, *Criminal Misconduct in Office: Law and Politics* (OUP 2018)

Horne A, 'Select Committee Powers of Enforcement' *U.K. Const. L. Blog* (23 March 2017)

House of Commons Reform Committee, First Report, *Rebuilding the House* (2008–09, HC 1117)

Howe of Aberavon (Lord), 'Procedure at the Scott Inquiry' (1996) PL 445

Howell TB (ed), *Howell's State Trials* (London 1809–1826)

Hulse C, 'In a Polarised Era, Will Impeachment Become a "New Normal"?' *The New York Times* (12 December 2019)

Hurwitz MS, 'The Impeachment of Federal District Judge Samuel B. Kent' (2009) 30(2) *The Justice System Journal* 223

Hutchinson GD, '"The Manager in Distress": Reaction to the Impeachment of Henry Dundas, 1805–7' (2017) 36(2) *Parliamentary History* 198

Illing S, 'President Trump Is Considering Pardoning Himself. I Asked 15 Experts If That's Legal' *Vox.com* (21 July 2017)

Isenbergh J, 'Impeachment and Presidential Immunity from Judicial Process' (1999) 18(53) *Yale Law and Policy Review* 53

ITV News, 'Iraq War: Everything You Need to Know About the Chilcot Inquiry' (5 July 2016)

Jack M (ed), *Erskine May: Parliamentary Practice* (24th edn, Lexis Nexis Butterworths 2011)

Jennings I, *The Law and the Constitution* (4th edn, University of London Press 1952)

Jennings I, *Parliament* (2nd edn, Cambridge University Press 1969)

Jensen JA, 'Denmark: The 150th Anniversary of the Danish Constitution and a Landmark Decision of the Supreme Court' (1999) 5(4) *European Public Law* 492

Jensen JA, 'Constitutional Chronicle – Denmark: The Separation of Power with Special Regard to the Role of the Judiciary' (2000) 12(1) *European Review of Public Law* 119

Jensen JA, 'Political Accountability in Denmark' in L Verhey, H Broeksteeg and I Van den Driessche (eds), *Political Accountability in Europe: Which Way Forward: A Traditional Concept of Parliamentary Democracy in a EU Context* (Europa Law Publishing 2008)

Johnston D, 'Hastings Ousted as Senate Vote Convicts Judge' *The New York Times* (21 October 1989)

Joint Committee on Parliamentary Privilege, First Report (1999, HL 43-I, HC 214-I)

Joint Committee on Parliamentary Privilege, Report of Session 2013–15, HL 30, HC 100

Katyal NK, 'Impeachment as Congressional Constitutional Interpretation' (2000) 63 *Law and Contemporary Problems* 169

Keeton GW, *The Passing of Parliament* (2nd edn, John de Graff 1954)

Kenyon JP, *The Stuart Constitution: Documents and Commentary* (2nd edn, Cambridge University Press 1989)

King A, *The British Constitution* (OUP 2007)

King A and I Crewe, *The Blunders of Our Governments* (Oneworld 2013)

Knights M (ed), *Faction Displayed: Reconsidering the Impeachment of Dr Henry Sacheverell: Parliamentary History* (Wiley-Blackwell 2012)

Knights M, 'Introduction: The View from 1710' in M Knights (ed), *Faction Displayed: Reconsidering the Impeachment of Dr Henry Sacheverell: Parliamentary History* (Wiley-Blackwell 2012)

Kucinich D, *The 35 Articles of Impeachment and the Case for Prosecuting George W Bush* (Feral House 2008)

Kyvig DE, *The Age of Impeachment: American Constitutional Culture Since 1960* (University Press of Kansas 2008)

Lambert P, 'The Lightning Impeachment of Paraguay's President Lugo' *E-International Relations* (9 August 2012)

Langford P, *A Polite and Commercial People: England 1727–1783, the New Oxford History of England* (Guild Publishing 1989)

Lawrence W, 'The Law of Impeachment' (1867) 15(11) *The American Law Register* 641

Laws S, 'The Supreme Court's Unjustified Lawmaking' *Judicial Power Project* (4 October 2019)

Lawson P and J Phillips, '"Our Execrable Banditti": Perceptions of Nabobs in Mid-Eighteenth Century England' (1984) 16(3) *Albion* 225

Lawton MC, Acting Assistant Attorney General, Office of Legal Counsel, 'Presidential or Legislative Pardon of the President' (5 August 1974)

Lee SM, 'Paull, James (1770–1808), *Trader and Politician*' in *Oxford Dictionary of National Biography* (OUP 2004, Online 23 September 2004)

Leigh D and R Evans, '"National Interest" Halts Arms Corruption Inquiry' *The Guardian* (15 December 2006)

Leigh I and R Masterman, *Making Rights Real: The Human Rights Act in Its First Decade* (Hart Publishing 2008)

Lemmings D, 'Erskine, Thomas, First Baron Erskine (1750–1823)' in *Oxford Dictionary of National Biography* (OUP 2004, Online 3 January 2008)

Lemmings D, 'Criminal Trial Procedure in Eighteenth-century England: The Impact of Lawyers' (2005) 26(1) *The Journal of Legal History* 73

Lester A and M Weait, 'The Use of Ministerial Powers Without Parliamentary Authority: The Ram Doctrine' (2003) (Autumn) *Public Law* 415

Levinson S, 'Transitions' (1999) *Yale Law Journal* 2215

Levy LW (ed), *Essays on the Making of the Constitution* (2nd edn, OUP 1987)

Lichtman AJ, *The Case for Impeachment* (William Collins 2017)

Lim H, 'A Closer Look at the Korean Constitutional Court's Ruling on Park Geun-Hye's Impeachment' *Yale Journal of International Law* (18 May 2017)

Logan J, *A Review of the Principal Charges Against Warren Hastings Esquire, Late Governor General of Bengal* (John Stockdale and John Murray 1788)

Lovat-Fraser JA, 'The Impeachment of Lord Melville' (1912–13) 24 *Jurid. Rev.* 235

Lyons R and W Chapman, 'Judiciary Committee Approves Article to Impeach President Nixon, 27 to 11' *The Washington Post* (28 July 1974)

Maitland FW, *The Constitutional History of England* (4th reprint, Cambridge University Press 1919)

Malik K, 'If We Want to Build Trust in Society, a New Treason Law Is No Way to Do It' *The Guardian* (29 July 2018)

Marshall G, *Constitution Conventions: The Rules and Forms of Political Accountability* (OUP 1984)

Marshall G (ed), *Ministerial Responsibility: Oxford Readings in Politics and Government* (OUP 1989)
Marshall G and GC Moodie, *Some Problems of the Constitution* (4th edn, Hutchinson University Library 1967)
Marshall PJ, 'Benfield, Paul' (1741–1810)' in *Oxford Dictionary of National Biography* (OUP 2004, Online 11 March 2021)
Marshall PJ, *The Impeachment of Warren Hastings* (OUP 1965)
Marsteintredet L, M Llanos and D Nolte, 'Paraguay and the Politics of Impeachment' (2013) 24(4) *Journal of Democracy* 110
Mastrangelo D, 'Ken Starr: Impeach Has Become a "Weapon to Be Wielded Against One's Political Opponent"' *Washington Examiner* (27 January 2020)
Matheson C, *The Life of Henry Dundas, First Viscount Melville 1742–1811* (Constable and Co Ltd 1933)
Matthews F, 'Majoritarianism Reinterpreted: Effective Representation and the Quality of Westminster Democracy' (2019) 71 *Parliamentary Affairs* 50
McCarthy A, *Faithless Execution: Building the Political Case for Obama's Impeachment* (Encounter Books 2014)
McCarthy T, 'John Roberts: Justice Once Labelled a "Disaster" by Trump to Oversee Impeachment Trial' *The Guardian* (3 January 2020)
McKay W and CW Johnson, *Parliament and Congress: Representation and Scrutiny in the Twenty-First Century* (OUP 2012)
McKisack M, *The Fourteenth Century 1307–1399: The Oxford History of England* (OUP 1959, reprinted 1988)
McLynn F, *Crime and Punishment in Eighteenth Century England* (Routledge 2013)
Merco Press, 'Paraguayan Supreme Court Receives Unconstitutional Appeal on Lugo's Removal' (12 July 2012)
Mindock C, 'Donald Trump's Sexual Assault Allegations: The Full List of Women Who Have Accused the President' *The Independent* (5 December 2017)
Ministerial Code, Cabinet Office, January 2018
Mitchell A, 'Clinton Is Acquitted Decisively by Senate on Both Charges' *The New York Times* (13 February 1999)
Moon P, *Warren Hastings and British India* (Hodder and Stoughton 1947)
Mortimer C, 'Donald Trump Says Pledge to Jail Hillary Clinton Played "Great Before the Election" but Now "We Don't Care"' *The Independent* (10 December 2016)
Mueller III RS, *Report on the Investigation into Russian Interference in the 2016 Presidential Election*, Volume I (March 2019)
Mulgan R, '"Accountability": An Ever-Expanding Concept' (2000) 78(3) *Public Administration* 555
Murphy S, 'Alex Allan: The Veteran Windsurfing Mandarin Who Quit Over Patel Row' *The Guardian* (20 November 2020)
Murray J, 'Company Rules: Burke, Hastings, and the Specter of the Modern Liberal State' (2007) 41(1) *Eighteenth-Century Studies* 55
Neate R, 'Iceland ex-PM Geir Haarde Cleared of Bank Negligence' *The Guardian* (23 April 2012)
Neuberger (Lord), 'UK Supreme Court Decisions on Private and Commercial Law: The Role of Public Policy and Public Interest' (Centre for Commercial Law Studies Conference 2015, 4 December 2015)
Neumann RK, 'The Revival of Impeachment as a Partisan Political Weapon' (2006–2007) 34(2) *Hastings Const. L.Q.* 162

Nevin M, 'Nixon Loyalists, Barry Goldwater and Republican Support for President Nixon During Watergate' (2017) 27(3) *Journal of Policy History* 403

The New York Times, 'President Trump Deserves a Real Trial' (19 December 2019)

The New York Times, 'A Dishonourable Senate: Republican Legislators Abdicated Their Duty by Refusing to Seek to the Truth' (31 January 2020)

Nicholson C and G Carnall (eds), *The Impeachment of Warren Hastings: Papers from a Bicentenary Commemoration* (Edinburgh University Press 1989)

Norton P, *Does Parliament Matter?* (Harvester Wheatsheaf 1993)

Norton P, *Parliament in British Politics* (2nd edn, Palgrave 2013)

Norton P, 'The Strathclyde Recommendations Are Based on a False Premise That There Is a Convention That the Lords Does Not Reject Statutory Instruments' *Constitution Unit* (14 January 2016)

Norton P, 'Parliament: The Best of Times, the Worst of Times' in J Jowell and C O'Cinneide (eds), *The Changing Constitution* (9th edn, OUP 2019)

Norton P, *Governing Britain: Parliament, Ministers and Our Ambiguous Constitution* (Manchester University Press 2020)

Obeidallah D, 'Nancy Pelosi Was Right About Trump's Impeachment and the Democrats Were Wrong' *NBC News* (20 December 2019)

Paley R, 'The Dying Embers of an Outdated Privilege: The 1935 Trial of Lord de Clifford in the House of Lords' (2013) *Parliamentary History* 169

Palmer JJN, 'The Parliament of 1385 and the Constitutional Crisis of 1386' (1971) 46(3) *Speculum* 477

Parliamentary Assembly of the Council of Europe, 'Keeping Political and Criminal Responsibility Separate' (Resolution 1950 (2013))

Payne S, 'Boris Johnson's Ethics Adviser Quits Over Patel Bullying Report' *Financial Times* (20 November 2020)

Peltonen M, 'Bacon, Francis, Viscount St Alban' in *Oxford Dictionary of National Biography* (OUP 2004, Online 4 October 2007)

Phillips A, 'A House Republican Already Wants to Impeach Hillary Clinton' *The Washington Post* (9 September 2016)

Phillips CH, 'The East India Company "Interest" and the English Government, 1783–4' (1937) 20 *Transactions of the Royal Historical Company* 83

Pincus S, 'Addison's Empire: Whig Conceptions of Empire in the Early 18th Century' in M Knights (ed), *Faction Displayed: Reconsidering the Impeachment of Dr Henry Sacheverell*, Parliamentary History (Wiley-Blackwell 2012)

Plucknett TFT, 'The Origin of Impeachment' (1942) 24 *Transactions of the Royal Historical Society* 47

Plucknett TFT, 'Impeachment and Attainder' (1953) Fifth Series (3) *Transactions of the Royal Historical Society* 145

Plumb JH, *The Growth of Political Stability in England 1675–1725* (MacMillan and Company Limited 1967)

Popp KA, 'The Impeachment of President Clinton: An Ugly Mix of Three Powerful Forces' (2002) 63(1–2) *Law and Contemporary Problems* 223

Porter R, *English Society in the Eighteenth Century* (Rev edn, Penguin 1991)

Potts CS, 'Impeachment as a Remedy' (1926) 12 *St Louis L Rev* 15

Presser SB, 'Would George Washington Have Wanted Bill Clinton Impeached?' (1999) 67 *Geo. Wash. L. Rev.* 666

Public Service Committee, *Ministerial Accountability and Responsibility*, Second Report (1995–96, HC 313)

Qvortrup M, 'Checks and Balances in a Unicameral Parliament: The Case of the Danish Minority Referendum' (2000) 6(3) *The Journal of Legislative Studies* 15

Rangwala G and D Plesch, 'A Case to Answer: A First Report on the Potential Impeachment of the Prime Minister for High Crimes and Misdemeanours in Relation to the Invasion of Iraq' (August 2004)

Rawlinson K, 'Renew Treason Laws to Jail Enemies of the State for Life, Says Think-tank' *The Guardian* (25 July 2018)

Riddell P, 'In Defence of Politicians: In Spite of Themselves' (2010) 63(3) *Parliamentary Affairs* 545

Ridley FF, 'There Is No British Constitution: A Dangerous Case of the Emperor's Clothes' (1988) *Parliamentary Affairs* 340

Roberts C, 'The Law of Impeachment in Stuart England: A Reply to Raoul Berger' (1975) 84(7) *Yale Law Journal* 1419, 1435–1436

Romero S, 'Dilma Rousseff Is Ousted as Brazil's President in Impeachment Vote' *The New York Times* (31 August 2016)

Rose M, 'Enough of His Excuses: Blair Must Be Impeached Over Iraq' *The Guardian* (10 January 2006)

Royal Commission on Tribunals of Inquiry 1966, *Report of the Commission Under the Chairmanship of The Rt. Hon. Lord Justice Salmon* (Cmnd, 3121)

Russell M, *The Contemporary House of Lords: Westminster Bicameralism Revived* (OUP 2013)

Russell M and P Cowley, 'The Policy Power of the Westminster Parliament: The "Parliamentary State" and the Empirical Evidence' (2015) 29(1) *Governance: An International Journal of Policy, Administration and Institutions* 121

Sang-Hun C, 'South Korea's Impeachment Process, Explained' *The New York Times* (27 November 2016)

Sang-Hun C, 'South Korea Removes President Park Geun-Hye' *The New York Times* (9 March 2017)

Scarman L, *English Law – The New Dimension, The Hamlyn Lectures* (Stevens & Sons 1974)

Schuck PH, 'Why Congress Can Impeach Obama: The Impeachment of Obama in Immigration May Be Legal – But It's Wrong' *The New York Times* (21 November 2014)

Sedley S, 'Judicial Independence Is a Fragile Thing' *The Financial Times* (27 January 2017)

Select Committee on Parliamentary Privilege, *Report* (1966–67, HC 34)

Select Committee on Reform of the House of Commons, *Rebuilding the House, First Report* (Session 2008–9, HC 1117)

Simson Caird J, 'Impeachment' (House of Commons Library, Briefing Paper CBP-7612)

Singh R and C Gearty, 'In the Matter of an Impeachment of the Prime Minister: Arising from the War Against Iraq' (Legal Opinion, 22 September 2004)

Skovgaard-Petersen H, 'Legal and Political Accountability in Denmark – an Overview' (received 3 October 2017)

Slack J, 'Enemies of the People: Fury Over "out of Touch" Judges Who Have "Declared War on Democracy" by Defying 17.4m Brexit Voters and Who Could Trigger Constitutional Crisis' *Daily Mail* (4 November 2016)

Sloss D, 'Domestic Application of Treaties' (2011) *Santa Clara Law Digital Commons*

Smith D, 'Boost for Trump as 45 Republican Senators Vote to Dismiss Impeachment' *The Guardian* (26 January 2021)

Smith D, 'The Crucial Differences in Trump's Second Impeachment Trial' *The Guardian* (7 February 2021)

Speck WA, 'Harley Robert, First Earl of Oxford and Mortimer' in *Oxford Dictionary of National Biography* (OUP 2004, Online 4 October 2007)

Speck WA, 'Sacheverell, Henry' in *Oxford Dictionary of National Biography* (OUP 2004, Online 23 September 2004)

Speck WA, 'The Current State of Sacheverell Scholarship' in M Knights (ed), *Faction Displayed: Reconsidering the Impeachment of Dr Henry Sacheverell*, Parliamentary History (Wiley-Blackwell 2012)

Stack L, 'Donald Trump Featured Paula Jones and 2 Other Women Who Accused Bill Clinton of Sexual Assault' *The New York Times* (9 October 2016)

Stacy WR, 'Impeachment, Attainder, and the "Revival" of Parliamentary Judicature Under the Early Stuarts' (1992) 11(1) *Parliamentary History* 40

Steinhauer J, 'Senate, for Just the 8th Time, Votes to Oust a Federal Judge' *The New York Times* (8 December 2010)

Stephen JF, *A History of the Criminal Law of England: Volume 1* (MacMillan and Co 1883)

Stevenson RW, 'The President's Acquittal: The Chief Justice; Rehnquist Goes with the Senate Flow, "Wiser, but Not a Sadder Man"' *The New York Times* (13 February 1999)

Sumption J, 'Judicial and Political Decision-Making: The Uncertain Boundary' (The FA Mann Lecture 2011)

Sutherland L, *East India Company in Eighteenth Century Politics* (OUP 1962)

Syal R, 'Tony Blair Faces Calls for Impeachment on Release of Chilcot Report' *The Guardian* (3 July 2016)

Tanner JR, *Constitutional Documents of the Reign of James I: 1603–1625* (Cambridge University Press 1930, reprinted 1961)

Taylor S, 'Walpole, Robert, First Earl of Orford' in *Oxford Dictionary of National Biography* (OUP 2004, Online 3 January 2008)

The Telegraph, 'Grenfell Tower Inquiry Chairman Heckled as He Is Met with Angry Response from Residents' (7 July 2017)

Thomas PDG, *The House of Commons in the Eighteenth Century* (Gregg Revivals 1992)

Tite CCG, *Impeachment and Parliamentary Judicature in Early Stuart England* (University of London: The Athlone Press 1974)

Todd A, *On Parliamentary Government in England: Its Origin, Development, and Political Operation*, Volume II (Longmans, Green, and Co. 1869)

Tomkins A, 'The Scott Report: The Hope and Failure of Parliament' (1996) *Political Quarterly* 349

Tomkins A, *The Constitution After Scott: Government Unwrapped* (OUP 1998)

Travers R, *Ideology and Empire in Eighteenth-Century India: The British in Bengal* (Cambridge University Press 2007) 142

Tribe LH, 'And the Winner Is. . .' *The New York Times* (12 February 1999)

Tribe LH and J Matz, *To End a Presidency: The Power of Impeachment* (Basic Books 2018)

Trotter LJ, *Warren Hustings: A Biography* (WH Allen & Co 1878)

Turley J, 'Congress as Grand Jury: The Role of the House of Representatives in the Impeachment of an American President' (1998–1999) 68(3) *Geo. Wash. L. Rev.* 735

Turpin C, 'Responsibility in Government' (1996) 11 *Public Policy and Administration* 35

United States Senate, 'Impeachment of President William Jefferson Clinton: Constitutional Provisions; Rules of Procedure and Practice in the Senate When Sitting on Impeachment Trials; Articles of Impeachment Against President William Jefferson Clinton; President Clinton's Answer; and Replication of the House of Representatives' 106th Congress, Document 106–2, 13 January 1999

Victor D, '"Access Hollywood" Reminds Trump: "The Tape Is Very Real"' *The New York Times* (28 November 2017)

Walker P, 'Davis Rebuked Over Brexit Impact Papers but Not Held in Contempt' *The Guardian* (14 December 2017)

Walker S, 'Rumour, Sedition and Popular Protest in the Reign of Henry IV' (2000) 166 *Past & Present* 31

Washington Post, 'Time Line' (13 September 1998)

Watt N, 'Lady Butler-Sloss Stands Down from Child-Abuse Inquiry' *The Guardian* (14 July 2014)

Watts, J, 'Brazil's Dilma Rousseff Impeached by Senate in Crushing Defeat' *The Guardian* (1 September 2016)

Weitzman S, *Warren Hastings and Philip Francis* (Manchester University Press 1929)

White SD, *Sir Edward Coke and the Grievances of the Commonwealth* (Manchester University Press 1979)

Wilkinson B, *Studies in the Constitutional History of the Thirteenth and Fourteenth Centuries* (Manchester University Press 1937)

Williams B, *The Whig Supremacy 1714–1760: The Oxford History of England* (2nd edn, OUP 1962, reprinted 1987)

Wilson W, *Congressional Government: A Study in American Politics* (2nd edn, Houghton, Mifflin and Company 1885)

Winetrobe BK, 'Forms of Investigatory Inquiry & the Scott Inquiry' (House of Commons Library, Research Paper 96/22, 9 February 1999)

Woodhouse D, *Ministers and Parliament: Accountability in Theory and Practice* (OUP 1994)

Woodhouse D, 'Individual Ministerial Responsibility and a "Dash of Principle"' in D Butler, V Bogdanor and R Summers (eds), *The Law, Politics and the Constitution: Essays in Honour of Geoffrey Marshall* (OUP 1999)

Wright T, 'The Politics of Accountability' in M Elliot and D Feldman (eds), *The Cambridge Companion to Public Law* (Cambridge University Press 2015)

Wyatt D and R Ekins, 'Reforming the Supreme Court' *Policy Exchange* (July 2020)

Wynne SM, 'Catherine [Catherine of Braganza, Catarina Henriqueta de Braganca]' in *Oxford Dictionary of National Biography* (OUP 2004, Online 3 January 2008)

Zurcher A, 'US Election 2016: Presidential Race Goes Down the Drain' *BBC News* (15 October 2016)

Index

Note: Page numbers followed by "n" indicate a note on the corresponding page.

For Product Safety Concerns and Information please contact our EU representative GPSR@taylorandfrancis.com
Taylor & Francis Verlag GmbH, Kaufingerstraße 24, 80331 München, Germany

www.ingramcontent.com/pod-product-compliance
Ingram Content Group UK Ltd.
Pitfield, Milton Keynes, MK11 3LW, UK
UKHW020146200926
475702UK00016B/2578
9781032215846